# The Right to Know and the Right Not to Know

The privacy concerns discussed in the 1990s in relation to the New Genetics failed to anticipate the relevant issues for individuals, families, geneticists and society. Consumers, for example, can now buy their personal genetic information and share it online. The challenges facing genetic privacy have evolved as new biotechnologies have developed, and personal privacy is increasingly challenged by the irrepressible flow of electronic data between the personal and public spheres and by surveillance for terrorism and security risks.

This book considers the right to know and the right not to know about our own and others' genomes. It discusses new privacy concerns and developments in ethical thinking, with the greater emphasis on solidarity and equity. The multidisciplinary approach covers current topics such as biobanks and forensic databases, DIY testing, group rights and accountability, the food we eat and the role of the press and the new digital media.

**Ruth Chadwick** is Professor of Bioethics at the University of Manchester. She directed the ESRC Centre for Economic and Social Aspects of Genomics (Cesagen) from 2002 to 2013.

**Mairi Levitt** is a senior lecturer in the Department of Politics, Philosophy and Religion at Lancaster University, where she works in empirical bioethics and researches ethical and social issues in genetics.

**Darren Shickle** is Professor of Public Health at the University of Leeds, where his research interests include public health ethics, public health genetics, ophthalmic public health, and HIV and sexual health.

D0916728

*Cambridge Bioethics and Law*

This series of books was founded by Cambridge University Press with Alexander McCall Smith as its first editor in 2003. It focuses on the law's complex and troubled relationship with medicine across both the developed and the developing world. Since the early 1990s, we have seen in many countries increasing resort to the courts by dissatisfied patients and a growing use of the courts to attempt to resolve intractable ethical dilemmas. At the same time, legislatures across the world have struggled to address the questions posed by both the successes and the failures of modern medicine, while international organisations such as the WHO and UNESCO now regularly address issues of medical law.

It follows that we would expect ethical and policy questions to be integral to the analysis of the legal issues discussed in this series. The series responds to the high profile of medical law in universities, in legal and medical practice, as well as in public and political affairs. We seek to reflect the evidence that many major health-related policy debates in the UK, Europe and the international community involve a strong medical law dimension. With that in mind, we seek to address how legal analysis might have a trans-jurisdictional and international relevance. Organ retention, embryonic stem cell research, physician-assisted suicide and the allocation of resources to fund health care are but a few examples among many. The emphasis of this series is thus on matters of public concern and/or practical significance. We look for books that could make a difference to the development of medical law and enhance the role of medico-legal debate in policy circles. That is not to say that we lack interest in the important theoretical dimensions of the subject, but we aim to ensure that theoretical debate is grounded in the realities of how the law does and should interact with medicine and health care.

*Series Editors*

Professor Margaret Brazier, *University of Manchester*
Professor Graeme Laurie, *University of Edinburgh*
Professor Richard Ashcroft, *Queen Mary, University of London*
Professor Eric M. Meslin, *Indiana University*

*Books in the series*

Marcus Radetzki, Marian Radetzki, Niklas Juth *Genes and Insurance: Ethical, Legal and Economic Issues*
Ruth Macklin *Double Standards in Medical Research in Developing Countries*
Donna Dickenson *Property in the Body: Feminist Perspectives*

# The Right to Know and the Right Not to Know

*Genetic Privacy and Responsibility*

Edited by

Ruth Chadwick, Mairi Levitt and Darren Shickle

CAMBRIDGE
UNIVERSITY PRESS

# CAMBRIDGE
UNIVERSITY PRESS

University Printing House, Cambridge CB2 8BS, United Kingdom

Cambridge University Press is part of the University of Cambridge.

It furthers the University's mission by disseminating knowledge in the pursuit of education, learning and research at the highest international levels of excellence.

www.cambridge.org
Information on this title: www.cambridge.org/9781107076075

© Cambridge University Press 2014

First edition published by Avebury 1997
Second edition Cambridge University Press 2014

Printed in the United Kingdom by Clays, St Ives plc

*A catalogue record for this publication is available from the British Library*

*Library of Congress Cataloguing in Publication data*
The right to know and the right not to know : genetic privacy and responsibility / edited by Ruth Chadwick, Mairi Levitt and Darren Shickle. – Second edition.
    pages   cm – (Cambridge bioethics and law)
First published: Aldershot; Brookfield, VT: Avebury, 1997.
Includes bibliographical references and index.
ISBN 978-1-107-07607-5 (hardback)
1. Human chromosome abnormalities–Diagnosis–Moral and ethical aspects.   2. Genetic disorders–Diagnosis–Moral and ethical aspects.   3. Privacy, Right of.   I. Chadwick, Ruth F., editor.   II. Levitt, Mairi, editor.   III. Shickle, Darren, editor.
RB155.6.R53 2014
174.2'96042–dc23
2014020711

ISBN 978-1-107-07607-5 Hardback
ISBN 978-1-107-42979-6 Paperback

# Contents

# Contributors

JOACHIM ALLGAIER is a sociologist and media and communications researcher. He is a senior scientist at the Institute of Science, Technology and Society Studies at the Alpen-Adria-Universität Klagenfurt in Austria. Previously he was an Honorary Fellow at the School of Journalism and Mass Communication at the University of Wisconsin-Madison, USA, and he was employed at the Research Center Jülich in Germany, the University of Vienna in Austria, and the Open University in the UK, where he was awarded a PhD in sociology. He studied sociology at LMU Munich in Germany, and Science and Technology Studies at Maastricht University in the Netherlands. His research interests are Science and Technology Studies, Public Communication of Science, Technology and Medicine, and (New) Media, Communication and Popular Culture.

RUTH CHADWICK is Professor of Bioethics at the University of Manchester and directed the ESRC Centre for Economic and Social Aspects of Genomics (Cesagen) from 2002 to 2013. She co-edits *Bioethics* and *Life Sciences, Society and Policy* and has served on the Council of the Human Genome Organisation, the Panel of Eminent Ethical Experts of the Food and Agriculture Organisation of the United Nations (FAO), and the UK Advisory Committee on Novel Foods and Processes (ACNFP). She is Academician of the Academy of Social Sciences and Fellow of the Hastings Center, New York; of the Royal Society of Arts; and of the Society of Biology. In 2005 she won the World Technology Network Award for Ethics.

ANCA GHEAUS holds a De Velling Willis fellowship in the Department of Philosophy at Sheffield University. Her research is in moral and political philosophy, with a special focus on the importance of caring relationships for theories of distributive justice. Recent publications include 'Care drain: who should provide for the children left behind?' in *Critical Review of International Social and Political Philosophy*, 'Is the family uniquely valuable?' in *Ethics and Social Welfare* and 'The right to parent one's biological baby' in *The Journal of Political Philosophy*.

JØRGEN HUSTED is Associate Professor of Philosophy at Aarhus University, Demark, and a former member of The Danish Council of Ethics. Among his recent publications are books on Kierkegaard, Wittgenstein and J. S. Mills. In the area of applied ethics he has published *Ethics, Morality and Values* (2006); *Ethics and Values in Social Work* (2009) and *Ethics and Values in Nursing* (2013).

MICHIEL KORTHALS (1949) studied Philosophy, Sociology and German at the University of Amsterdam and the Karl Ruprecht University in Heidelberg (FRG). He analysed the Frankfurt School (Marx, Adorno and Horkheimer, Marcuse and Habermas) and issues of moral education and societal development. As Professor of Applied Philosophy, Wageningen University, he contributes to the philosophy of food and agriculture, of both local and global significance. Main publications include *Pragmatist Ethics for a Technological Culture* (with Keulartz *et al.* 2002); *Before Dinner. Philosophy and Ethics of Food* (2004); *Pépé Grégoire, A Philosophical Interpretation of his Sculptures* (2006); *Genomics, Obesity and the Struggle over Responsibilities* (2011).

GRAEME LAURIE is Professor of Medical Jurisprudence in the School of Law, University of Edinburgh. His research interests relate to the regulation and promotion of medicine, science and technology. Among his publications relevant to this collection are *Genetic Privacy: A Challenge to Medico-Legal Norms* (Cambridge University Press, 2002), and his co-authorship of *Law and Medical Ethics* (with J. K. Mason), now in its 9th edition (Oxford University Press, 2013). His policy work has included Chairmanships of the UK Biobank Ethics and Governance Council (2006–2010) and the Privacy Advisory Committee in Scotland (2005–2013).

MAIRI LEVITT is Senior Lecturer in the Department of Politics, Philosophy and Religion at Lancaster University. She is a social scientist working in empirical bioethics with a particular interest in researching ethical and social issues in genetics through engagement with different publics, from children to pensioners and from legal professionals to readers of a local newspaper. Her current research is looking at the implications of behavioural genetics for notions of responsibility, blame and fairness. Earlier projects include a schools-based project on the ethics of 'Making humans better and making better humans'; 'Barcoded children' (on the National DNA Database); commercial genetic screening; and young people's ideas of risk and safety in biotechnological applications in different European countries.

JEANTINE LUNSHOF studied Philosophy and Health Law in Hamburg and in Amsterdam. She obtained her PhD from VU University Amsterdam. As a philosopher and bioethicist, her research focus is on the conceptual and normative aspects of systems and synthetic biology. Based with Molecular Cell Physiology at VU University Amsterdam, she works as a Marie Curie Fellow at Harvard Medical School, conducting research on systems biology-based concepts of health and disease, and the development of a systems approach for ethics. In 2006, she developed the innovative model of 'open consent' that forms the normative backbone of the Personal Genome Project.

BARBARA PRAINSACK is a Professor at the Department of Social Science, Health & Medicine, King's College London. A political scientist by background, Barbara has published widely on the societal, regulatory, and ethical dimensions of genetic and genomic science and technology in medicine and forensics. From 2011 to 2013, she chaired the ESF 'Forward Look on Personalised Medicine for the European Citizen' alongside Stephen Holgate and Aarno Palotie. Barbara is also a member of the Austrian National Bioethics Commission, and of the British Royal Society of Arts.

DARREN SHICKLE is Professor of Public Health at the University of Leeds. He has previously worked at the University of Sheffield and University of Wales College of Medicine. As part of a Harkness Fellowship in 1996/7 he was based at the Bioethics Institute at the Johns Hopkins School of Public Health and the Kennedy Institute of Ethics at Georgetown University, USA. He has worked for the Department of Health and Human Services in Washington DC and the Department of Health in London on a range of ethics issues related to genetics, privacy and end-of-life. He is also a research ethics expert for the European Commission and the European Research Council Executive Agency. His research interests are public health ethics, public health genetics, ophthalmic public health, and HIV/ sexual health.

KADRI SIMM is an Associate Professor in Practical Philosophy at the Institute of Philosophy and Semiotics, University of Tartu, in Estonia. Having graduated from history, gender studies and philosophy, her main research interests and publications relate to bioethics (especially biobanking and ethical and social implications of genetics), political philosophy (theories of justice) and feminist theory.

HENK TEN HAVE is Director of the Center for Healthcare Ethics at Duquesne University in Pittsburgh, USA. He studied medicine and philosophy in the Netherlands and worked as professor in the Faculty of Medicine of the Universities of Maastricht and Nijmegen. From 2003 until 2010 he joined UNESCO in Paris as Director of the Division of Ethics of Science and Technology. His recent publications include *Contemporary Catholic Healthcare Ethics* (with David Kelly and Gerard Magill, Georgetown University Press, 2013) and *Handbook of Global Bioethics* (with co-editor Bert Gordijn, Springer, 2013). He is Editor-in-Chief of the journal *Medicine, Health Care and Philosophy*.

RICHARD WATERMEYER is Research Fellow in Impact and Engagement studies at the School of Social Sciences, Cardiff University, and Director of PIER Logistics – an academic consultancy specialising in impact evaluation and evidence review in Higher Education contexts. He is currently seconded to the Chief Scientific Adviser for Wales as a Science Policy Research Analyst, leading research responding to the policy priorities of *Science for Wales* and *Innovation Wales*. Research is focused on academics' strategy in exploiting the economic and social impact of their research, specifically in science domains; and STEM careers guidance by secondary science teachers and the interface with ITT, teachers' CPD and science enrichment and engagement activity.

MATTHIAS WIENROTH studies cross-epistemic identities and relationships of new and emergent technosciences. He is a post-doctoral Research Fellow at the Faculty of Health & Life Sciences at Northumbria University and in the FP7 European Forensic Genetics Network of Excellence. Here, he explores prevalent narratives and practices around emergent forensic genetics technologies and their uses. Previous work includes analysis of the production of the field of nanotechnology through identity building and collaboration; the governance of scientific conduct and research outcomes; collaboration across knowledge boundaries; and failure of technology. He is currently lead-editing a book on social convergences in the new biotechnologies.

ROBIN WILLIAMS is Professor Emeritus in the School of Applied Social Sciences at Durham University, Professor in the Faculty of Health & Life Sciences at Northumbria University, and a Visiting Professor at the Policy, Ethics and Life Sciences Research Centre, Newcastle University. He has published widely on the police uses of forensic science, is the Northumbria University lead investigator on the FP7 European Forensic Genetics Network of Excellence, and also holds a Wellcome Trust grant for a study of the use of 'familial searching' in support of criminal investigations in the UK and USA.

# Acknowledgements

The editors would like to thank all the contributors and the contacts at Cambridge University Press for their assistance with this volume.

# Introduction

*Ruth Chadwick, Mairi Levitt and Darren Shickle*

The first edition of *The Right to Know and the Right Not to Know* was published in 1997 as an output of the Euroscreen projects (1994–6; 1996–9), funded by the European Commission. The idea for the book emerged over dinner at a conference in Turku, where Ruth Chadwick had given a talk on the topic of the right to know and the right not to know, and discussion in the management team of Euroscreen concluded that there were so many interesting associated issues that a volume could and should be prepared. As the publication was an output of a project on genetic screening, it did not seem necessary to specify in the title that the issues were to be understood in the genetic context. At the time, it was a hot topic in genetics: in the 1990s there had been much discussion about disclosure (or not) in the clinic. At the beginning of the decade, for example, the Royal College of Physicians published its *Ethical Issues in Clinical Genetics* (1991), which identified a number of possible scenarios, and in the same year the results of the empirical survey of disclosure dilemmas, conducted by Dorothy Wertz and John Fletcher, was published in the journal *Bioethics* (Wertz and Fletcher 1991).

There had been developments, however, in the 1980s, which paved the way for discussions related to wider population screening (Shickle and Harvey 1993). The Nuffield Council on Bioethics published its report on genetic screening in 1993. Of the two Euroscreen projects that were funded by the European Commission, the first (1994–6) examined ethical issues in predictive medicine. The second was concerned with insurance, commercial testing and public awareness. Clearly, issues of rights to know and not to know were implicated in all of these, in different ways.

In the clinic the principal issues discussed concerned potential tensions between the interests of family members, and the right (not) to know about late onset disorders. A commonly discussed scenario was where one member of a family wished to undergo genetic testing but another (their parent, for example) did not, the implication being that disclosure for the one would also give an indication of the genetic status

1

of the parent. Findings of non-paternity in genetic testing in the clinic also gave rise to potentially difficult situations.

In relation to late onset disorders, some people would prefer to know about their risk of developing diseases such as cancer or dementia, even though the onset might be decades into the future, so that they could structure their lives accordingly (even though the predictions would be fraught with more or less uncertainty, depending on the condition in question). For some individuals with a strong family history of genetic disease, the uncertainty of not knowing was difficult to bear, and hence a genetic test that helped to provide more clarity helped to alleviate these anxieties, even if the recalculated risk was higher. The contrary position, held by other individuals, was a preference *not* to know, and to live in the hope of a long and healthy life. There were also particularly challenging issues about genetic testing of children (Clarke 1994). These issues remain.

The wider issues addressed in projects such as Euroscreen 2 included the rights of third parties such as insurers and employers to what they perceived as information relevant to insurability or employability; the rights of individuals to access genetic information in the marketplace rather than in the clinical context (and without the professional safeguards associated with a clinic); and the right of society (including but not confined to patient groups) both to be informed about the direction of science and to have a voice.

In this book we aim to update the debate by further critiquing philosophical principles of privacy and autonomy, reviewing changes in the genetic privacy debate since the 1990s and discussing new arenas of the privacy concern.

## Part I: Philosophical and legal issues

Part 1 sets the scene with an overview of the philosophical and legal debate around the right to know and the right not to know. In the first chapter the editors explore developments since the first edition of the book in 1997. There have been changes in context with the completion of the Human Genome Project, the establishment of large-scale population biobanks and social and political change, with an increase in surveillance and an explosion in social media, emerging issues and trends in ethical approaches. Genomic research has opened up the potential of personalised health advice, in the context of medication (pharmacogenomics) and nutrition (nutrigenomics). Whole genome sequencing has meant that rather than disclosing just single incidental findings there is now the prospect of knowing everything in the genome. Thinking about the ownership of genetic information has expanded from the implications of the right to know and right not to know for the individual's sense of identity to include the implications for collective identity. In ethical approaches there is now a greater emphasis on solidarity and equity and a trend towards rethinking the concept of privacy, over and above developments in data protection.

Next, in the only chapter reprinted from the last edition, Jørgen Husted focuses on the specific issue of unsolicited disclosure of genetic information to hitherto unsuspecting relatives, who thereby irreversibly lose their 'genetic innocence' and thus their right not to know. In thinking about the moral acceptability of this – about whether it can be justified in terms of a right to know – he distinguishes between two senses of autonomy: a thin and a thick conception. From the point of view of the thin conception the disclosure appears to enhance autonomy by providing information to facilitate decision making. This analysis is flawed, however, if a thick conception allowing for autonomy as self-*definition* is acknowledged, because it takes away from the individual the very decision of whether to know or not to know. There are dangers here of moralism as well as paternalism.

Graeme Laurie's analysis of privacy and the right not to know is in contrast to that of Husted. He argues that while the right to know is typically underpinned by an autonomy argument, the right not to know cannot be so underpinned, except in situations where an individual has expressed a prior wish not to know. For Laurie the difficult cases of disclosure concern those instances where there is no prior expression of preference, and to disclose the option of knowing/not knowing will in itself make clear that there is something to know. Here the interests at stake are best construed as privacy interests. Privacy here is explained as a genuine state of separateness from others, which also includes *psychological separateness* from others. The chapter proceeds to examine what legal protection of such interests is possible and concludes that the role of the law here should be approached with caution: 'Professional discretion, rather than legally imposed duty, is likely to be the optimal way to navigate this particular maze'.

## Part II: Issues in genetics

The second part contains five chapters on contemporary issues in genetics. Kadri Simm reviews the ethical debates when large population biobanks were being established and the lack of discussion at that time of the possibility of incidental findings, that is, the discovery of DNA information that might be relevant to a donor but was not the aim of the research. Simm discusses why 'incidentalome' has now become a hot topic in biobanking. As genetic research is more commonplace and biobanks share information across global networks the challenge of feedback looms large and researchers and institutions consider what is the right thing to do and who should do it. Whereas most biobanks had no mechanisms for the feedback of personal information to donors when they were set up, sociological research has indicated that donors would like such feedback. Simm considers the arguments for and against the disclosure of relevant research results to donors and the proposals for guidelines in this area. The focus is now on the 'how and when' of feedback, rather than 'if and whether' it should be given. In a future where whole genome sequencing becomes cheaper and part of routine medical care, it cannot be assumed that individuals will act on the information that is disclosed and that their quality of life will improve.

Robin Williams and Matthias Wienroth focus on forensic databases and who has the right to commission, deploy and share this information. Having considered the complex and divergent legislation that limits the uses of forensic DNA profiles in different jurisdictions, the authors look at recent controversial developments that promise the ability to infer relatedness through familial searching, population group origins and physical attributes of the person whose sample has been analysed. It might be presumed that legally sanctioned criminal investigations have a right to know but whether such intrusive interventions may be considered legitimate depends on who is to have access to the knowledge and their overall value orientation, the purposes for which it will be used and the categories of people to be subject to these interventions. The authors conclude with a discussion of the claims of the individual either to be known or to be forgotten.

Mairi Levitt argues that in order to exercise a right to know or a right not to know, it is necessary to have the right information to facilitate this choice. The problem is that in many areas of everyday life, choices have proliferated: some choices may be trivial, others have more importance. At the more significant end of the spectrum, patients and parents are bombarded with information about health and child rearing. The assumption is frequently made that an individual will be empowered by choice and in turn that empowerment is a means to improving the quality of individuals' lives. Choice has also been portrayed by governments as the key mechanism in driving quality and value for money in public services. However, as Levitt points out, individuals who are economically deprived may also be relatively choice deprived. Levitt describes the effects on the chooser, both positive and negative, of an ever-increasing range of choices. In particular, there are psychological consequences for making decisions under uncertainty and where there are implications for health and well-being of self and family. In recognition of this, many societies evolve socially acceptable ways of doing things that remove the need for individuals to decide how to act in every situation. Levitt concludes by discussing the implications of an increasing range of options arising from genetic technologies and how third parties may seek to influence these choices through more or less subtle messages about what the good parent or the responsible person should do.

One expanded area of choice is the emergence of commercial companies offering knowledge of one's own genome. Barbara Prainsack discusses seven instances of knowing, sharing and storing data on one's own genome; from genetic analysis within a clinical context to making one's own genomic data public. Although the right to know one's own genetic constitution might be seen as relatively unproblematic, there are new issues to consider, including the portability of genetic data and the availability of raw data that individuals might analyse, make sense of using online tools, share with others or make accessible for research. Prainsack discusses the risks inherent in these practices and comes to the conclusion that there are no compelling reasons to deny a person the right to know his or her own genome. Individuals should be able to enforce a right not to know in relation to institutions, but they should not be able to enforce this right vis-à-vis other individuals who may disclose information that, at least partially, applies also to them.

The last chapter in this part sets out to investigate the intricate relationship between science, ethics and accountability against the background of developments in the genomic sciences. To whom are scientists accountable with respect to the content and outcomes of their work? Highly 'inconvenient truths' may result from meticulous empirical observation and rigorous theoretical analysis. What to do if carefully derived, robust research findings clash with the deep convictions and key components of people's traditional knowledge – in particular if it concerns vulnerable populations? Can people be expected to consent to the confrontation with 'enlightenment'? Respect for persons and populations requires respect for choosing to adhere to tradition and narrative. The case study of the Havasupai is used to explore the ways in which scientific findings about communities can clash with fundamental beliefs they have about themselves. Scientists should adhere to the values of science that, according to Ismail Serageldin, presuppose 'freedom to enquire, to challenge, to think, and to envision the unimagined' and they may thereby reveal some inconvenient truths.

### Part III: Emerging issues

In the third and final part Henk ten Have sets the scene for the discussion of emerging issues by a consideration of the rise of the genetic framework for human existence, used not only for viewing health and disease but also for human behaviours and interactions. He shows that this geneticisation is one part of a dominant ideology which has often remained unanalysed in bioethics but is becoming subject to criticism in some areas of science. Within this dominant ideology of neo-liberalism, globalisation is focused on empowering autonomous individuals, who should be free to choose what they want, rather than on the interconnectedness of humans with each other and the environment. As bioethics becomes global bioethics, ten Have discusses the consequences of this change, drawing on Foucault's concept of biopolitics that subjects autonomous individuals to new and pervasive forms of discipline, monitoring and surveillance, self-regulation, nudging and incentives. In this context of individual responsibility the protective role of the state is deliberately decreased, and economic and social determinants of health become irrelevant. In the second part of the chapter, ten Have finds areas where neo-liberalism is under critique as the public domain is being redefined and expanded. He discusses changes in the patenting system, increases in data sharing and open access publishing as evidence of the emergence of a new ethos of science. However, as a more open science maximises the right to know, it is important to reflect on the implications for the protection of privacy and whether privacy is viewed from an individual or social perspective. In conclusion, ten Have discusses the critical role of bioethics today.

The next four chapters focus on four emerging issues. First, Anca Gheaus discusses 'designer babies' and the possibility of harm in knowing that one has been selected or enhanced. Parents may speculate what their unborn children will be like when they grow up – what will they look like? will they be clever? what occupation will they have? – but Anca Gheaus explores the consequences for the parent–child relationship if children were selected for particular traits or genetically enhanced. She argues that they might feel as though the love that they receive from their parents is conditional on them growing up to manifest the selected traits. Gheaus's argument is underpinned by an understanding of adequate parental love which includes several characteristics: parents should not make children feel they are loved conditionally for features such as intelligence, looks or temperament; they should not burden children with parental expectations concerning particular achievements; and parental love is often expressed in spontaneous enjoyment and discovery of children's features. Gheaus concludes by arguing that this understanding of parental love provides a reason to question the legitimacy of parental use of selection and enhancement and to explain why parents should not engage on a quest for the 'best child'.

The next two chapters consider the role of traditional and digital media in the right to know and the right not to know debate. First Joachim Allgaier considers what have been the main sources of information about medical and scientific development: television and the press. These have framed the public debate about the ethical and legal issues associated with such technologies. However, the inter-relationship and inter-dependence of scientists, journalists and public are complex, requiring deeper investigation. Allgaier notes that genetic manipulation and biotechnology became a topic of mass interest in the mid-1990s, most notably in the context of genetically modified food and cloning. This time was also marked by a divergence in the debate around biotechnology, with a separation between agri-food (green) and biomedical (red) biotechnology. This distinction has consequences for how the different technologies were portrayed in the mass media, and consequently how they were perceived by the public. Allgaier analyses the media coverage of these different manifestations of biotechnology and genetics over the last twenty years and presents data on how public opinion and attitudes towards genetic biotechnology have also evolved.

Richard Watermeyer argues that in the age of the Internet, information is both ubiquitous and instant – instantly populated, repopulated and retrieved. Science dialogue has been opened up to social actors with disparate socio-political orientations. The public are able to interact directly with scientists, bypassing the mediation of science journalists. The fluidity of online interactions provides for a more integrated, informed and efficient republic of choice makers compared to traditional forms of public consultation. This represents a unique opportunity for the online citizen to emerge as a scientific citizen or citizen scientist, beyond the control of dialogue sponsors and regulators who may wish to inhibit, contain or direct public debate. However, Watermeyer recognises that online public dialogue in science is not without risk or drawback. User-generated scientific information is particularly susceptible to inconsistency or factual error caused by unscientific, subjective interpretations, but also to manipulation by online authors seeking to align scientific 'truths' or re-imagine 'facts' in line with their particular agenda or interests. The dialogue, or as Watermeyer calls it, the 'polylogue', may be inchoate and fragmentary and the multitude of perspectives may still coalesce around the same concerns as arise from face-to-face dialogue. Indeed, the sheer abundance and heterogeneity of digital publics may actually inhibit public debate and decision making. The onus is on participants to make fair and credible assessments, particularly where public knowledge of new science is limited. The question remains of how to mobilise 'uninvited' dialogue in ways that might bear pressure on organisational and governing powers. The public are becoming increasingly adept at navigating their way online and, for the current younger generation, to 'exist offline' is for the majority fantastical and absurd. However, less technologically savvy older generations might be excluded from such polylogues. For Watermeyer, the important questions are not about our right to know or not to know in the digital age, but how we make sense of what we know, what we need to know and what we do not need to know.

In the final chapter Michiel Korthals discusses the food we eat. Everyone needs to eat, but in modern societies there is a gap between food production and food consumption, resulting in people becoming both alienated from food and subordinated to corporate production of food. Consumers lose their trust in the food sector. In the food sector, the right to know and to be informed about the aspects of food one is interested in has prominence over the right not to know. Those who do not wish to know about their foodstuffs can simply ignore the information. Korthals discusses consumer rights and the ethical considerations that underpin them, and the pros and cons of labelling. The right to know has its mirror in the duty to inform, and here companies, governments and civil societies play a role. However, the food sector is an incredibly complex bowl of spaghetti, full of black holes, sometimes due to the strategies of producers to make information inaccessible and to defend their interests. It is a 'bizarre bazaar'. Perhaps the gap between consumers and food production can be bridged by labelling and certification schemes, but these are in many cases not sufficient to structure the food sector into a fair sector that acts responsively to consumers' and citizens' interests. Market-driven and third-party certifiers (labelling organisations) are often not living up to their promises. The right to be informed can also be given shape by consumers and their organisations in developing knowledge and information schemes (as a kind of crowd communication system) by using modern mass media such as apps. Moreover, in participating in agricultural processes, for example in Community Supported Agriculture, consumers can organise their own knowledge about what they think is ethically legitimate to eat.

## References

Chadwick, Ruth, Levitt, Mairi and Shickle, Darren (eds.) 1997. *The Right to Know and the Right Not to Know*. Aldershot: Avebury.

Clarke, Angus 1994. 'The genetic testing of children. Report of a Working Party of the Clinical Genetics Society (UK)', *Journal of Medical Genetics* 31(10): 785–97.

Nuffield Council on Bioethics 1993. *Genetic Screening: Ethical issues.* Nuffield Council on Bioethics: London.

Royal College of Physicians 1991. *Ethical Issues in Clinical Genetics.* London: Royal College of Physicians.

Shickle, Darren and Harvey, Ian 1993. '"Inside-out", back-to-front: a model for clinical population genetic screening', *Journal of Medical Genetics* 30: 580–2.

Wertz, Dorothy and Fletcher, John 1991. 'Privacy and disclosure in medical genetics examined in an ethics of care', *Bioethics* 5(3): 212–32.

*Part I*

Philosophical and legal issues

# 1    The right to know and the right not to know: the emerging debate

*Ruth Chadwick, Mairi Levitt and Darren Shickle*

In this chapter we aim to outline some of the ways in which the debate over the right to know and the right not to know has moved on since this book was first published in 1997. The issues in genetics and genomics have moved even further out of the clinic, notably in the context of population-wide genomics research and commercial testing.

At the time of the first edition of this volume, 'the right to know/not to know' was a prominent framing of issues in genetics. Today, this framing is less overt, though still relevant. Other rights are increasingly discussed, such as the right to be forgotten, discussed here in Chapter 5. But beyond framings using rights language, debates in genetics, genomics and other areas are frequently discussed in relation to privacy and data protection, concepts closely related to the right (not) to know.

Privacy is a wider concept than data protection and includes spatial and decisional privacy as well as privacy in relation to personal information, the aspect of privacy most clearly implicated in genetics. In the 1990s the EU Directive on Data Protection came into force, recognising that data needs to flow across the European Union (and beyond), but that safeguards are necessary. Since the Directive, privacy and data protection have come increasingly under challenge, and the challenges are of different types. There are, first, *intentional* encroachments upon privacy in a society concerned with surveillance and security, by governments and corporations. These are justified by a 'trade-off' argument: some privacy is surrendered in exchange for benefits. The second type of challenge occurs as a seemingly unavoidable *side effect* of new technologies: mobile phones reveal our location; and it is claimed, for example, that privacy can no longer be guaranteed in the light of technological developments (see, e.g., Lunshof *et al.* 2008). Thirdly there is *cultural change* in the form of what may be called the 'new exhibitionism', which we have seen in the explosion of social media.

In the light of such developments, at the time of writing there is under way discussion of the revision to the existing EU data protection rules (European Commission 2012).

Privacy in genomics has always been at the centre of the debate, but it is interesting to reflect why so many concerns have arisen here, while in other contexts it appears there has been more acceptance of possible threats to individual privacy in exchange for purported benefits – both convenience, in the case of mobile phones, and greater security, as in the case of surveillance and airport procedures. It is tempting to think that genomics has unjustifiably had a bad press, but this may be due to historical legacies related to public (dis)trust of science. On the other hand, maybe the appropriate norms of information flow *do* differ according to context, as Helen Nissenbaum has argued (Nissenbaum 2009); maybe there is variation between different publics, such as generational differences in how much information we are willing to reveal about ourselves and in what arena. Facebook, for example, appears to be challenging old conceptions of 'friendship', but how people relate to their genetic information still gives rise to controversy.

It may be the case that there is a need to think differently about privacy in today's world and this is not necessarily a matter of surprise or regret. Values change and thinking about ethics develops, just as scientific paradigms shift. What is needed is a real sense of what interests (of different kinds) are at stake, and how the appropriate balances can be struck. In examining developments relevant to these issues since 1997 we will consider changes in **context**, emerging **issues** and finally trends in **ethical approaches**.

### Changes in context

The first contextual change since 1997 that must be mentioned is the completion of the mapping and sequencing of the human genome, which paved the way for developments such as whole genome sequencing. This is important for the right to know and the right not to know in at least two ways. First, attention has turned to the significance of the information that has been produced, and has also returned to issues of genetic determinism. The discovery that humans have far fewer genes than had previously been supposed led initially to the suggestion that genetic determinism had been proved false, in so far as the genes themselves could not explain the complexity of human beings. Since then, however, determinism has arguably reappeared in a new guise. In the immediate aftermath of the Human Genome Project, it was claimed that genetic determinism was dead. This was due to the discovery that there were far fewer genes in the human genome than had been expected, around 23,000 rather than 100,000. Surely, such a small number of genes could not account for the complexity of the beings that we are. If there is determinism, it must lie elsewhere than in the genes *per se*.

Of course, there had been critical discussions of genetic determinism that predated this discovery. There had been debate about the difference between the ways in which a gene can *influence* rather than *determine*. Even in the case of a single gene disorder, there is variation in penetrance and severity. It is also important to remember that these discussions of determinism relate to the nuclear genome: disorders in the mitochondrial genome, inherited down the female line, produce very variable results. Much more is now understood about such things as copy number variation and epigenetics (Chadwick and O'Connor 2013). With the advent of whole genome sequencing, however, genetic determinism is heavily implicated in an imagined future in which it is possible to predict people's future talents and behavioural traits and to use these predictions to inform not only biomedical but also training and educational needs.

Is this re-emerging genetic determinism determinism *in the same sense* as the genetic determinism that was rejected at the turn of the century? We think not. What was being rejected in that debate was primarily based on the outdated 'gene for x' model. The genetic determinism that is emerging now is the idea that the *genome* in all its complexity is deterministic, taking into account the volume of data that can be made available on the precise sequence in an individual's genome, including all the myriad ways in which he or she differs from other individuals.

So we need to be clear about the *form* that genetic determinism is now taking, in addition to the ethical implications of its employment. It is still counteracted by other considerations, including arguments about gene–environment interaction. Such interaction, however, has to take into account not only the environment external to the body, which can be both physical and social, but also the environment internal to the body.

A contextual factor which has arguably affected the debate since 1997 as much as any other has been the development of large-scale population genetic research involving the establishment of biobanks. Alongside the much-discussed national initiatives in Iceland, Estonia and the United Kingdom, there has been increasing recognition of the scale of biobanking of different kinds, including disease-specific collections, regional collections and international initiatives.

Biobanking has brought with it new challenges to data protection and privacy, particularly in an era of data sharing and cross-border flow of samples and data. In this situation there are two broad types of response, not mutually exclusive. The first is to seek enhanced forms of data protection, at both a technological and regulatory level. The other is to re-examine what our thinking about privacy is and should be. If re-identification is always possible, at least in principle (Lunshof *et al.* 2008; Gymrek *et al.* 2013), it is misleading to ask people to consent to donate samples in exchange for a promise of privacy: privacy is no more.

A less strong view is that privacy *as we knew it* is no more. Mireille Hildebrandt has argued, for example, that privacy regarded as sovereignty over one's data is not tenable, and this is particularly the case when the issues concern how conclusions may be drawn about an individual through data mining and profiling (Hildebrandt 2008). Group privacy has become a real issue alongside individual privacy, as is shown in Chapter 8 in this volume. These developments have at the very least added a new dimension to the right to know and the right not to know discussion. The ongoing tension between the interests of the individual and the collective has been played out afresh in relation to biobanks, with the motivations for participation, for example.

Beyond the genome, there have been important social and political developments affecting the issues. In the post 9/11 world, concerns about security have had a significant impact upon debates about privacy. The extent to which there can and should be a trade-off between privacy and other values such as security is a live issue not only in genomics but also in relation to such developments as biometric identification technologies. Developments in relation to both WikiLeaks and the Edward Snowden affair have also given rise to increased concerns about personal data.

Further, the extent to which debates about science have become public debates has increased over the last ten years, with the increasing recognition that public engagement should move upstream. This phenomenon is related to the right to know/not to know debate in so far as the public or different publics might claim a right to know what options are on the table at a much earlier stage than the downstream offer of a test. Rather, it might be argued that their awareness of, and input to, the discussion of the relevant issues should take place at the stage when decisions are being taken about research that will ultimately lead to the offer of particular tests. The so-called 'democratisation of science' issues become increasingly complicated in the light of commercial offers of testing direct to consumers that may reveal sensitive health-related information, bypassing the traditional safeguards of the biomedical context.

Perhaps most strikingly, the explosion in social media, the implications of which are discussed in Chapter 12, has brought with it extensive revelation of personal information in exchange for perceived benefits of social inclusion and various services, which contrasts starkly with the fears in the genomics context of disclosure leading to potential *exclusion* and *loss* of services such as insurance. Perhaps this difference can be traced at least in part to the fact that in biomedicine privacy comes with a lot of 'baggage' related to disclosure issues, which may need to be cast overboard in some contemporary situations.

### Emerging issues

Despite all these changes in context, it would be inaccurate to say that there has been a wholesale change in the issues now being confronted regarding the right to know and the right not to know: some of the dilemmas remain in place, particularly in the context of the clinic, as indicated above. It is important to recognise, however, the areas in which new issues have emerged.

#### Biobanks and the right to know

In relation to population genomic research involving biobanks, one of the most prominent emerging issues has been the extent to which individuals have the right to feedback regarding results from research on their samples. There are at least two distinct questions: the actual policies of biobank initiatives, on the one hand, and the principles involved, on the other. Biobanks in different social contexts have taken different stances on this, so the discussion here will be limited to the kinds of argument appealed to. Considerations in favour of the view that individuals either do not or should not be regarded as having such a right include, first, that the information is likely to be of little value to the individual. Raw research data may not provide information of any real benefit: it may be unclear what the significance is. From an ethical point of view, an argument against a right also follows from the informed consent involved – if individuals have agreed to participate knowing that there is to be no feedback, then they do not have a right to it – there is no legitimate expectation of a contractual or quasi-contractual sort. Based on considerations of this sort, there is a view that information provided about research on samples provided to biobanks should be limited to general research results, and not to specific information.

On the other hand, whatever the facts of the informed consent, there is a moral argument for a residual obligation to offer feedback of the following sort. If A has information which could be potentially life-saving to, or even significantly relevant to the future health of, person B, then A has a moral obligation to offer that information. While this could be argued against by appealing, for example, to a purported moral difference between harming B and not going out of one's way to help B, the context in which the information is sought and possessed arguably affects the issues. Where individuals have volunteered to participate for the public good and information is discovered that is material to their welfare, to withhold it could be construed not only as an omission but also as a harm. If they are displaying solidarity to their community, are there not moral considerations of solidarity for supporting them in return? There is a view, however, that participants should themselves take the initiative in accessing data through online platforms, for example (Nuffield Council on Bioethics 2011: xviii). In this volume, Kadri Simm takes the debate further, to look at the 'how and when' rather than just the 'if and whether'.

This discussion is linked to issues concerning how information gathered by biobanking initiatives is held and stored, including the specifics of anonymisation and coding. Much has been written about the very confusing terminology surrounding these questions (Knoppers and Saginur 2005). Simply, the main issues relevant to the right to know and the right not to know debate turn on the extent to which it is possible to link data to identifiable individuals. If it is not possible, then the previous issue concerning feedback would not even arise, for it would not be possible to trace the particular individual involved.

If samples are completely anonymised, and it is not possible to link the data to be gleaned from them to individuals, then their value in research terms is considerably reduced. But as has already been pointed out, where DNA is concerned there is no such thing as a complete loss of identifiability. DNA is, after all, despite ongoing debates about its usefulness in the forensic context (including the UK National DNA Database as discussed in Chapter 5), one of the primary identifiers, if not *the* primary one. Where there is less than complete anonymisation, however, another issue arises, beyond that of the individual's right or otherwise to feedback on their data, and this is the question of who else has the right to access the data. The questions of commercial companies' and other third parties' access to data take on a new twist in relation to the value of collections in so far as they may be regarded as resources for the common good.

What of the right *not* to know in relation to population research? This might appear to be a non-issue – arguably the burden of proof is upon those who would seek to know, or seek to disclose, rather than the other way round. However, this is not clear cut. When population genetic research produces results which characterise groups in particular ways, individuals, identifying themselves with a group in question, may be made aware of factors they would have preferred not to know about. Science may reveal 'inconvenient truths' (see Chapter 8).

*Identity*

These considerations raise the very large issue of the role of identity in the right to know and right not to know debates. It was suggested in the 1997 volume that there may be a right not to know genetic information on the grounds that it may constitute a threat to the individual's sense of identity (see, e.g., Husted, reprinted here, Chapter 2). Developments since 1997 have arguably added new ways in which, and increased the extent to which, this is the case.

Collective identity, for example, may be affected in a variety of ways. A prominent example has been the arguments put forward by disability rights organisations in opposition to the characterisation of particular conditions as disorders, combined with the seeking of measures to 'cure' them. There are at least two strands of thought to be disentangled here. The first is the concern that attempts to eliminate or cure genetic conditions will lead to a society that is less tolerant of disability. This is typically countered by an argument that the object of these attempts is not the people but the conditions (Chadwick 1999). At this point the second strand comes into play, which is that it is not possible to distinguish these two elements, because their identity is dependent upon their genetic condition. Beyond the relatively familiar debates surrounding genetic conditions of a health-affecting sort, however, other developments such as behavioural genomics and genetic ancestry tracing can have far-reaching implications for individuals' sense of self and have the potential to affect social and political rights in addition to their relevance to the right to know and not to know. Comparative genomics has further identity implications: for our self-identity *as a species* in relation to others. This may be perceived as threatening in some way, as is the prospect, for some, of hybrid embryos.

*Personal health*

One promised outcome of population genomic research has been personalised health advice, in the context of both medication and nutrition. Pharmacogenomics aims to identify the genetic factors involved in drug response and to facilitate the avoidance of adverse drug reactions. Nutrigenomics plays an analogous role in relation to food and food ingredients, enabling personalised nutritional advice for optimum health. In the case of pharmacogenomics the argument for a right to know is clear: it makes sense to say that if someone's genetic make-up is such that they have a higher than normal risk of responding adversely to a particular drug, then they have a right to know that they should not take it. It has also been argued that this kind of genetic information is less sensitive than other types of genetic information – the fact that someone should not take drug B has less potential to be damaging, if disclosed inappropriately, than information that they have a genetic predisposition to developing a late onset condition, for example. However, this argument depends on the assumption that the drug-related information is not linked or linkable to other more sensitive information.

Some of the worries about personalised medicine arise in connection with its implementation. Different scenarios are considered here in Barbara Prainsack's Chapter 7. The rise of companies offering direct-to-consumer tests has led to criticisms over how the results might be interpreted, conveyed and misused. There are also concerns about what tests are offered, and the time at which tests may be offered. Whereas it may be considered acceptable for an autonomous adult to decide to undertake genetic testing, on the grounds of a right to know, what of whole genome sequencing at birth, or even prenatally, for the purposes of personalised predictive medicine?

In principle, in the context of nutrigenomics, there is also an argument for a right to know diet-related genetic information in so far as it could be of benefit to health prospects. However, there is more scepticism about the value of the information in nutrigenomics (Müller and Kersten 2003). In the nutrition context, also, as Korthals points out in Chapter 13, the relevant rights issues range far beyond genomics, to include questions about the source, production and content of what we are eating. Nevertheless there are some issues analogous to pharmacogenomics. Whereas drugs are well-characterised substances acting on specific targets in the body, foodstuffs are far more complicated, and the difficulty of establishing reliable associations is therefore greater. Even in the pharmacogenomics context, however, there has been concern about achieving sufficient statistical power to ensure the reliability and replicability of association studies, and calls for oversight of these (Human Genome Organisation 2007).

Although the prospect of tailored dietary advice may seem attractive, there are also arguments for a right not to know here. While some may see the provision of such personal information as empowering, there may be concerns about political agendas behind it, such as putting responsibility for health squarely on the shoulders of individuals. This is an issue, for example, in the light of the purported obesity problem. Providing individuals with information, including genetic information, may be promoted in the name of choice, but there is a question as to whether what is at stake is the freedom to make *any* choice or whether there is a presupposition that there is a 'right' choice, leading to individuals being held responsible for wrong choices in particular.

*Whole genome sequencing*

The new generation of sequencing technologies massively increases the density of analyses that can be performed in a single run, as compared with conventional sequencing. The prospect of whole genome sequencing changes the whole scope of the right to know and right not to know debate. While there have always been issues concerning disclosure of incidental findings (e.g., non-paternity), the possibilities of whole genome sequencing open up the prospect of knowing everything in the genome. There is of course a question about the extent to which the volume of information will be meaningful, at least in the early stages of this development, but are there grounds for thinking that the privacy concerns are increased? If there is concern about access to the knowledge about one's genome, does the volume of information that may be accessed give rise to a parallel increase in the concerns about privacy? Even if to know someone's genome is not to know everything about a person, perceptions may suggest otherwise.

## Trends in ethical approaches

It is not necessary to subscribe to full-blown genetic exceptionalism to take the view that there have been developments in ethical thinking alongside the developments in genomics and in the social and political contexts in which these have taken place. The primacy of autonomy as an ethical principle has come increasingly under challenge, at least partly because it cannot do all the work in genomics. Different interpretations of autonomy (for example, relational autonomy) also continue to be discussed. In the 1997 volume Jørgen Husted identified two conceptions of autonomy relevant to the right (not) to know debate, a 'thin' one which was typically used to support the benefits of genetic information; and a 'thick' one which supported a right not to know (Husted 1997, reprinted in this volume as Chapter 2).

Since then solidarity has become more prominent as a principle in bio- and global ethics (Nuffield Council on Bioethics, 2011). In genomics it has been regularly appealed to through the first decade of the twenty-first century. A piece in *Science* (Knoppers and Chadwick 1994) identified the principles that were then informing genetic research, and a decade later the same authors claimed that there were 'emerging trends' in ethics, speaking of a turn towards equity, mutuality, reciprocity and solidarity (Knoppers and Chadwick 2005). It should be emphasised that these principles are not new, but draw on older traditions of ethical thought. The point is that it is *not possible* to rely on individual informed consent to do all the ethical work in the context of developments such as genetic databases. Ethical considerations relating to participation in research and sharing the benefits require alternative frameworks (see, e.g., Chadwick and Berg 2001). Despite evidence of a 'communitarian turn' in this context (Chadwick 2011), there is a view that just as autonomy cannot do all the work in all circumstances, neither can solidarity (see Chapters 6 and 7 by Levitt and Prainsack). Ethics is still developing in this area, alongside the science.

The trend towards rethinking the concept of privacy has already been mentioned and the need to be clear about what is involved is discussed in this volume by Laurie. In the 1997 volume Tony McGleenan asked if there should be a genetic privacy law. It is now clearer than ever that if we could rely on public institutions to adhere completely to regulations on data protection, there is still a need to look at the issues in different ways. In the genomics context, there has been a suggestion that emphasis on privacy should be replaced by the concept of open consent (Lunshof et al. 2008). The concept of open consent is used in the context of the Personal Genome Project, which aims to build a framework for the development and evaluation of personal genome technologies. Towards this end, open consent implies that research participants accept that their data may be included in an open-access database with no guarantees of privacy and confidentiality. At the time of writing, the trend, however, at the level of discussion of the draft European Regulation on Data Protection, appears to be towards a more conservative view (European Commission 2012).

### Prospects for the future

So how is the debate on the right to know and the right not to know likely to develop? The pace of development of the technologies is very fast: ethical thinking is faced with the move towards greater 'personalisation', on the one hand, and more global developments on the other, in relation both to the facilitating of international biobanks (requiring consideration of the harmonisation of standards and ethics) and to claims for sharing the benefits that genomics has to offer on a global scale. The discussion of rights to know and not to know has to be continually renegotiated in the light of these interests in tension.

### References

Chadwick, Ruth 1999. 'Gene therapy and personal identity', in Gerhold K. Becker (ed.) *The Moral Status of Persons: Perspectives on bioethics*. Amsterdam: Rodopi, pp. 183–94.

Chadwick, Ruth 2011. 'The communitarian turn: myth or reality?', *Cambridge Quarterly of Healthcare Ethics* 20(4): 546–53.

Chadwick, Ruth and Berg, Kåre 2001. 'Solidarity and equity: new ethical frameworks for genetic databases', *Nature Reviews Genetics* 2: 318–21.

Chadwick, Ruth and O'Connor, Alan 2013. 'Epigenetics and personalized medicine: prospects and ethical issues', *Personalized Medicine* 10(5): 463–71.

European Commission 2012. Proposal for the EU General Data Protection Regulation. Available at: http://ec.europa.eu/justice/data-protection/document/review2012/com_2012_11_en.pdf (accessed 8 July 2013).

Gymrek, M., McGuire, A. L., Golan, D., Halperin, E. and Erlich, Y. 2013. 'Identifying personal genomes by surname inference', *Science* 339(6117): 321–4.

Hildebrandt, Mireille 2008. 'Defining profiling: a new type of knowledge?' in M. Hildebrandt and S. Gutwirth (eds.) *Profiling the European Citizen: Cross-disciplinary perspectives.* Dordrecht: Springer, pp. 17–45.

Human Genome Organisation 2007. *Statement on Pharmacogenomics, Solidarity and Equity.*

Husted, Jørgen 1997. 'Autonomy and a right not to know', in Ruth Chadwick, Mairi Levitt and Darren Shickle (eds.) *The Right to Know and the Right Not to Know.* Aldershot: Avebury, pp. 55–68.

Knoppers, Bartha and Chadwick, Ruth 1994. 'The human genome project: under the international ethical microscope', *Science* 265: 2035–2036.

Knoppers, Bartha and Chadwick, Ruth 2005. 'Human genetic research: emerging trends in ethics', *Nature Reviews Genetics* 6: 75–79.

Knoppers, Bartha M. and Saginur, M. 2005. 'The Babel of genetic data terminology', *Nature Biotechnology* 23(8): 925–7.

Lunshof, Jeantine, Chadwick, Ruth, Vorhaus, Daniel B. and Church, George M. 2008. 'From genetic privacy to open consent', *Nature Reviews Genetics* 9: 406–11.

McGleenan, Tony 1997. 'Should there be a genetic privacy law?' in Chadwick *et al.* (eds.), pp. 43–54.

Müller, M. and Kersten, S. 2003. 'Nutrigenomics, goals and strategies', *Nature Reviews Genetics* 4: 315–22.

Nissenbaum, Helen 2009. *Privacy in Context: Technology, policy, and the integrity of social life.* Stanford University Press.

Nuffield Council on Bioethics 2011. *Solidarity: Reflections on an emerging concept in Bioethics.* London.

## 2    Autonomy and a right not to know

*Jørgen Husted*

### A problem out of a problem

Genetics and diseases of genetic origin inescapably involve families. Thus genetic information obtained by testing one person may contain information of the same kind on one or more other persons. These other persons are, so to speak, being tested indirectly by the original test. Now, the justification for testing the first person is the recognition that this person has an interest in knowing the relevant information. The knowledge may be sought to gain a better background for reproductive decisions or for undertaking measures preventive of future health problems caused by genetic disease or susceptibility. This leads to the conclusion that each of the other persons concerned has the same interest in knowing the information about herself or himself.

But suppose the person who has undergone the test does not want the findings to be passed on to the other family members? In its report on the ethical issues of genetic screening the Nuffield Council on Bioethics offers the following example:

A man diagnosed with a mild form of adrenoleukodystrophy (ALD), an X-linked condition that can be carried by healthy females, did not wish his diagnosis or the genetic implications to be discussed with his family. Seven years later, his niece gave birth to two successive boys who have a more severe form of ALD. The illness only came to light in them when the elder boy started to display symptoms. The mother's sister, the man's other niece, has also given birth to a son subsequently diagnosed with ALD. Both families are bitterly resentful that the medical services did not warn them of their genetic risk.

(Nuffield Council on Bioethics 1993, p. 42)

In this kind of situation an ethical dilemma arises between the right of the individual to personal privacy on the one hand and the interest of family members to be made fully aware of available information which would play a part in making important life decisions on the other. More directly it presents itself to the doctor as a conflict between the duty of confidentiality owed to the patient and the regard for the third parties who are likely to be harmed or at least forego a major benefit due to non-disclosure. The doctor's duty of confidentiality is strongly supported by two considerations: the individual's right to privacy and the upholding of trust and confidence in the doctor/patient relationship generally. However, as the Nuffield Council on Bioethics (1993) and also Ruth Macklin (1992) point out, this duty is not absolute. In very special circumstances it may be overruled in the public interest or for preventing injury or severe health damage to other individuals. Both argue that the same kind of exceptional overruling may apply to the genetic context as well. No general rule can be given and the doctor has to perform a very delicate exercise in balancing the risks and harms of non-disclosure against those of disclosure. Ruth Macklin suggests that there are cases, albeit few, in which an actual duty to disclose genetic information emerges (1992, p. 163). The Nuffield Report concludes that the third party's interest is to be considered strong enough to support 'a legitimate right to know' and it even discusses, though finally rejecting it primarily out of pragmatic reasons, whether there should be a legally enforceable duty of disclosure to family members placed on people who have been tested and on their medical service (Nuffield Council on Bioethics 1993, p. 53).

Now, within this ethical problem another one seems to be lurking in the background. If the person who has been tested or that person's doctor, perhaps overruling the duty of confidentiality, approaches the unsuspecting family member with the finding, this latter person is quite defenceless. As it seems, the alleged right to know does not comprise a right not to know. But by the very approach the 'cat has been let out of the bag'. Either this person comes to know the new personal information or, at least, comes to know that there is something to know that is considered quite urgent for her or him to know. A wholly new situation has been created: the irreversible loss of genetic informational innocence is a *fait accompli*.

### Paternalism revived?

A first reaction to this problem could be to acknowledge that there is a significant difference in status between the two persons involved. Whereas the first person has given informed consent both to being tested and to being informed of the findings, the latter person definitely has not. However, the requirement of obtaining informed consent is meant to ensure voluntariness and adequate understanding – that is, to rule out any form of compulsion, deceit, misinformation and manipulation – as a necessary condition for performing a medical intervention on a person.

This requirement clearly applied to the first person, this being a case of a person who has to decide whether to undergo a medical intervention or not. In the case of the unwitting family member there is no medical intervention and the relative or the doctor is only offering to impart some already available information that the person has a clear interest in knowing.

If one is to take the principle of informed consent seriously this reaction will not do. The principle grew out of the critique of medical paternalism according to which the doctor is justified to act, with or without consent, to promote what is perceived from the medical point of view as the patient's best interest. As the doctor is taken to be in the best position to know what is best for the individual patient the so-called therapeutical privilege gives the doctor the right of usurping the decision making, even in relation to fully competent adult persons. One major point against medical paternalism was simply that since a person can have different and competing interests, what is in this person's overall best interest might very well be different from what is perceived as such from the narrow medical point of view. In itself this point strongly supports the requirement of informed consent. Now, the justification for performing the genetic test on the first family member was not that this person has an interest in knowing the relevant information (the interest shared with the family member). The justification was that this person after mature and well-informed consideration decided to give priority to this interest. However, the very fact that the other family member has the same interest in no way justifies the assumption that she or he would reach the same decision. Thus the unsolicited disclosure, whether by the relative following the doctor's strong suggestion or by the doctor acting independently, seems to be a clear-cut case of strong medical paternalism. Acting solely from the medical point of view, the decision 'To know or not to know?' is taken out of the hands of the unsuspecting individual, for her or his own good, of course.

A more sophisticated response grants the above but seeks to put the matter in the right light by linking informed consent directly to the concept of (personal) autonomy. According to this the very point of insisting on the principle of informed consent in the medical context is to uphold in this area a general right to autonomy, that is, a right for persons to make important decisions defining their own lives for themselves. What is wrong with medical paternalism is not so much the assumption that the doctor knows best as the usurpation of decision making. Ethics demands fundamentally that adults of normal competence be respected as responsible decision makers in matters pertaining to themselves. The important thing is not that the best decision is found, but that the person concerned reaches a decision that she or he considers the best. Denying people this right to autonomy, even out of the most benevolent motives, is denying them respect for their dignity as persons, as beings who are able to think and choose for themselves. Now, in the case of unsolicited disclosure, the decision to know or not to know is of course being taken out of the hands of the person concerned. This case is, however, significantly different from the much-criticised cases of paternalism where the doctor decides on irreversible interventions without consulting the patient about her or his view on the alternatives. This constitutes a clear reduction of autonomy, a closing of options, and is being done in the name of values other than autonomy, such as welfare, health or survival. In the case of unsolicited disclosure, on the other hand, what initially seems to be a denial of autonomy is just the opposite: it is done in the name of autonomy and the result is an enhancement of autonomy, an opening of options. As the important information has become available and is there to be made use of or not, is it not quite clear that a respect for persons as decision makers demands that they be given and not denied this information? Maybe some persons will resent the disclosure, at least as a first reaction, and will come to worry and agonise about new challenges and fears. But all this is part and parcel of being a responsible decision maker. Thus the challenge of paternalism can be evaded. Unsolicited disclosure violates autonomy in a formal sense, but respects and enhances it in a substantial sense – the very one that makes the formal one so important. In her discussion of a duty to disclose Ruth Macklin puts this way of thinking quite clearly:

If such information (viz. genetic information that can substantially affect a patient's relatives) is disclosed, it can enable them to make reproductive decisions and other life plans in accordance with the newly revealed information. Without adequate information, people cannot make informed choices and decisions related to their own health and well-being.

(Macklin 1992, p. 163)

Put this way, unsolicited disclosure to relatives seems quite unproblematic from an ethical point of view.

The Nuffield Report dwells on several psychological problems, arising especially where some family members do not wish to be presented with the information, and notes 'this would become a much more serious problem if widespread screening were introduced for X-linked or autosomal dominant diseases' (Nuffield Council on Bioethics 1993, p. 49).

In view of this latter remark and the astonishing speed of the development of genetic research it is important to investigate further the above reasoning that tends to give unsolicited disclosure to unwitting relatives a firmly established and ethically unproblematic place in clinical practice.

Since the concept of autonomy is pivotal in justifying the reasoning, this is where we will proceed next.

## Autonomy: the thin conception

Although there is only one concept of autonomy there are, when it comes to explaining it, several conceptions of autonomy. For the purpose at hand the following two will suffice. Both agree that autonomy is the running of one's own life according to one's own lights: people are said to be autonomous to the extent to which they are able to fashion their own lives, and to some extent their own destiny, by the exercise of their own faculties in successive choices during their lives. The first – thin – conception of autonomy aims to explain the autonomous person and the autonomous life by way of explaining the kind of choice characteristically made by the former and defining the latter, that is, the autonomous individual choice. The idea is that an agent's decision will be maximally autonomous where:

1  there are no apparent defects in the individual's ability to control either his or her desires or actions or both;
2  there are no apparent defects in reasoning, or no defects in reasoning which would bear on the validity of the conclusions upon which the agent's decisions are based;
3  there are no apparent defects in the information available to the agent and which are germane to the decision at hand (Harris 1985, p. 201).

The usual background for this thin account of autonomy is a preference or desire satisfaction theory of the good for persons. According to this, what is good for persons is for them to have their desires or preferences satisfied to the maximum extent possible over their lifetimes. So on the one hand there is the person's wishes or preferences. Some of these are short-term, others are long-term wishes, perhaps even a life plan. Among the latter could be wishes for the following: a happy family life, good health, beauty, wealth, power, social prestige, deep involvements with other people, personal independence, self-realisation, to see the world, to lead a quiet and pleasant life, enjoying oneself as much as possible, strong and varied excitements, intellectual achievement, a successful career in a certain walk of life, and social and spiritual security. Given his or her long-term preferences the person successively develops short-term preferences, the satisfaction of which is considered conducive to the satisfaction of the long-term ones, such as having at least three healthy children, taking up a career in dentistry, keeping fit, travelling and so on. The person's wishes or preferences are something given about him or her: the person finds himself or herself as a person with this kind of inclination. They are the person's own wishes, part of the individual's set-up. Also, they can only be criticised rationally in so far as they can be shown to be either clearly unrealistic or based on false beliefs. On the other hand there is the person's decisions and actions. Their whole point is the instrumental one of contributing to the person's good by serving the satisfaction of his or her short-term and long-term preferences. Thus they can be criticised rationally as more or less well informed, well considered, realistic or well suited to achieve various goals. An important consideration here is of course whether they are autonomous in the above sense.

This approach offers a very clear justification of the principle of informed consent in health care, at least as soon as it is recognised that the goal is the promotion of the individual's good, not just his or her health. Thus R. M. Hare writes:

on the whole people are the best judges of what will be best for them in the future. They are likely to predict more correctly than any doctor what will be best for *themselves*. For people's ideas of what is a good life vary enormously, and doctors are, these days, seldom in a position to know a patient well enough to predict them. The doctor can usually predict better than the patient what the consequences of a particular treatment will be; but he is not expert on how the patient will like these consequences. Therefore, in deciding on a treatment, the doctor should be guided by the patient's idea of the best life, and not impose his own.

(Hare 1994, p. 154)

Since people generally are the best judges of their own good their autonomous decisions relating to that matter should be respected. A doctor is always in the wrong if he or she goes against a person's autonomous decision of this kind. First, the doctor actually wrongs this person by acting against the person's good and, second, the doctor jeopardises the whole relationship between doctors and the public, as much harm is likely to ensue both for the profession as a whole and for individual patients, if autonomy comes to be disregarded.

Now, seen from this ethical perspective, the above, preliminary characterisation of unsolicited disclosure as ethically quite unproblematic can be endorsed. First of all, in such cases there is clearly no question of doing the wrong thing, that is, going against a person's autonomous decision relating to his or her own good. Also, the information revealed is information of great importance for the individual's ability to make decisions and consider short-term preferences with a view to achieving the maximal satisfaction of long-term preferences. Thus, revealing the information is, very literally, for the person's own good.

Though everything now seems all well and good there remains a problem and this points towards the second – thick – conception of autonomy. A person may decide to undergo a genetic test, the result of which is very likely to be devastating by revealing an incurable condition that will mean within a few years the end of his or her life and all his or her aspirations. His or her reason for doing this is to provide vital information for a number of his or her close relatives. As he or she is the first to admit, it is definitely not done for his or her own good in the above sense. On the contrary, the person decides against his or her own good, sacrificing it out of a deeply felt moral obligation overruling all of his or her personal preferences. The problem now is that, according to the principle of informed consent, his or her decision should be respected even though, by his or her own admission, it is not an autonomous decision of the kind that was crucially appealed to in the above justification for this principle, that is, an autonomous decision in the area where the person concerned is the best judge – pertaining to promoting his or her own good. Going against a person's decision of that kind would be wrong although it would not be an instance of going against a person's autonomous choice relating to his or her own good. There are many well-known cases of this kind, such as people who decide to forego necessary medical treatment either because they believe other people need it more or because they want the expenses avoided in order to save the money for the benefit of a child's education, for example. What they show is that the justification of the principle of informed consent is not fully explained by reference to the claim that people are the best judges of their own good. This claim has to be supplemented by independent considerations.[1]

### Autonomy: the thick conception

In the following quotation the gist of this way of thinking is eloquently expressed by Sir Isaiah Berlin:

I wish my life and decision to depend on myself, not on external forces of whatever kind. I wish to be the instrument of my own, not of other men's acts of will. I wish to be a subject, not an object; to be moved by reasons, by conscious purposes, which are my own, not by causes which affect me, as it were, from outside. I wish to be somebody, not anybody; a doer – deciding not being decided for, self-directed and not acted upon by external nature or by other men... I wish, above all, to be conscious of myself as a thinking, willing, active being, bearing responsibility for his choices and able to explain them by reference to his own ideas and purposes.

(Berlin 1969, p. 123)

---

[1] cf. R. Dworkin's discussion of this point (Dworkin 1993, chapter 8).

The ideal of the person outlined here is the ideal of personal autonomy as self-determination, or self-definition.[2] It is readily contrasted with the preference satisfaction theory of the good for persons. First, a person's decisions and actions are not seen as of primarily an instrumental function and value, as the means for achieving the satisfaction of already given preferences. Instead human well-being is thought of under the category of activity, as the successful pursuit of freely chosen goals, the thought being that what persons are is, in significant respects, what they become through successive choices and actions during their lives – their lives are a continuous process of self-creation. What makes a life *ours* is that it is fashioned by our choices, is selected from alternatives by a human being taking his or her life seriously and wanting to be, and be recognised by others as, the kind of person who makes decisions and accepts responsibility for them.

Also, a person's preferences or goals are not to be considered as given and outside the reach of critical evaluation. What makes self-determination possible is the unique capacity of the human person for reflective self-evaluation, for considering what they want their motivation to be, for forming higher-order wants and preferences defining what they for themselves find it *worth being* and *worth doing* in life and trying, sometimes successfully, sometimes not, to change their given preferences and inclinations in light of what they have come to care about, their higher-order goals and values. By exercising this capacity, people determine their lives and themselves, create meaning and coherence and take responsibility for their lives and character.

It is here of great importance to distinguish between autonomy as an achievement, the autonomous life created by the person, and autonomy as a capacity. To lead an autonomous life a person needs to have certain conditions fulfilled. These are the various mental and linguistic abilities needed to exercise self-evaluation and self-control, independence in the sense of absence of external interference with decision processes and with actions, and a reasonable range of valuable options in the important self-defining situations throughout the various periods of life. Personal autonomy in the primary sense is first here, the idea of an autonomous life. Also what primarily has value is the autonomous life, the value of autonomy in the capacity sense being only contributional to this, not of value independently of its use. Autonomous decisions are, ideally, decisions that fit into an autonomous life, a life freely chosen. And as Joseph Raz puts it:

---

[2] For further discussions of autonomy as self-determination cf. R. Dworkin (1993, chapter 8), G. Dworkin (1988), Raz (1986, chapter 14), and Lindley (1986).

It is a life which is here primarily judged as autonomous or not, and it is so judged by its history ... the autonomous life is discerned not by what there is in it but by how it came to be. It is discerned, if you like, by what it might have been and by why it is not other than it is.

(Raz 1986, p. 371)

In this connection Raz argues very convincingly that autonomy and the kind of autonomous choosing that is constitutive of self-determination requires not only a free choice but a choice between valuable or good options. In a sense the choice between good and evil is no choice at all. Someone with the choice between becoming an electrician and having to murder someone else is not choosing autonomously if he or she chooses to become an electrician. His or her choice is forced: if he or she wants to be moral, he or she has no choice, being forced to fight for 'moral survival':

Autonomy requires a choice of goods. A choice between good and evil is not good enough. Remember that it is personal, not moral autonomy we are concerned with. No doubt is cast on the fact that the person in the example is a moral and fully responsible person. So are the inmates of concentration camps. But they do not have personal autonomy.

(Raz 1986, p. 379)

Now the general point of the right to autonomy can be explained in a new and, it seems, more satisfactory way. Respecting an individual right to autonomy is an important part of making self-creation possible. The point of the right is to protect and encourage the capacity to take responsibility for one's life and express one's personality, commitments, convictions and vision of the good in the life one leads. And when people insist on their right to autonomy this is often done in the name of self-determination. They value being able to decide for themselves because they value being, and being recognised by others as, the kind of person who is capable of determining and taking responsibility for his or her destiny. To them the ideal of self-determination offers an attractive vision of what human beings can be and they hold this ideal for noninstrumental reasons. Being recognised as a person capable of choosing and taking responsibility for her or his choices, and of course actually making choices of this kind, has intrinsic value quite apart from the consequences and satisfactions flowing from it.

The principle of informed consent can now be seen as an application to the medical context of the right to autonomy explained in this way (Brock 1993, chapter 1). What is wrong about medical paternalism is not primarily or solely that the doctor by deciding for the patient may be wrong, or more likely to be wrong than the patient, in the estimation of the patient's good. What is wrong is the usurpation of decision making as such. Many of the decisions to be made in clinical practice, for example between alternative forms of treatment or between treatment and non-treatment, are neither simple technical decisions nor decisions of the relatively simple kind where the task is to find the best solution given one or more rather clear personal preferences. Often the very idea of determining what is best is quite out of place. There is no question of who is the better judge of the patient's good, the doctor or the patient. A decision is called for, to choose this future or this other very different kind of future, to take responsibility for following this path ahead rather than another. Here the patient has to choose among values and the doctor's role is to help clarify the values, possibilities and consequences and, as far as possible, create valuable options suited to the individual's unique situation. In other words, many of the decisions to be made in clinical practice clearly belong to the self-defining kinds of decision that the right to autonomy is meant to protect and encourage.

From this new perspective the matter of the unsolicited disclosure of genetic findings to unsuspecting relatives begins to present itself as quite problematic. Taking the decision of whether to know or not to know out of the person's hands is a case of doing the wrong thing, being a clear case of usurpation of decision making. Also, the response that this violation of formal autonomy is justified by the enhancement of autonomy in a substantial sense is no good any more. The fact that the person receives new and relevant information does not in itself justify a claim of enhancement of autonomy. Before turning more directly to the latter point it is worth noting that if the response were uncontroversial it would be quite difficult to make sense of the existing ethical codes for genetic testing, stipulating the requirements of genetic counselling prior to testing, informed consent and non-directiveness in genetic counselling. The point of these requirements cannot just be to ensure voluntariness (no compulsion, manipulation, etc.) and a proper level of information. Their point must be to make choice possible, recognising that the choice to undergo a genetic test may have serious consequences of a kind that may make it fully understandable for a responsible and rational person to end up declining the offer of genetic testing. If the response appealing to the alleged enhancement of autonomy in the case of unsuspecting relatives were uncontroversial it would by the same token be quite uncontroversial for the doctor just to seek *assent* and not *informed consent* from the person invited to undergo a genetic test.

## A mixed blessing?

As already mentioned, in their discussion of the dilemma between the doctor's duty of confidentiality and the relative's interest in knowing, need to know, or even the right to know, both the Nuffield Council on Bioethics and Ruth Macklin cite cases to show that the duty of confidentiality is not absolute. The relevant cases stem from outside the field of applied human genetics, dealing with very dangerous mentally ill patients or patients with dangerous infectious diseases. Here the third party needs to be warned that somebody is out to kill or grievously harm her or him in one way or another. In the genetic context the kind of information to be received by the unwitting relative is of course of a totally different character. Here a person may learn things of the following kind about himself or herself:

1. that the person is a carrier so that having children by another carrier might result in children with serious health problems;
2. that the person is a carrier who risks having children with serious health problems and/or passing this very unwanted condition on to future generations;
3. that the person has a disease likely to be passed on to eventual offspring and future generations;
4. that the person has a presymptomatic condition that is likely to develop into a condition with serious symptoms unless the person undertakes certain draconian measures (radical change of lifestyle, frequent medical check-ups, preventive surgery, etc.);
5. that the person has a genetic predisposition that may develop into a serious disease unless precautions are taken – and may develop despite precautions;
6. that the person has a genetic susceptibility for a serious multifactorial disease that may be triggered by various environmental, psychological and other more or less unknown factors that the person should guard himself or herself against;
7. that the person suffers from a genetic disease, the manifest outbreak of which may be postponed and made less severe if the person changes his or her life in various drastic ways.

Now, in stark contrast to the cases involving a warning about highly dangerous persons and infectious diseases, information of this kind is likely to have a great impact not only on people's feelings but on their lives as a whole. Reactions such as the following are to be expected:

1. a decision not to marry and thus not to seek deep emotional involvement with members of the opposite sex;
2. a married couple's decision not to have children of their own;
3. trying to avoid any kind of dependants or deep involvement with other people;
4. a married couple's decision not to have any further children;

5.  terminating one's one and only pregnancy by selective abortion;
6.  giving up a career one has built the major part of one's life around;
7.  not marrying the person with whom one is deeply in love and trying to find a genetically more suitable partner for life and having a family;
8.  giving up the chance of an attractive career or education for which one clearly has the ability;
9.  giving up most of the things in one's life that one enjoys and finds worth doing;
10. trying to avoid all kinds of life challenges that are bound to tax one's resources and, if one is to succeed, put one under great and long-term strain.

Of course, there are alternatives to all such decisions of paramount importance to the individual's self-definition. The person can always choose to ignore the benevolent genetic warnings and just go ahead with the life she or he has embarked, or is embarking, on. The person may marry the one they love, have the children God gives, pursue the career and lifestyle of his or her choice with full vigour, become deeply entwined in other people's lives, accepting all the worthy challenges that life throws in the way, hoping, dreaming, planning and striving for the kind of life a human being is entitled at least to hope for. However, due to the disclosure of the genetic information on him or her, nothing will ever be the same again.

If and when the problems predicted by the genetic warning show themselves in that person's life they are now her or his responsibility in a different way than if they had shown up without any kind of genetic forewarning, namely as the normal hazards of life. If, for example, a pregnant woman belonging to a special risk group chooses not to accept the offer of foetal diagnosis and selective abortion, 'then the disabled child, to whom she eventually gives birth, is not only her responsibility being the child's mother: she is, in her own as well as in other people's eyes, responsible not only for the disabled child, but for having a child that has a disability. It could have been avoided. As she did not use the option created by the genetic service the new situation is her own choice' (Dworkin 1988, chapter 5). Much the same goes for all the other kinds of life problems met by persons who either choose to ignore the genetic warnings or find themselves unable to follow the instructions coming with the warning.

Thus it seems quite controversial whether the disclosure of genetic findings to unsuspecting persons is to be thought of as an enhancement of autonomy. In many cases of the kinds considered here it is rather misleading to think of them as cases where a person has a number of long-term preferences for herself or himself and then receives some useful, although maybe also worrying, information, with the help of which he or she is put in a situation better to steer a safe way towards preference satisfaction, avoiding some blind ends, uncharted cliffs and unhelpful projects. One could instead argue that in many such cases what were initially very valuable options for the person to choose (for one set of reasons) or not to choose (for a different set of reasons) were being closed due to the disclosure. Of course, the option still remained open for the person, but the reason why he or she did not choose it was not that another one was considered more valuable. The reason was that she or he could not take the responsibility for choosing it, i.e. choosing it being aware of the genetic warning, because it would be a morally wrong thing to do, starting a family, for example, knowing in advance what kind of suffering this is bound to create for other people. Where the person concerned was formerly pondering the various options for trying to make something worthwhile out of life, accepting the normal hazards of life, she or he may now be struggling for moral survival. And as a result of this the history of that person's life may very well not be the history of an autonomous life, a life whose contents, for a significant part, are freely chosen among different and morally valuable alternatives. The history of that person's life might rather come to resemble the life of the person who had to become an electrician in order not to have to murder someone else – a life of morally forced choices.

### Moralism as well as paternalism?

In their discussions of the duty to disclose and the right to know, both the Nuffield Council on Bioethics and Ruth Macklin give pride of place to the interest of family members to be made fully aware of available information which would play a part in making important life decisions. However, it now seems that there might also be quite another interest of family members: the interest of making important life decisions without the interference of genetic information on themselves and their prospects in life. Perhaps it could even be argued, appealing to the right of autonomy, that people have a right not to know, not to be told and not to be approached unwittingly by benevolent relatives or medical services.

Remarkably, the Nuffield Report as well as Ruth Macklin take for granted that the relative should be presented with the information that has become available. They argue that health professionals should seek to persuade individuals, if persuasion should be necessary, to allow the disclosure of relevant genetic information to other family members (Macklin 1992, p. 164; Nuffield Council on Bioethics 1993, p. 53). In its list of key ethical principles of genetic counselling, the Nuffield Report first insists that counselling at each stage of the process should be non-directive, as far as possible. It then goes on to stipulate as one of the key ethical principles that the assurance of confidentiality should be coupled with an emphasis on the responsibility of individuals with a positive (abnormal) result to inform partners and family members (Nuffield Council on Bioethics 1993, p. 37). The background of this principle is the following consideration:

> As a starting point, we adopt the view that a person acting responsibly would normally wish to communicate important genetic information to other family members who may have an interest in that information, and that a responsible person would normally wish to receive that information, particularly where it may have a bearing on decisions which he or she may be called upon to take in the future.
>
> (Nuffield Council on Bioethics 1993, p. 49)

It has already been argued that the conclusion to take the decision whether to know or not to know out of the unwitting family member's hands can be characterised as strongly paternalistic in relation to that person. It now seems difficult to avoid the impression that moralism is added to paternalism. According to the above, the health professional should tell the patient what her or his moral duty is in relation to a third person. If necessary, the health professional should enlighten the patient on what the concept of a responsible person amounts to in the context of applied human genetics. So, on the one hand the professional should avoid any kind of directiveness in counselling on medical options, possibilities or probabilities and, on the other hand, should be strongly directive in her or his counselling on general ethical matters and specific human relations in which the professional has no professional expertise at all.

### References

Berlin, J. (1969). *Two Concepts of Liberty*. Oxford: Clarendon Press.

Brock, D. (1993). *Life and Death*. Cambridge University Press.

Dworkin, G. (1988). *The Theory and Practice of Autonomy*. Cambridge University Press.

Dworkin, R. (1993). *Life's Dominion*. London: Harper Collins Publishers.

Hare, R. M. (1994). 'Utilitarianism and Deontological Principles', in Gillon, R. (ed.), *Principles of Health Care Ethics*. Chichester: John Wiley and Sons, pp. 149–59.

Harris, J. (1985). *The Value of Life*. London: Routledge.

Lindley, R. (1986). *Autonomy*. London: MacMillan.

Macklin, R. (1992). 'Privacy and Control of Genetic Information', in Annas, G. J. and Elias, S. (eds.), *Gene Mapping*. Oxford University Press.

Nuffield Council on Bioethics (1993). *Genetic Screening: Ethical issues*. London: Nuffield Council on Bioethics.

Raz, J. (1986). *The Morality of Freedom*. Oxford University Press.

# 3 Privacy and the right not to know: a plea for conceptual clarity

*Graeme Laurie*

## Introduction

The contribution of this chapter is two-fold. First, it argues for conceptual clarity in the debates about the right to know and the right not to know by suggesting that the most appropriate framing mechanism to conduct such discussions – and ultimately to give effect to any such rights – is through an understanding of the symbiotic relationship between notions of personal autonomy and privacy. Importantly, the claim is made that the right to know and the right not to know should not be seen simply as two sides of the same conceptual coin. Different interests are at stake with each putative 'right', and, albeit overlapping, we cannot give proper effect to either right without this deeper understanding.

The second contribution of this chapter is to ask whether and how *legal* effect might be given to the most contentious of the two claims, that is, the right not to know. It is argued that current legal paradigms, nationally and internationally, fail to recognise the conceptual distinctiveness of this kind of right-claim and, accordingly, there is little chance of effective legal remedy for unwarranted disclosure of personal information to a person about themselves. This, however, should not be lamented given the subtle considerations and judgments that are in play. Discretion and not duty should be the watchword when it comes to recognising any so-called 'right' not to know.

## What is at stake?

The triumph of autonomy in the medico-legal sphere is as intimidating as it is impressive.[1] Within the space of a few short decades, national, regional and international legal regimes have come to embrace the mantra of the crucial importance of self-determination as the principal defining feature of a plethora of patients' rights, and have accordingly positioned the concept as the central feature of the regulatory and legal

---

[1] See the healthy scepticism of Foster (2009).

landscapes governing patient/health-care professional relationships. It is easy to forget contributions such as that made by Sheila McLean in the 1980s in *A Patient's Right to Know* (McLean, 1989), which was entirely consumed with the challenge of achieving due recognition in law and professional practice of the importance of respect for patient autonomy and the pursuit of patient-centred and appropriate informed consent.

Since then, and despite no explicit mention of autonomy in the original text of the European Convention on Human Rights (ECHR 1950), the fundamentality of the concept in giving proper effect to the collection of human rights embodied in the instrument was recognised by the European Court of Human Rights in 2002 in *Pretty* v. *UK*,[2] in which it said of the ECHR that 'the notion of personal autonomy is an important principle underlying the interpretation of its guarantees'.[3] This recognition was largely afforded as an aspect of Article 8(1) ECHR: the right to respect for private and family life.

More recently still, the Council of Europe and other international bodies have extended autonomy-based claims with respect to the right to know also to the right not to know, as illustrated by these two examples:

> The Council of Europe Oviedo Convention on Human Rights and Biomedicine (1997), Article 10(2) states: 'Everyone is entitled to know any information collected about his health. However, the wishes of an individual *not* to be so informed shall be observed.' [emphasis added]
>
> The UNESCO Universal Declaration on the Human Genome and Human Rights (1997), Article 5c provides: 'The right of every individual to decide whether or *not* to be informed of the results of genetic examination and the resulting consequences should be respected.' [emphasis added]

These attempts to cast the right *not* to know in law do so in a way that suggests that this 'un-right' is unproblematically connected to the right to know, linked as an aspect of one's autonomy and the right to self-determination.

Similar attempts to cast the right not to know as a feature of autonomy appeared in the first edition of this book. For example, Husted (reprinted in this edition) supported it on the basis of a thick conception of autonomy as 'self-definition':

What makes a life ours is that it is fashioned by our choices, is selected from alternatives by a human being taking his or her life seriously and wanting to be,

---

[2] *Pretty* v. *UK* 2002 35 EHRR 1.
[3] *Ibid.*, para. 61.

and be recognised as by others as, the kind of person who makes decisions and accepts responsibility for them.

(Husted 2014, p. 31)

He concluded that: '[t]aking the decision of whether to know or not to know out of the person's hands is a case of doing the wrong thing, being a clear case of usurpation of decision making' (Husted 2014, p. 33).

I would like to take issue with this assumption that claims to know or not know are necessarily or even helpfully linked to our understandings about autonomy, be they thick or thin.

In Husted's analysis, it appears that the violation with which we should be concerned is the removal of (unfettered) choice. I suggest that this is questionable for three central reasons. First, this view tells nothing to the bearer of the dilemma about whether information should be revealed or not, save perhaps to support non-disclosure in all cases since only then can they remain unimplicated in the usurpation of decision making. But, of course, doing nothing is also an example of doing something, and so the quandary remains unresolved from the perspective of individual choice. This reveals a second problem with such an autonomy-based approach: it fails to distinguish between situations involving prior-expressed choices not to know and no choices at all. That is, while prior-expressed autonomy might well be undermined by later disrespectful disclosure of information in defiance of those earlier wishes, it is less clear that a 'usurpation of decision making' takes place when entirely unsolicited information is offered to someone who has never attempted to exercise their autonomy over the information in question, probably because they do not know that there is anything to know. This, in turn, leads to the third concern with this kind of approach. It is eloquently expressed by Wertz and Fletcher:

[T]here is no way…to exercise the choice of not knowing, because in the very process of asking 'Do you want to know whether you are at risk…?', the geneticist has already made the essence of the information known.

(Wertz and Fletcher 1991, p. 221)

The apparent unassailable link in contemporary bioethics and biolaw between autonomy and choice – and importantly *informed* choice – suggests that any attempt to facilitate autonomy, or to avoid usurping autonomous decision making, could result in violation of the 'right' not to know. Conversely, with the right to know the link between autonomy, information and choice is clear and promoted by giving effect to the right. Precisely the opposite is the case with the right not to know. By giving information, seeking consent and promoting autonomy the very essence or *state* of not knowing is compromised.

It is for these reasons that I have argued elsewhere (Laurie 1999; Laurie 2002) that the affront in these circumstances is the invasion of the private sphere of life of the individuals who are approached.[4] Put more simply, the interest with which we are concerned is a privacy interest, and more specifically it is a psychological privacy interest defined as being in a state of (psychological) separateness from others. I suggest that this conceptualisation of privacy reveals a core reason why the disclose/do not disclose debate involves a genuine dilemma. It explains why – if we appreciate the limits of autonomy and control in the discussion – we nonetheless still have reason to wonder if there is good reason not to disclose. That reason is related to an intuitive recognition of the presumptive inviolability of the private sphere around individuals. We recognise that disclosure will have consequences for individuals (and others), and the source of the dilemmas here – and where autonomy cannot assist – is that the individual who is the focus of our attention is the very person who is removed from having a say in the outcome. This conceptualisation allows us to recognise a core sense of self that can be fundamentally affected – potentially in an adverse way – by information disclosure.

This having been said, the dilemma is compounded by precisely the opposite likelihood, that is, that the person's situation and well-being might be improved through disclosure. But this consideration speaks more to the kinds of factor to take into account in weighing up the pros and cons of disclosure, such as whether there is an effective intervention for a medical condition, rather than the central concern of this chapter, which is to argue for recognition of the fundamental human interest at stake being one related to our privacy and not necessarily to our autonomy.

A final important consideration that also supports this analysis of privacy as a *state* of separateness is that this conceptualisation does not adopt a value-laden presumption that a state of separateness from others is necessarily a good thing. The very language of the 'right' to know or the 'right' not to know implies entitlement. These are normatively-heavy claims that might not stand up under close scrutiny. To suggest that human beings are in a state of (psychological) separateness from others is not to make a normative claim *ab initio* as to whether that state should be entered.

If we want to argue for the value and importance of this state of being this must be done robustly. It can be constructed in various ways, including the importance of psychological integrity for one's own personality development and/or the psychological or even psychiatric harm which

---

[4] cf. Cannelopoulou Bottis (2000).

could result from receiving 'bad news'. This is not to argue, however, that such a state of privacy should never be entered. Like all privacy claims, it is not a claim to absolute protection. Rather, this conceptualisation helps us to understand both what might be at stake – less a matter of one's own choices and more a concern with unwarranted intrusion – and how privacy and autonomy can and should be seen as overlapping and yet distinct human values and interests (Parent 1983). It is very fitting that both can be subsumed under the human rights rubric of the 'right to respect for private and family life', but this umbrella term gives shade to a very wide gamut of human rights and concerns, of which the right not to know might be one deserving of fuller – and more independently conceptualised – recognition.

The decision whether or not to recognise a 'right' not to know is ultimately a value preference. But it is important here, in light of the above analysis, to take into account the undoubted connection between the concepts of privacy and autonomy, and our commitment to them and to their protection. Each is concerned with core human interests, often given effect through law and in the form of rights. The triumph of autonomy has been questioned above not because autonomy is not important, but because autonomy cannot do all of the work in protecting all possible human interests. Moreover, and despite the above analysis, it is important to recognise that autonomy *does* have a role to play in protecting certain forms of the claim not to know, namely, when it is possible (and meaningful) to express a prior wish. This is no different to advance decisions about treatment. What the above account suggests, however, is that individuals might have an interest in not knowing when they do not know that there is something to know, and that in such circumstances it would be a mistake to suggest that this interest can be given effect by an appeal to autonomy alone. Privacy is a more coherent construct in such cases. And, the connection between autonomy and privacy here is this: if we are willing to accept that individuals have a right to know and a limited set of interests not to know through prior wishes – all as aspects of autonomy – does our commitment to the protection and promotion of fundamental and common human interests not also commit us to recognition of the privacy interest in *not* knowing?

## Protecting privacy in law

The preceding argument suggests that autonomy and privacy must work together if we wish to give full and proper effect to claims cast as the right to know and the right not to know information about ourselves. The triumph of autonomy in the medico-legal sphere has firmly committed legal systems to protection of a patient's right to know and, increasingly, recognition of, and protection of, advance decisions with respect to future interventions on their behalf. Thus, for example, in England and Wales ss. 24–26 of the Mental Capacity Act 2005 give formal statutory effect to advance refusals of treatment. While these provisions do not extend explicitly to advance refusals of information, the principled commitment to such exercises of autonomy would be entirely in keeping with the spirit of the law. Furthermore, the international examples given above of the Oviedo Convention and the UNESCO Declaration attempts to embody the right not to know can now be seen as particular forms of the commitment to individual autonomy.

This author is unaware, however, of any legal system that has imposed legal rights not to know as an aspect of privacy protection. This is a further reason to support conceptual clarity around the putative rights that are the subject of this book. In law, any claim to a right must be supported by an appropriate remedy; and remedies are different for different rights. Moreover, the nature and scope of a given remedy is concerned with recognition of the particular kind of legal harm that has been caused, the objective being to return the claimant as far as possible to the position prior to the wrongful act – or if this is not possible – to provide monetary compensation to reflect the degree of harm caused. In addition, an exceptionally useful remedy is prior restraint in the form of injunctive relief. This involves court-ordered prohibition against certain behaviour deemed to constitute a wrong if carried out, and for which an individual can petition a court. Finally, the role of the declarator is of particular importance in the medico-legal sphere because often the law is silent or unclear as to whether a particular course of action is lawful or permissible. It is possible, therefore, to petition a court for a declarator of legality in advance of any conduct for a determination in this regard.

A moment's thought will reveal that this does not leave an individual with many options if she or he is concerned with an interest in not knowing. While damages might be payable once disclosure is made, this is predicated on finding an appropriate remedy to plead. Injunctions and declarators are both anticipatory orders – prior to any wrongful conduct – but they clearly require knowledge of what might occur. The individual who is in a genuine state of ignorance about his or her own health status clearly cannot benefit from either of these. Damages for *ex post* disclosure harm would be the only viable option. Health care professionals facing the dilemma of disclosure are in a slightly better position in that they could petition a court for a declarator of legality on whether or not it is prudent and lawful to proceed to disclose. But this, again, would only be competent if it were accepted that a legal right was at stake, and that a legal wrong might be committed.

This brings us to consider whether and how existing legal protections of privacy might be played in aid of the recognition of the right not to know. There are four options in the European context and for a country with a Common Law tradition:

1. the common law action of breach of confidence;
2. the European provisions that promote data protection;
3. the common law action of negligence;
4. the European Convention on Human Rights.

### Breach of confidence

The duty of medical confidence has been called a 'cornerstone' of medical ethics (Ngwena and Chadwick, 1993) and it enjoys widespread support as a matter of professional principle and legal duty. Indeed, in the jurisdictions of the United Kingdom the common law duty of confidence was the closest that citizens came to direct protection of their privacy before the passing of the Human Rights Act 1998. However, confidentiality and privacy protection are not synonymous. The latter is a far wider concept, as demonstrated by the Article 8(1) ECHR jurisprudence on the meaning of 'private life',[5] while in its origins the duty of confidence required a pre-existing 'confidential relationship', such as that between priest/penitent, lawyer/client, or doctor/patient. Absent such a relationship, the UK courts were historically reluctant to recognise that information per se could have the 'necessary quality of confidence'.[6] This, however, has changed over the years to become a situation where manifestly confidential information – i.e. assessed on an objective analysis and by reference to the reasonable man – can be the basis of a duty of confidence. Yet further shifts have occurred since the Human Rights Act 1998, whereby Article 8(1) can be relied upon by claimants to argue that they had a 'reasonable expectation of confidentality'[7] with respect to their private information. But, none of these legal shifts changes the fundamental limitation of the common law action of breach of confidence with respect to the right not to know. This is linked to its origins in protecting the confidential relationship and its

---

[5] See, for example, the discussion of the scope of private life in *Pretty*, n. 2 above.
[6] cf. *Attorney General v. Guardian Newspapers Ltd (No 2)* [1990] AC 109, [1988] 3 All ER 545.
[7] *Campbell v. Mirror Group Newspapers Ltd* [2004] 2 AC 457, [2004] 2 All ER 995.

central concern to keep information confidential *within* the relationship. In other words, a breach of duty of confidence only occurs when information is disclosed outside the relationship to a third party in the public domain. The concern in our scenario is precisely the opposite: the disclosure dilemma is within the relationship itself – between health-care professional and patient. There is no third party and no release of information into the public domain. The legal construct does not permit a remedy in such cases.

### Data protection

The Data Protection Act 1998 implemented a 1995 EC Directive (European Directive 95/46/EC) to advance two equally important objectives within the European Union: (i) the adequate protection of personal data of citizens when this was processed for legitimate purposes, and (ii) the promotion of the free flow of information in the European single market. Key features of the law are that it protects the privacy rights of individuals in respect of the processing of their 'personal data', defined in Article 2 of the Directive as 'any information relating to an identified or identifiable natural person; an identifiable person is one who can be identified, directly or indirectly, in particular by reference to an identification number or to one or more factors specific to his physical, physiological, mental, economic, cultural or social identity'. This is regulated by reference to eight principles that ensure, *inter alia*, that data are only processed when it is fair and lawful to do so, that data are processed and kept only so far as is necessary for the purposes for which they were obtained, that the data are accurate and kept up to date, and that they should not be transferred to any jurisdiction where there are inadequate data protection provisions. 'Processing' of data enjoys a very wide interpretation, including:

> any operation or set of operations which is performed upon personal data, whether or not by automatic means, such as collection, recording, organization, storage, adaptation or alteration, retrieval, consultation, use, disclosure by transmission, dissemination or otherwise making available, alignment or combination, blocking, erasure or destruction.
>
> (European Directive 95/46/EC, Art 2(b))

For present purposes, this can be taken to cover any use or disclosure of personal data, in any direction and for any purpose. As such, it has far wider regulatory capture than the common law duty of confidence. But, would disclosure of personal data to an individual themselves provide a legal remedy? On the helpful side, the legitimate purposes of processing of sensitive health data do not require individual consent (Data Protection Act 1998, Schedules 2 and 3). This is but one of a range of legitimate purposes, and another is the vital interests of the patient himself. But this, of course, is to protect the health-care professional rather than the patient. As for explicit remedies, the construct of the legislation is rather less helpful. Section 10 of the Data Protection Act 1998 provides a right 'to prevent processing likely to cause damage or distress', and the provision is silent as to the nature of that processing, i.e. it need simply be caught by the above definition. There is no explicit requirement that processing be to third parties, for example. Furthermore, the claimant need only show that:

(a)  the processing of those data or their processing for that purpose or in that manner is causing or is likely to cause substantial damage or substantial distress to him or to another, and

(b)  that damage or distress is or would be unwarranted.

(Data Protection Act 1998, s. 10(1))

While the injunctive route would not be open for reasons already given, these provisions might be helpful to a claimant so long as they could show that the disclosure to them met the threshold of 'substantial distress'. While no case has yet been brought, a possible hurdle here relates to the origins of the Directive itself and the explicit objective to promote the free flow of data. A court would have to be persuaded of the importance of the privacy interests at stake – as articulated herein – before it would accept the kind of interpretation of the remedy offered above.

### Negligence

To return to the common law, and moving beyond the realm of remedies that are explicitly concerned with privacy protection, it is important to consider the action of negligence and to ask whether the scope of a professional duty of care might encompass a duty not to disclose. Space does not permit a rehearsal of the well-known elements of a successful negligence action,[8] but in circumstances where a disclosure dilemma arises within a doctor/patient relationship then the question of the existence of a duty of care simply does not arise. There is clearly a duty of care. The issue is whether or not the standard of care extends to non-disclosure in certain circumstances, and whether a failure to respect this – i.e. to disclose, would amount to a legally recognised harm.

---

[8] For which, see Mason and Laurie (2013, chapter 5).

This kind of scenario is not new in discussions about professional duties of care. Long before the triumph of autonomy – largely brought about through successful negligence action by patients arguing an entitlement to information – there was much discussion (and some judicial recognition) of the so-called 'therapeutic privilege'. Thus, in the immediate post-war period of the 1940s, we have commentaries in the United States such as this from Smith:

> There are two main situations in which it is justified to withhold the truth from a patient … if the physician has compelling evidence that disclosure will cause real and predictable harm, truthful disclosure may be withheld. Examples might include disclosure that would make a depressed patient actively suicidal. This judgment, often referred to as the 'therapeutic privilege,' is important but also subject to abuse. Hence it is important to invoke this only in those instances when the harm seems very likely, not merely hypothetical. The second circumstance is if the patient him- or herself states an informed preference not to be told the truth. Some patients might ask that the physician instead consult family members, for instance. In these cases, it is critical that the patient give thought to the implications of abdicating their role in decision making. If they chose to make an informed decision not to be informed, however, this preference should be respected.
>
> (Smith 1945–47: 349)

This quote embodies both autonomy-based and privacy-based reasons not to disclose information to a patient. It will probably also provoke a reaction in the reader as to the manifest paternalism of its tone. It is certainly undeniable that a decision not to disclose information to a patient – for fear that it will do them more harm than good – is a paternalistic act. But, it is often overlooked that the act of disclosure in the belief that it will do more good than harm is also paternalistic. What comes to be known cannot then be unknown. And, if the above analysis about the limits of autonomy is accepted, it is not a credible justification to claim that disclosure facilitates autonomy; at least, not if the concern is with unwarranted intrusions of privacy.

Would a patient nevertheless have a remedy in negligence for an unwarranted disclosure? There would be two key considerations to take into account here in the contemporary context. First, and to return to a UK-focused perspective, the courts are likely to take their steer from practices accepted as proper by a responsible body of medical opinion.[9] In this regard, the guidance from the General Medical Council might hold considerable sway. The latest version (2013) of Good Medical Practice is illustrative in this regard:

---

[9] See *Bolam* v. *Friern Hospital Management Committee* [1957] 2 All ER 118, [1957] 1 WLR 582 and *Bolitho* v. *Hackney Health Authority* [1998] AC 232, [1997] 4 All ER 771, HL.

49. You must work in partnership with patients, sharing with them the information they will need to make decisions about their care, including:

a. their condition, its likely progression and the options for treatment, including associated risks and uncertainties
b. the progress of their care, and your role and responsibilities in the team
c. who is responsible for each aspect of patient care, and how information is shared within teams and among those who will be providing their care
d. any other information patients need if they are asked to agree to be involved in teaching or research.

(General Medical Council 2013, para. 49)

The notion of 'partnership' is of crucial importance here. It suggests the need to establish and build relationships that will reveal patient preferences, expectations and tolerances of information flows. The general tenor of this guidance tends towards disclosure, but discretion is also a clear element of effective professional communication.

Finally, if a patient were aggrieved by an unwarranted disclosure, would this yield a successful negligence action? This would require not only that a court be satisfied that disclosure amounted to a breach of the requisite standard of care, but also that the patient was caused recognised legal harm as a result. In the context of privacy-based claims this would have to be psychological harm, and it is well established in tort that this must reach the level of psychiatric injury. Mere upset would not be enough.[10] This suggests that there would be a very real practical barrier to legal remedy in such cases.

### Human rights

As a final consideration, we must examine the contemporary human rights paradigm. It has already been argued that to conceive of the right to know and the right not to know as aspects both of autonomy and of privacy can be caught by the very wide human right protection provided by Article 8(1) ECHR: the right to respect for private and family life. The decision in *Pretty* v. *UK* confirmed the expansive nature of this Article, extending it to autonomy claims. Just as importantly, however, the European Court in that decision accepted the state argument that it could legitimately interfere with the citizen's rights by relying on Article 8(2), which provides:

There shall be no interference by a public authority with the exercise of this right except such as is in accordance with the law and is necessary in a democratic

---

[10] Note too, however, that in data protection law the threshold level is 'substantial distress', see s. 10, Data Protection Act 1998.

society in the interests of national security, public safety or the economic well-being of the country, for the prevention of disorder or crime, for the protection of health or morals, or for the protection of the rights and freedoms of others.

This would need to be considered in any legal claim to protect a right not to know. Thus, even if it were accepted that a privacy right were engaged, disclosure could be justified if it were shown to be a necessary and proportionate response to the dilemma that was faced, and even if this were upsetting to the individual involved.

This example also reveals a universal (legal) truth about privacy protection. In no legal system are privacy rights absolute. While the legal parameters for what counts as 'good cause' vary from jurisdiction to jurisdiction, this is nonetheless important because it suggests that healthcare professionals and others who face a disclosure dilemma and who are able to demonstrate sound reasons and processes for choosing to disclose are unlikely to be the subject of successful legal action.

There might in fact be a range of clinical reasons to justify stepping into the private sphere with knowledge about a person's own health or at least that will help in the assessment of where any tipping point might lie in favour of (non)-disclosure. These are likely to include:

- the availability of a cure or effective intervention;
- the severity of the condition and likelihood of onset;
- the nature of the health condition itself, genetic or otherwise;
- the nature of any further testing or intervention that might be required;
- the nature of the information to be disclosed;
- the nature of the request (e.g., testing for an individual's health or for diagnostic purposes for a relative);
- the question of whether and how far disclosure can further a legitimate public interest, which can include familial interests;
- and the question of how the individual might react if offered unsolicited information (e.g., whether any advance decision has been made and is applicable in the circumstances).[11]

The above framework provides one possible approach to defend against any legal action.

### Conclusion

This chapter challenges the central role that autonomy has come to play in the medico-legal sphere by arguing that claims to know or not

---

[11] Discussed further in Mason and Laurie (2013, chapter 7).

to know information cannot all be accommodated within this paradigm. Respect for personal autonomy is about recognising capacity for self-determination and respecting choices. But we do not and cannot control all aspects of our lives, as perfectly illustrated by the example of unsolicited approaches with information about ourselves. If this information is given, then something is irrevocably changed. Disclosure here generates a genuine dilemma for those in possession of the information. Any decision to approach or not approach the subject is a morally and socially significant act. This is so because it is an entry into our private space. To be in a state of privacy – a genuine state of separateness from others – is also to enjoy psychological separateness from others. The conceptualisation offered in this chapter allows us to understand more clearly what is at stake, and also to examine more deeply whether and how legal protection might be forthcoming. In the final analysis, and true to the nature of the decisions being ethical in nature, the role of the law here should be approached with caution. Professional discretion, rather than legally imposed duty, is likely to be the optimal way to navigate this particular maze.

### References

Cannelopoulou Bottis, M. 2000. 'Comment on a view favouring ignorance of genetic information: confidentiality, autonomy, beneficence, and the right not to know', *European Journal of Health Law* 7: 173–83.

*European Directive 95/46/EC on the Protection of Individuals with Regard to the Processing of Personal Data and on the Free Movement of Such Data*, 1995.

Foster, C. 2009. *Choosing Life, Choosing Death: The tyranny of autonomy in medical ethics and law*. Oxford: Hart Publishing.

General Medical Council 2013. *Good Medical Practice*. Available at: www.gmc-uk.org/guidance/good_medical_practice.asp (accessed 31 March, 2014).

Husted, J. 1997. 'Autonomy and the right not to know', in R. Chadwick, M. Levitt and D. Shickle (eds.) *The Right to Know and the Right Not to Know*. Aldershot: Ashgate Publishing, reprinted in this volume as Chapter 2.

Laurie, G. 1999. 'In defence of ignorance: genetic information and the right not to know', *European Journal of Health Law* 6: 119–32.

Laurie, G. 2002. *Genetic Privacy: A challenge to medico-legal norms*. Cambridge University Press.

Mason, J. K. and Laurie, G. T. 2013. *Law and Medical Ethics*. Oxford University Press.

McLean, S. A. M. 1989. *A Patient's Right to Know*. Aldershot: Dartmouth Publishing.

Ngwena, C. and Chadwick, R. 1993. 'Genetic diagnostic information and the duty of confidentiality: ethics and law', *Medical Law International* 1: 73–95.

Parent, W. 1983. 'Privacy, morality and the law', *Philosophy and Public Affairs* 12: 269–88.

Smith, H. W. 1945–47 'Therapeutic privilege to withhold specific diagnosis from patient sick with serious or fatal illness', *Tennessee Law Review* 19: 349.

Wertz, D. C. and Fletcher, J. C. 1991. 'Privacy and disclosure in medical genetics in an ethics of care', *Bioethics* 5(3): 212–32.

*Part II*

# Issues in genetics

# 4    Biobanks and feedback

*Kadri Simm*

'Genes now tell doctors secrets they can't utter' was the dramatic title of the *New York Times* article from August 2012 that described the problem of incidental findings in genetic research. Indeed, the issue of whether or not to disclose significant genetic information to participants of research that generally do not expect it, is a much-discussed topic in medical ethics and genetic journals and has now spilled over into general media. The right to know or not to know discussion in relation to biobank research is now almost entirely dominated by the so-called 'incidentalome' debate. Incidental findings are a well-known phenomenon in clinical care where, for example, a radiologist might find something unexpected from an image in addition to the information she was looking for. Genetic research, which is often based on biobank collections, is now similarly faced with such findings when researchers stumble upon DNA information that, while not the aim of the research itself, might be potentially very relevant to the donors. But while it might have been relatively straightforward for the radiologist to contact the patient or patient's physician regarding incidental finds, the matter is much more complicated for researchers far removed (both institutionally and geographically) from the biological owners of the mostly anonymized samples.

The possibility of disclosing unplanned, unexpected and yet important genetic information to biobank donors raises numerous scientific, ethical, legal and practical issues. Leaving aside the legal aspects, this chapter gives an overview of these challenges and situates the debate within a larger, long-anticipated phenomenon of personalized medicine. I will start by looking back at the debates we had ten to fifteen years ago in relation to biobanks and potential feedback and will then proceed to discuss the recent arguments regarding feedback in the context of population biobanks and other large-scale genomic research.

### Looking back – the debates from the dawn of biobanking

The so-called ELSA aspects of genetic research and the establishment and governance of biobanks, especially population biobanks, were amongst the most debated issues on the bioethics and medical ethics pages ten to fifteen years ago. Population biobanks are large collections of biological samples that often also include medical data and records, lifestyle information and other data linked to the genetic sample. Lots was expected of genetic research. Genetic information was simultaneously perceived as promising (of improved health) and threatening (to our identities and futures). Some of the more specific topics concerned informed consent (and its alternatives for biobank research like broad consent or open consent), privacy (and how biobanks might threaten this), commercialization (can genes be patented or are they truly human heritage?), insurance (how genetic information might jeopardize its affordability) as well as unease about the hype and deterministic outlook of much of genetics-based speculation.

Right to know and not to know debates were linked to questions about autonomy, choice and responsibility. There was anticipation of personalized medicine, where drugs and clinical care would be tailored according to patients' DNA. But there was little discussion of the possibility of incidentalome. While the prospect of a greatly heightened need for genetic counselling was indeed envisioned, it was mostly linked to clinical care, not research.

Questions regarding the right to know or not to know can be raised on several levels – the individual, the familial and the social – and these have remained relevant in the context of incidental findings and biobank feedback. The public health perspective that was perhaps the most underrepresented at the start of the so-called genetic revolution has also stressed the right of societies to know – whether it is for public health planning purposes or as a duty to promote scientific freedom. Largely epidemiological in nature, it would rely on anonymized samples.

Whereas the various dilemmas of returning unexpected information to patients were certainly considered, these mostly pertained to genetic testing and screening taking place within clinical care or direct-to-consumer testing. The likelihood of disclosing information to research participants, especially on the scale of population biobanks, was to become an issue only later.

### Why has feedback become such a hot topic?

Increased non-profit research capacities, including cheaper and faster genome sequencing technologies as well as the linking up of biobanks into global research networks, have resulted in researchers stumbling upon genetic findings that they might or might not have been looking for. Some of these findings are likely to have important consequences for health, treatment or reproductive decisions of donors. This information can be life-saving or at least gravely affect quality of life. However, in research settings researchers are mostly working with anonymized samples and most donors have signed consent forms stating that they will not be contacted. And thus researchers and the institutions involved are faced with an age-old moral dilemma: what is the right thing to do? And who should do it? Francis Collins, Director of the NIH, has called this 'one of the thorniest current challenges in clinical research' (Kolata 2012).

This 'thorny challenge' has numerous causes. Firstly, genetic research, especially of the kind based on biobanks or other collections, has become much more commonplace. Clinical genetics or incorporation of genetic information into routine medical care has become if not yet an everyday reality, then a more common practice. Genetic information about oneself is more readily available and is sometimes being quite publicly shared along with other medical information. Contrary to the worries about their privacy being threatened by potential leakages of genetic and medical information, many choose to go public with that data themselves. A website (patientslikeme.com) offers a virtual meeting ground for patients with similar diagnoses and people are willing to identify themselves personally on those sites through their Facebook account or similar. Another site – Quantified Self – offers the possibility of sharing various self-tracking data (including genetic information) with others and has actual meeting groups in over eighty cities across the world. Genetic information in those sites has usually originated from direct-to-consumer testing or clinical care. The personal genomics industry has latched onto the genetic testing wagon and its activities and engagements are often pushing public authorities to scramble for new policies (Wallace and Kent 2011).

Secondly, the feedback challenge relates to the way in which most biobanks were set up. Biobanks themselves are and always were a complex and varied group with many dissimilarities. Yet, over the past decades the complexities have increased. Besides the more traditional categories of national, commercial and the various public–private partnership models, or the disease-specific, population-specific large-scale population biobanks, there are whole new combinations. Biobanks are increasingly also globally networked and their governance is therefore a legally and ethically complicated affair. Pooling biobank data has been seen as crucial for breakthroughs on common complex diseases and recently global alliances have being established to start working towards a common framework for sharing genomic data and clinical information.

Approximately ten to fifteen years ago most new biobanks saw altruism and the benefits of the future generations as appropriate motivational mechanisms for collecting data. The personal benefit of participating in a biobank was largely limited to some testing at the initial joining (for example, taking blood pressure). The good old gift relationship was largely hoped to be applicable still, even though criticisms about its appropriateness in the context of commercial or public–private biomedical research arrangements had already been raised (Tutton 2002). A few biobanks promising donors general access to their genetic information and counselling (like the Estonian Genome Center) were chastized for going along with the neoliberal focus on private gains at the expense of solidaristic and selfless donations for the benefit of humankind. Thinking at the time is exemplified by the US National Bioethics Advisory Committee guidelines from 1999 on *Research Involving Human Biological Materials*. While they suggested that the issue of disclosure of results should already be addressed in research plans, they were also of the opinion that reporting results back should be limited and disclosure should be exceptional (National Bioethics Advisory Committee 1999: 72). Disclosing individual findings would also 'place the researcher in an inappropriate clinical relationship with research participants' (Samet and Bailey 1997: 207).

Furthermore, most donors signed informed consent forms agreeing that they would not receive any (personal) information back from the biobank. For example, the UK biobank consent form states that the undersigned agrees to the following: 'I understand that none of my results will be given to me (except for some measurements during this visit) and that I will not benefit financially from taking part (e.g., if research leads to commercial development of a new treatment)' (UK Biobank consent form, available online).

Thus for large-scale population biobanks the norm at the time was to rely on the altruistic public health model. In contrast, the Estonian Genome Center's consent form states both that:

• I have the right to be aware of my genetic data and other data about me stored in the Gene Bank, except my genealogy. I have the right to genetic counseling upon accessing my data stored in the Gene Bank. I can access my data stored in the Gene Bank free of charge, and that
• I have the right not to be aware of my genetic data, hereditary characteristic and genetic risks obtained as a result of genetic research.

(Estonian Genome Center, available online)

The Estonian case (and a few others) aside, feedback, if any, would be provided in most general terms (for example, online publication of general research results). Would people have signed different consent forms, ones that promised feedback? Sociological data suggests that quite likely they would (although we cannot infer anything normative from this). Of the potential participants of the Estonian biobank, 83 per cent wanted to get the promised personal 'gene card' (Sutrop and Simm 2004). More recently a strong majority has wanted disclosure of both general and individual research results (Bovenberg *et al.* 2009).

Most biobanks had no mechanisms in place for disclosing information to donors and a recent study of eighty-five biobanks concluded that the issue of return of results was not addressed in their public documents (Johnson *et al.* 2012). Since the incidentalome has become more prominent many biobanks and research programmes have started to ask donors whether they would like to have feedback and what kind of feedback they would like. But all of this has come too late for biobanks and research collections that were set up without explicit disclosure policies. The incidentalome looks to be the initiation rite into the era of personalized medicine – and while the latter was much talked about it was apparently still not expected to actually arrive so soon. The arguments against disclosure that I will turn to now can perhaps provide some insights into why biobanks were reluctant to promise personal feedback.

### Arguments against feedback

The duty to disclose relevant results to participants of clinical research involving genetic information has been well established in numerous international documents (Knoppers *et al.* 2006). Things are more complicated with biobanking. If feedback concerns significant health-related information then few would dispute that there is a moral duty to disclose information. Researchers tend to agree that sharing information with donors is justified in cases of preventable or treatable diseases (Meulenkamp *et al.* 2012). Any of the numerous principles that have been evoked in these debates – whether it is avoidance of harm, duty of beneficence or respect for autonomy – would grant that. But that still leaves open the question of whose duty this is and what are its limits.

Potential duty to disclose health-related information has traditionally been located within the domain of medical doctors. One of the strongest arguments against providing personal feedback relies on the tradition of separating the domains of clinical care and research. These domains have had different objectives, care focusing on the individual's needs and benefits, research aiming to generate new knowledge for the benefits of future generations or at least populations more widely. Because of those differences these domains have also been governed by distinct ethical principles – beneficence and avoidance of harm relevant for clinical care, creation of new knowledge and public health values for research. Thus, the argument goes, it would be unnecessary and in breach of principles governing research to start providing personal feedback. Furthermore, such activities would lead to the strengthening of therapeutic misconception: a mistaken perception of the research participants that they are being cured and cared for.

Duties of beneficence and non-maleficence traditionally characterize clinical care. The principle of respect for autonomy is more difficult to categorize and could arguably be relevant for researchers as well – in this case weakening the delineation of the two spheres. But since the duty of feedback can be thought quite demanding on researchers, it is likely to be considered supererogatory.

Argument for the maintenance of trust is one that can be played both ways. For many biobanks feedback would be contradictory to what was promised and any breach of initial agreement could affect trust negatively. On the other hand, public awareness of researchers holding on to information that can greatly benefit donors can also lead to a loss of trust towards the biobank and its governance framework.

Besides ethical arguments, potential feedback also presents scientific challenges. Quality of research findings can be problematic as a lot of the information uncovered is of indeterminate and possibly unreliable clinical significance. Much of biobank research is done by secondary researchers on anonymized samples in different countries and the biobank itself tends not to control the quality of the research (Bledsoe *et al.* 2012). In the USA, laboratories need to be certified to provide clinically relevant data but there are many research laboratories without this certification. Therefore the clinical relevance of a laboratory finding still needs to be determined (Hansson 2012). Genetic information is complex and continuing research is likely to increase, not decrease this complexity.[1] Yet it is also worrying that with the 'hype' around genetic information continuing, considerations of environmental and socio-economic determinants of health might be overshadowed by tendencies towards the logic of genetic determinism.

Finally, there are a number of practical issues: providing individual feedback of research results can be very expensive and it is uncertain who is responsible for the cost. Although the use of IT can help to lower

---

[1] Tim Spector estimated that 90 per cent of the research articles published at the height of the hype in the 1990s turned out to be wrong (McKie 2013).

the costs, if professional genetic counselling is included, this is bound to be costly. Also, the cumbersome duty to give feedback might be a disincentive for the establishment of new biobanks (Bledsoe *et al.* 2012). And let's not forget about the potential psychological burdens that disclosure may create – for genetic conditions numerous generations of a family might have to undergo a 'lifetime of medical surveillance' that might or might not have actual health-related results (Rothstein 2013: 65).

## Arguments for disclosure

Traditional ethical principles of health care figure prominently in the pro-disclosure arguments. But for their relevance in biobank research the strict clinical ethics/research ethics differentiation needs to be deconstructed. This might not be so difficult, especially for newer biobanks. For example, in novel participant-centred initiatives relying on large international biobank consortia the regular contact and communication between participants and researchers is already central (Kaye *et al.* 2013). Participants can choose to support certain research projects, manage their consent and decide what sort of feedback they would like to have (or not).

Indeed I would argue that the entire issue of biobank feedback is an illustration of an entirely new social, political and scientific trend. The conventional roles and responsibilities of medical care and research vis-à-vis the patient and the public at large are undergoing change as the need for democratizing research and better science governance is emphasized. Policy initiatives (for example, from the EU) provide support for participatory science, for transparency and for engagement with the public and stakeholders throughout the research cycle from setting research priorities and making funding decisions to implementing research results. Novel ethical frameworks have been proposed to deal with the breaking down of the research/care delineation and the need to openly embrace mutual learning as part of the clinical practice (Faden *et al.* 2013). Medical innovation is increasingly happening in clinical settings. The reciprocity embedded in disclosure policies is a necessary part of any such participatory medicine.

The care/research differentiation is also challenged through changes in clinical care. Medical professionals have always stressed the importance of prevention in health care and genetics is likely now to offer an evidence-based way of doing exactly that as genetic information becomes a more routine part of care. It has been suggested that researchers already have a duty to actively look for mutations in all samples (Green *et al.* 2013) or that this is likely to be a future obligation

(Gliwa and Berkman 2013). If the train of personalized medicine is ever to truly leave the station, the overlapping of medical care and research must intensify.

Although it is true that the aims of research differ from those of clinical care, this does not necessarily mean that both objectives cannot be simultaneously enacted. People can participate in research while also potentially benefiting from personal feedback. Therapeutic misconception is problematic in clinical trials where the patient, instead of benefiting from treatment, might actually be harmed (e.g., by being in the placebo arm of a successful trial). In genetic research therapeutic misconception is problematic because personal care is simply neglected, not because it is somehow impossible to provide it. There is no logical inconsistency in striving to do both, although it might clearly be more costly.

If the care/research differentiation is not as solid as it perhaps used to be, we can proceed to discuss the ethical principles of health care that have been considered relevant in feedback debates. Health care is a value- and principle-laden field. We know of the principles of biomedical ethics (beneficence, non-maleficence, autonomy and justice) with or without their additions (the so-called European principles of solidarity, reciprocity, precaution, etc.) as well as of the important values of public health ethics (generalizable knowledge and benefits for future generations). What is obvious is that these values and principles can and do conflict. Much has been written about the tensions between individualistic ethics of principlism and the more communitarian priorities in public health ethics or even about the paradoxes of medical practice where communicating a difficult diagnosis supports a patient's autonomy while it might simultaneously bring harm (principle of non-maleficence).

A public health perspective would favour an efficient and just use of resources and might not support individual feedback. The most prominent arguments for disclosure have been associated with the principles of autonomy and beneficence. Disclosure of significant health-related information is crucial for allowing a person to make autonomous, informed decisions about his or her life. Duty of beneficence requires the promotion of human well-being. Decisions regarding whether to give feedback necessarily struggle with paternalism and autonomy. To respect autonomy we need to avoid paternalism, yet, unless we are dealing with a biobank that had detailed feedback procedures in place from the very start, decisions to disclose genetic information or not necessarily involve paternalistic decision-making regarding people's genetic information. Duty of beneficence and avoidance of harm seem straightforward but they might have potentially paternalistic undertones, especially when avoidance of harm is used as an argument against disclosure (Costain *et al.* 2012). Or alternatively, paternalistically we throw away people's informed consent and assume that everyone wants to know.

Both camps of the for and against disclosure are essentially juggling with the same set of principles and values, just ranking them differently. The most common route out of those conflicts usually points to the necessity of contextual decision making as opposed to more absolutist and universal resolutions. As these numerous conflicts show, we have a pluralistic situation where multiple important and yet incommensurable values exist side by side and weighing those values while sensitive to particular contexts is likely to produce well-justified solutions. Nevertheless, work towards normative guidelines in this area has also been ongoing for years and has resulted in various proposals (Green *et al.* 2013; Wolf *et al.* 2012).

## Proposals for regulating feedback

In many ways the challenges regarding potential feedback from clinical care and research were known more than a decade ago (Schulte 2004). The criteria of clinical validity and of clinical utility, the creation of pre-symptomatic patients, the shared character of genetic information and the challenges this entails to privacy and confidentiality were all discussed. Yet the information to be disclosed has become more complex and the scale – the mere quantity of analysed DNA – has increased.

By now the debate has largely left behind the 'if and whether' stages and has concentrated already on how to give feedback, what information to return, when to do it and who should do it. There is no question any more of whether there will be incidental findings but rather how many and which ones to focus on (Abdul-Karim *et al.* 2013: 565). There is relatively little general disagreement about the criteria that should characterize information that ought to be disclosed. Analytic validity, clinical validity, avoidance of significant harm (potentially life-saving), clinical utility and actionability are some of the more widely shared standards (Bredenoord *et al.* 2011; Wolf *et al.* 2012). But while the overall importance of these criteria is not disputed, the specific qualifications of each remain uncertain. Clinical validity, for example, is not usually established by researchers in laboratories but results from various long-term investigations and trials, ideally also peer-reviewed. Learning more and more about genetics necessarily brings a realization that we know very little of the 'big picture' – or as Socrates insisted a few thousand years ago – the more we learn, the more we also learn how little we know. The threats and the assurances of today's genetic science and counselling can and likely will be in a state of flux as research advances. We are already leaving behind the comfortable plains of monogenetic conditions for the heart-land of complex diseases. There are many helpful analyses and pragmatic recommendations that attempt to create order in this tsunami of ques-tions and concerns associated with feedback (Anastasova et al. 2013; Berg et al. 2013; Bovenberg et al. 2009; Wolf et al. 2012).

One potential mismatch between disclosure recommendations and empirical research on biobank participants' preferences concerns action-ability – whether it is possible clinically to treat or prevent a condition. Researchers have tended to strongly support the position that genetic mutations with unclear implications for health should not be disclosed (in a Netherlands study 95 per cent support among geneticists) and only treatable or preventable conditions should be disclosed (74 per cent sup-port among the same group) (Bovenberg et al. 2009: 232).[2] Thus, for example, Huntington's disease would not qualify for disclosure because prevention is not possible (Chan et al. 2012). This is contentious, espe-cially if one is to consult public opinion in this matter. In one study 60 per cent of research biobank participants were willing to learn about even the unclear implications (Bovenberg et al. 2009) and in another study over 80 per cent of participants in direct-to-consumer testing wanted to know about unpreventable conditions (Bloss et al. 2010). Other research has confirmed that knowledge itself can be deemed beneficial even without the subsequent benefits towards health (Costain et al. 2012).

In this chapter I have considered mostly cases where we do not know whether people would like to receive feedback. Most biobank partici-pants signed consent forms stating that no feedback would be provided but at the time this was the only option for participation; people did not actually have a choice in these matters. There is a general tendency to assume that people would want to know because this would allow them to make better-informed decisions. The right not to know is, in some sense, inherently problematic for the domain of health care since the lat-ter is normative, prescriptive of health while the principle of autonomy as an ethical ideal tries to be open and value-neutral as regards life choices. Of course, philosophers recognize very few rights as absolute (if any), so even a right not to know is conditional and in biobank research it seems to be tied up with responsibilities for significant others – our children and relatives – rather than with personal choices.

As genetic information is always shared, feedback will concern other people besides the participants who will be directly involved. When and

---

[2] Although, interestingly, in earlier studies of geneticists' views they appeared to support the position that information should be disclosed regardless of whether a condition is treatable or not (Wertz and Fletcher 1989).

how is this information to be shared? Passive disclosure has been advocated as appropriate for relatives, meaning that they themselves ought to ask for information (Chan *et al.* 2012). Yet the nature of 'passivity' in that context has been questioned, especially since relatives are often not aware of such data existing (Nijsingh 2012) and the original participant might be deceased. While keeping important information from relatives can contradict with a duty not to harm, non-disclosure of genetic information to relatives cannot be construed as producing direct harm but rather seen as a lesser offence of a failure to help (Powers 2002: 375). An interesting subsection regarding the sharing of information concerns pediatric collections where it has been suggested that parents do *not* have a right not to know crucial, potentially life-saving, genetic information about their children (Hens *et al.* 2011). If this were accepted it raises questions about the special status of genetic information in a parental relationship. Pediatric research might also produce results that are not immediately relevant for the child but rather for her parents – for example, the discovery of a BRCA gene (Abdul-Karim *et al.* 2013: 568).

Qualitative research has shown that sharing genetic information among relatives is often based on a different logic or at least discourse than the abstract, principle-laden debates of ethics and research communities. The nature of the relationships between people seems to matter more than prospects for prevention and actionability (Gilbar 2007). Substituting the concept of integrity instead of autonomy has opened up the nuances of familial communication in these matters (Boddington and Gregory 2008). Talk of rights can seem inappropriate in familial settings where justice has less to do with rights-talk and more with notions of care and need. We have to be careful to ensure that the conceptual framework driving policy change in this area is responsive to the actual needs and concerns of research participants.

While standard informed consent procedures are intended to provide individual guaranteed rights to withdraw, people seem to have a broader perspective. They ask policy questions, such as how biobank research is going to benefit the health-care system or how the research priorities of biobanks are to be decided (Levitt and Weldon 2005, Ursin *et al.* 2008).

## Final thoughts

In conclusion, I believe that the expression 'incidental findings' increasingly makes only limited sense in the context of biobank research, or rather, it is only meaningful from the perspective of the researcher. For a participant who has given broad consent for almost any type of biomedical research to be undertaken on her sample, any finding can be considered incidental as participants usually do not have control over or even knowledge of what research gets done – at most they might simply be informed of ongoing research projects.

Perhaps surprisingly, studies with direct-to-consumer testing indicate that the sharing of genetic test results with one's GP might be less common than expected (Darst *et al.* 2013), and very few take advantage of the free genetic counselling that is offered (Bloss *et al.* 2011). This raises questions about the implications of genetic testing for medical care. But, to speculate further, it could well be that the incidentalome associated with research is likely to lessen over the next decade as whole genome sequencing becomes cheaper and more accessible as a routine part of medical care. Then the significant risks are likely to be uncovered and discussed within a more traditional doctor–patient relationship.[3]

I would also like to draw attention to a somewhat questionable premise to the entire feedback discussion, namely that people will act upon the disclosed information – they will take better care of themselves and ultimately their quality of life will be better. While this is an entirely reasonable assumption to make, there are some hints that the picture might be more complicated than that. For example, there is a surprising lack of belief (among biobank researchers) that knowledge of genetic information will motivate changes in lifestyle and a rather heightened sense that it may harm them or their insurance prospects (Meulenkamp *et al.* 2012: 261). While research on the long-term effects of genetic information on lifestyle choices and health is ongoing (e.g., the Scripps Genomic Health Initiative, the Coriell personalized medicine collaborative) there are some results from direct-to-consumer testing that demonstrate a lack of behavioural change (Bloss *et al.* 2011: 532). As genetic information deals with likelihoods and risks, disclosure of genetic information will often simply confirm already known risks that are present in family history or associated with lifestyle. We all know that smoking and being overweight affects our well-being and health and yet awareness of that information has often not led to behavioural change. Why this is so is beyond the aims of this chapter but these tendencies should be taken seriously when we discuss the future of medicine, and especially that of the personalized kind.

---

[3] This, however, is only likely to be true for affluent countries and not for the vast majority of the world population. Were the ancillary duties of researchers to be strengthened towards biobank participants, then samples sourced from developing countries would likely still require attention and care from researchers.

## Acknowledgements

I would like to thank Kristi Lõuk, Liis Leitsalu, Francesco Orsi, Alex Davies and members of the departmental philosophy seminar at the University of Tartu for useful comments. I also thank ISCH COST Action on Bio-objects and their boundaries for inspiring discussions.

## References

Abdul-Karim, Ruqayyah, Berkman, Benjamin E., Wendler, David, Rid, Annette, Khan, Javed, Badgett, Tom and Chandros Hull, Sara 2013. 'Disclosure of incidental findings from next-generation sequencing in pediatric genomic research', *Pediatrics* 131: 564–71.

Anastasova, Velizara, Mahalatchimy, Aurélie, Rial-Sebbag, Emmanuelle, Antó Boqué J. M., Keil, Thomas, Sunyer, Jordi, Bosquet, Jean and Cambon-Thomsen, Anne 2013. 'Communication of results and disclosure of incidental findings in longitudinal paediatric research', *Pediatric Allergy and Immunology* 24: 389–94.

Berg, Jonathan S., Adams, Michael, Nassar, Nassib, Bizon, Chris, Lee, Kristy, Schmitt, Charles P., Wilhelmsen, Kirk C. and Evans, James P. 2013. 'An informatics approach to analyzing the incidentalome', *Genetics in Medicine* 15: 36–44.

Bledsoe, Marianna J., Grizzle, William E., Clark, Brian J. and Zeps, Nikolajs 2012. 'Practical implementation issues and challenges for biobanks in the return of individual research results', *Genetics in Medicine* 14: 478–83.

Bloss, Cinnamon S., Ornowski, Laura, Silver, Elana, Cargill, Michele, Vanier, Vance, Schork, Nicholas J. and Topol, Eric J. 2010. 'Consumer perceptions of direct-to-consumer personalized genomic risk assessments', *Genetics in Medicine* 12: 556–66.

Bloss, Cinnamon S., Schork, Nicholas J. and Topol, Eric J. 2011. 'Effect of direct-to-consumer genomewide profiling to assess disease risk', *NEJM* 364: 524–34.

Boddington, Paula and Gregory, Maggie 2008. 'Communicating genetic information in the family: Enriching the debate through the notion of integrity', *Med Health Care Philos* 11: 445–54.

Bovenberg, Jasper, Meulenkamp, Tineke, Smets, Ellen and Gevers, Sjef 2009. 'Biobank research: Reporting results to individual participants', *European Journal of Health Law* 16: 229–47.

Bredenoord, Annelien L., Kroes, Hester Y., Cuppen, Edwin, Parker, Michael and van Delden, Johannes J. M. 2011. 'Disclosure of individual genetic data to research participants: The debate reconsidered', *Trends in Genetics* 27: 41–7.

Chan, Ben, Facio, Flavia M., Eidem, Haley, Chandros Hull, Sara, Biesecker, Leslie G. and Berkman, Benjamin E. 2012. 'Genomic inheritances: Disclosing individual research results from whole-exome sequencing to deceased participants' relatives', *American Journal of Bioethics* 12: 1–8.

Costain, Gregory and Bassett, Anne S. 2012. 'The ever-evolving concept of clinical significance and the potential for sins of omission in genetic research', *American Journal of Bioethics* 12: 22–4.

Darst, Burcu F., Madlensky, Lisa, Schork, Nicholas J., Topol, Eric J. and Bloss, Cinnamon S. 2013. 'Characteristics of genomic test consumers who spontaneously share results with their health care provider', *Health Communication* 1–4.

Estonian Genome Center. *Gene Donor Consent Form*. Available at: www.geeni varamu.ee/et/doonorile/geenidoonoriks-saamise-nousoleku-vorm-naidis (accessed 19 June 2013).

Faden, Ruth, Kass, Nancy E., Goodman, Steven N., Pronovost, Peter, Tunis, Sean and Beauchamp, Tom L. 2013. 'An ethics framework for a learning health care system: A departure from traditional research ethics and clinical ethics', Ethical Oversight of Learning Health Care Systems, *Hastings Center Report* 43: S16–S27.

Gilbar, Roy 2007. 'Communicating genetic information in the family: The familial relationship as the forgotten factor', *J Med Ethics* 33: 390–3.

Gliwa, Catherine and Berkman, Benjamin E. 2013. 'Do researchers have an obligation to actively look for genetic incidental findings?', *American Journal of Bioethics* 13: 32–42.

Green, Robert C., Berg, Jonathan S., Grody, Wayne W., Kalia, Sarah S., Korf, Bruce R., Martin, Christa L., McGuire, Amy L., Nussbaum, Robert L., O'Daniel, Julianne M., Ormond, Kelly E., Rehm, Heidi L., Watson, Michael S., Williams, Marc S. and Biesecker, Leslie G. 2013. 'ACMG recommendations for reporting of incidental findings in clinical exome and genome sequencing', *Genetics in Medicine* 15: 565–574.

Hansson, Mats G. 2012. 'Validate DNA-findings before telling donors', *Nature* 484: 455.

Hens, Kristien, Nys, Herman, Cassiman, Jean-Jacques and Dierickx, Kris 2011. 'The return of individual research findings in paediatric genetic research', *J Med Ethics* 37: 179–83.

Johnson, Gina, Lawrenz, Frances and Thao, Mao 2012. 'An empirical examination of the management of return of individual research results and incidental findings in genomic biobanks', *Genetics in Medicine* 14: 444–50.

Kaye, Jane, Curren, Liam, Anderson, Nick, Edwards, Kelly, Fullerton, Stephanie M., Kanellopoulou, Nadja, Lund, David, MacArthur, Daniel G., Mascalzoni, Deborah, Shepherd, James, Taylor, Patrick L., Terry, Sharon F. and Winter, Stefan F. 2013. 'From patients to partners: Participant-centric initiatives in biomedical research', *Nature Reviews Genetics* 13: 371–6.

Knoppers, Bartha Maria, Joly, Yann, Simard, Jacques and Durocher, Francine 2006. 'The emergence of an ethical duty to disclose genetic research results: An international perspective', *European Journal of Human Genetics* 14: 1170–8.

Kolata, Gina 2012. 'Genes now tell doctors secrets they can't utter', *New York Times* August 25.

Levitt, Mairi and Weldon, Sue 2005. 'A well placed trust?: Public perceptions of the governance of DNA databases', *Critical Public Health* 15: 311–21.

McKie, Robin 2013. 'Why do identical twins end up having such different lives?' *The Observer* June 2. Available at: www.guardian.co.uk/science/2013/jun/02/twins-identical-genes-different-health-study?INTCMP=SRCH (accessed 1 April 2014).

Meulenkamp, Tineke M., Gevers, Sjef J. K., Bovenberg, Jasper A. and Smets, Ellen M. A. 2012. 'Researchers' opinions towards the communication of results of biobank research: A survey study', *European Journal of Human Genetics* 20: 258–62.

National Bioethics Advisory Committee (USA) 1999. *Research Involving Human Biological Materials: Ethical Issues and Policy Guidance.* Available at: http://bioethics.georgetown.edu/nbac/hbm.pdf (accessed 27 June 2013).

Nijsingh, Niels 2012. 'Blurring boundaries', *American Journal of Bioethics* 12: 26–7.

Powers, Madison 2002. 'Privacy and genetics', in Burley and Harris (eds.) *A Companion to Genethics.* Oxford: Blackwell, pp. 364–78.

Rothstein, Mark 2013. 'Should researchers disclose results to descendants?' *American Journal of Bioethics* 13: 64–5.

Samet, Jonathan M. and Bailey, Linda A. 1997. 'Environmental population screening', in Rothstein (ed.) *Genetic Secrets: Protecting Privacy and Confidentiality in the Genetic Era.* Yale University Press, pp. 197–211.

Schulte, Paul A. 2004. 'Interpretation of genetic data for medical and public health uses', in Árnason, Nordal and Árnason (eds.) *Blood and Data. Ethical, Legal and Social Aspects of Human Genetic Databases.* Reykjavík: University of Iceland Press, pp. 277–82.

Sutrop, Margit and Simm, Kadri 2004. 'The Estonian healthcare system and the genetic database project: From limited resources to big hopes', *Cambridge Quarterly of Healthcare Ethics* 13: 254–62.

Tutton, Richard 2002. 'Gift relationships in genetic research', *Science as Culture* 11: 523–42.

UK Biobank consent form. Available at: www.ukbiobank.ac.uk/resources/ (accessed 27 June 2013).

Ursin, Lars Øysten, Hoeyer, Klaus and Skolbekken, John-Arne 2008. 'The informed consenters: Governing biobanks in Scandinavia', in Gottweis, Petersen (ed.) *Biobanks. Governance in Comparative Perspective.* Abingdon: Routledge, pp. 177–93.

Wallace, Susan E. and Kent, Alastair 2011. 'Population biobanks and returning individual research results: mission impossible or new directions?' *Hum Genet* 130: 393–401.

Wertz, Dorothy and Fletcher, John C. 1989. 'An international survey of attitudes of medical geneticists towards mass screening and access to results', *Public Health Reports* 104: 35–44.

Wolf, Susan M., Crock Brittney N., Van Ness Brian, Kahn, Lawrence, Frances, Jeffrey P., Beskow, Laura M., Cho, Mildred K., Christman, Michael F., Green, Robert C., Hall, Ralph, Illes, Judy, Keane, Moira, Knoppers, Bartha M., Koenig, Barbara A., Kohane, Isaac S., LeRoy, Bonnie, Maschke, Karen J., McGeveran, William, Ossorio, Pilar, Parker, Lisa S., Petersen, Gloria M., Richardson, Henry S., Scott, Joan A., Terry, Sharon F. and Wilfond, Benjamin S. 2012. 'Managing incidental findings and research results in genomic research involving biobanks and archived data sets', *Genetics in Medicine* 14: 361–84.

# 5    Suspects, victims and others: producing and sharing forensic genetic knowledge

*Robin Williams and Matthias Wienroth*

## Introduction

This chapter examines several related non-medical contexts in which genotyping is carried out and where questions arise over who has the right to commission, deploy and share with whom the results of that genotyping. There are three such contexts on which we focus attention. The first – and dominant one – is the application of genetic technologies to biological material recovered from crime scenes, from the victims of crime, from criminal suspects and from others for 'elimination purposes' in the course of criminal inquiries. The second is when genetic analysis is carried out on bodies recovered at 'mass disasters' in an effort to identify the dead. The third is the sampling and profiling of individuals involved in paternity and maternity disputes, or in other circumstances where it is deemed necessary to prove close genetic affiliation. We refer to all three of them as 'forensic' on the grounds that the primary purpose of each is to support legal process of various kinds, including the deliberations of civil, coronial, local, national and international criminal courts. Each genotyping knowledge context raises slightly different issues because of variations in the identities of the persons from whom samples are taken, the nature of the genetic information produced by preferred technologies, the primary purposes which its production serves and varying expectations of how much of this information should be shared with whom and under what circumstances.

A complicating factor is that close examination of some of these contexts suggests that the seemingly clear boundary between forensic genetic applications and the use of genetic knowledge within clinical medicine (or medical research) is often opaque in practice. This may be due to genetic inquiries crossing contexts of use (e.g., medical issues might be relevant for a criminal investigation or a paternity determination). It may be because medical information and genetic information have to be used in combination (e.g., to determine the robust identification of bodies), and it may also occur because some data generated by the application of particular genotyping methods are useful in both medical and non-medical contexts (e.g., analysis of ancestral lineage is relevant for biomedical research and for forensic identification).

In addition, important supplementary questions about the production, retention and dissemination of genetic knowledge are generated in the course of police or judicial inquiries, over and above those found in medical settings. Some arise from well-established considerations of privacy and confidentiality, whilst others arise from considerations of more recent claims concerning individuals' 'rights to be known' and its opposite, a 'right to be forgotten'. This chapter will consider all of these features, but before doing so will outline the varying forms of genetic knowledge that are typically sought in the course of forensic inquiries, the goals that such knowledge is intended to support, and the categories of people who may be subject to the application of forensic genetic knowledge in practice.[1]

## Forensic genetics: forms of knowledge and their application

The historical trajectory of forensic genetics has already been described in a number of texts (e.g., Hindmarsh and Prainsack 2010; Kaye 2010; Lazer 2004; Lynch et al. 2008; Williams and Johnson 2008). One feature of this trajectory is especially significant for the current discussion: its growing informativity. When first introduced, forensic DNA profiles were characterised appropriately as 'empty signifiers' (Pugliese 2010) insofar as the information captured first by Restriction Fragment Length Polymorphisms and subsequently by Short Tandem Repeat (STR) multiplexes were chosen from what were understood to be non-coding regions of the genome – so-called 'extragenic DNA'. This assertion was – and in part still is – heavily relied upon to defend the introduction or expansion of criminal justice DNA profiling and databasing whenever critics of the technology oppose it on the grounds of its risk to genetic privacy. Since the allelic combinations that make up STR profiles provide no information about functional genetic properties, then phenotypical or medical knowledge of the person whose profile has been constructed cannot directly be inferred from inspecting such profiles.[2] Medical, employment

---

[1] Most of this chapter's observations on issues in forensic genetics will refer to recent legislation and practice in England and Wales. However, from time to time we draw on material from other civil and criminal jurisdictions to illustrate particular points.

[2] Despite this fact, most court judgments relating to the sampling and profiling of DNA in support of criminal investigations still treat DNA profiles as 'sensitive personal information'. Data protection authorities normally share the same view, although such

and insurance agencies can learn nothing from an examination of the content of such profiles about the person from whom such data were derived, and it is difficult to think of any circumstances in which they would want to have this content anyway.[3] Nevertheless, and in line with common precautionary approaches, in all jurisdictions in which forensic DNA profiles are constructed from samples taken from individuals and from crime scenes, legislation normally limits their uses to policing and criminal justice purposes; knowledge of even these minimal details must not be shared with other agencies, including those with civil authority in paternity cases.[4]

The retention of samples following their successful profiling raises a more significant threat to the privacy of the individuals from whom such samples originated since their prospective informational content is genetically exhaustive. For this reason, forensic genetic legislation tends to strictly limit the control and uses of samples taken from suspects, offenders and others. In some cases, samples may be retained for varying periods of time, but in almost all cases, there are significant restrictions on any analysis that can be carried out on them and strict rules concerning their destruction. For example, the most recent UK legislation – the Protection of Freedoms Act 2012 – has radically reconfigured the previous retention regime in England and Wales by establishing different retention rules for DNA taken from convicted persons and that taken from unconvicted persons. It also establishes different retention periods for profiles taken from those convicted as adults and those convicted below the age of eighteen. Finally, it creates for the first time in this jurisdiction differences in the allowable retention period for those arrested and charged with 'qualifying offences' (serious, violent or sexual offences, terrorism and burglary offences) and those arrested and charged with other offences.[5]

Anyone whose DNA sample has been taken and whose profile has been constructed and retained following a criminal investigation in England and Wales has the right to know their profile information (under the

authorities have powers only over the information derived from samples and not samples themselves.

[3] This is, of course, entirely separate from circumstances in which medically relevant biological samples or genetic information about individuals might be of interest to forensic investigators. This could happen in criminal cases and in disaster victim identification and, along with other rare possibilities, does raise significant legal and ethical questions.

[4] However, it is worth noting that the range of organisations that come under the heading of 'authorised police or criminal justice agency' – and therefore have legitimate access to these genetic data – can be quite great.

[5] Full details of this legislation can be found at www.gov.uk/government/publications/protection-of-freedoms-act-2012-dna-and-fingerprint-provisions/protection-of-freedoms-act-2012-how-dna-and-fingerprint-evidence-is-protected-in-law (accessed 3 June 2014).

current SGM+™ profile system, consisting of their alleles at ten stand-ardised loci), although it is not clear why they would want it or what use they could make of it. The consequences of having such samples taken and retained depend less on the nature of the genetic information in the profile, but more on what is known (or believed) about the specific circumstances of sample collection, the uses that can be made of the retained sample and the profile derived from it, and on what the fact of databased profile retention is thought to connote about the individual. Depending on the particular forensic DNA legislation in place, reten-tion may signify only that the person sampled has, at least once, been arrested on suspicion of involvement in a crime. In other jurisdictions it may mean that the person sampled has been, at least once, charged with a crime. Under still other regimes it will show that they have been convicted of a crime. Each of these particulars – of growing 'involvement' in the criminal justice process – carries stigmatising connotations when they become known to a range of agencies and other actors.

The identity consequences and practical significance of having one's DNA profile retained on a legally governed database can only properly be determined once the full details of the regime in question are known. In addition, the significance of this potentially stigmatising retention and recording process varies according to the likelihood of others knowing this fact about the individual whose DNA has been retained. In Goffman's (1968) terms, such a fact might be discreditable for the individual con-cerned, but becomes discrediting only when known to others. For this, and other related reasons, the establishment, expansion and uses of such foren-sic DNA databases are the subject of constant deliberation in many juris-dictions, and there are many differences between jurisdictions concerning which categories of persons can be compulsorily sampled and profiled, against what existing profiles these 'subject' profiles should be specula-tively searched and whether, and for how long, subject profiles should be retained on such databases. The situation globally is complex and diver-gent. For example, in the UK and in some US states, DNA can be taken from any arrested person; in France, DNA samples from persons not charged or convicted can only be obtained voluntarily; and in Germany, DNA material can only be taken from charged or convicted persons.

Political sensitivity to these complicated issues of privacy, identity and stigma is often reflected in the terms used to denote forensic DNA databases. In the UK case, for example, the National DNA Database (NDNAD) was originally designated as a database that would hold 'the active criminal population' of England and Wales. It was then re-described, following the legislative changes that permitted the retention of profiles from the unconvicted, as a database of the 'active suspect population' of this jurisdiction, but even this modified nomenclature was both inaccurate and stigmatising. Not all profiles held on it were from criminal suspects since anyone who was sampled as part of an intelligence-led mass screening was asked if they would consent to the indefinite retention of their samples and profiles. In addition, some people whose profiles had been retained may have once been suspects, but subsequently cleared of involvement in a crime.

Questions of knowledge production and sharing arising from the collection, analysis and databasing of samples subjected to standardised STR profiling have been supplemented by additional questions that arise from more recent developments in forensic DNA analysis. Especially important are those developments designed to increase the capacity of investigators to infer information about an individual whose biological material was collected from a crime scene where an STR profile has been obtained from such material but has not matched a profile of a known individual.

These developments variously promise the capacity to infer from genetic analysis common but differentiated personal properties: of relatedness to others (by 'familial searching'), of features of visual appearance (through the genetic underpinning of visible characteristics) or of 'biogeographic origin'. Such promises remind us, of course, that forensic genetics has always sought to distinguish itself from the assertions of some other forensic fields to search for 'discernible uniqueness' by instead always asserting the presence of 'genotypes', 'haplotypes' and 'phenotypes' (Amorim 2012) with known frequencies in which individuals may be placed. Emerging innovations based on Single Nucleotide Polymorphisms (SNPs), such as biogeographic Ancestry Informative Markers (AIMs) and the genotyping of phenotypical information (Externally Visible Characteristics, EVCs) have raised expectations that in the near future forensic techniques can, with a convincing degree of certainty, determine the population group origins of a human DNA sample as well as provide information on some of the physical attributes – such as eye, hair and skin pigmentation; body and face morphology; and age – of the person whose sample has been analysed. Already, some studies have reported a degree of progress that gives cause for optimism about the capacity of such emergent technologies (e.g., Kayser and Schneider 2009; Ruiz et al. 2013; Spichenok et al. 2011; Walsh et al. 2011).

The use of these technologies represents a clear departure from earlier responses to privacy critics that forensic genetics only uses so-called 'non-coding' parts of the genome that do not hold any significant information about the individual and his or her relatives. Some (e.g., M'charek, Toom and Prainsack 2012; Toom 2012) have described this as a significant extension of jurisdictional intrusion into bodies and the information derived from them in support of criminal justice ambitions. In the case of ancestry informative markers and the enquiry into biogeographic ancestry in the context of criminal investigations, approaches to the interpretation of genetic data are unavoidably linked to prior social assumptions and categories. This means that forensic geneticists are by default steeped in a controversial history of classifying human individuals and groups through their genetic properties. Concerns about the use of 'racial' categories in forensic genetics, and their possible relationship to race issues in criminal justice generally have been reiterated recently (Chow-White and Duster 2011; Genewatch UK 2005; Ossorio and Duster 2005), with some even warning of a creeping scientificated politics of 'eugenics' (Duster 2003) or, more specifically, a 'racialisation' of forensic genetics (Skinner 2012) through the production of genetic 'facts' based on culturally misconceived and unreflective assumptions. The operational consequences of utilising technologies which offer the possibility of inferring genetic ancestry have been mixed. In the Dutch investigation of the murder of Marianne Vaastra, results from the analysis of the suspects' 'ethnic origins' successfully changed the focus of the investigation – and public prejudice – away from North African asylum seekers housed in a hostel near to the crime scene (Sankar 2010). However, the actions of the Metropolitan Police, following the ancestral profiling of suspect DNA in the British 'Operation Minstead' had negative effects on police–community relations and led to critical questioning in the House of Commons (Hansard Col 168W, October 2005).

Some of these techniques continue to face opposition in legal terms, following the *European Council Resolution 2001/C 187/01* of 25 June 2001 (Amorim 2012). Challenges to the informative value of AIMs and their relation to ethnic identity have been raised for scientific, social and practice-related reasons. A recurrent argument attends to the differences between genetic ethnic identification and self-identification of a donor, or even the attributed ethnicity of a donor through the person collecting samples. Cho and Sankar (2004) argue that in policing practice it is often assumed that a pre-conceived reference population and the suspect correspond, yet methods of assigning race or ethnicity have not yet undergone a process of standardisation, and are more often than not dependent on the individual conducting the assignment, and her interpretation of local reference populations. There is also considerable concern wherever concepts of 'race' and 'ethnicity' are used interchangeably in ways that neglect their differing social and scientific connotations (Bostanci 2011). Populations (groups and subgroups) are the basis for 'knowing' genetically, yet categories such as ethnic identity are socially constructed, indeed are a vital part of active identification of individuals and communities (Chow-White and Duster 2011; M'charek 2000; Skinner 2012). Even biological categories – and reference populations – are products of human classification and a necessary reduction of a complex world for efficacious and efficient engagement with it. Using these to make factual statements, critics anticipate, could lead DNA profiling to enforce, or at least support, existing unreflective social assumptions about race and ethnicity.

The boundary between the development and uses of ancestry-informative SNPs and the development and uses of phenotype-informative SNPs can be difficult to discern. AIMs are short sequences of DNA known to vary in frequency between geographically dispersed populations with no concern necessarily given to phenotypical differences between such populations. Markers used to predict EVCs may also be associated with biogeographic ancestry. Some studies are concerned to provide descriptors that are neutral with respect to ancestral features, while also being concerned to focus on SNPs 'located in and nearby genes known for their important role in pigmentation' in order to predict skin and eye colour (Spichenok et al. 2011). Other studies involving coloration – in this case eye colour – point to the difficulty caused by the existence of a 'complex and continuous range of intermediate phenotypes distinct from blue and brown eye colours' (Ruiz et al. 2013).

These more recent forensic innovations clearly raise issues of genetic knowledge production, dissemination and use that are different from those encountered in the earlier history of forensic genetics. Their introduction into policing has usually been supported by an underlying commitment to 'investigative pragmatics', a commitment which gives weight to their potential usefulness in investigations where other approaches have proved unproductive, and also to the claim that they are simply variants on more traditional ways of generating potentially useful information to support criminal investigations. These arguments stress the intelligence – rather than evidential – uses of such innovations, the necessity for careful explanations of their potential to investigators and a degree of sensitivity about their operational deployment. It is argued that phenotypical analysis provides only the genetic correspondences of externally visible and directly knowable physical characteristics of whoever is the source of biological material recovered from crime scenes. It hardly seems worth reminding the reader that knowledge of their own visual physical characteristics cannot be new knowledge to the (presumably unwitting) sample donor. In addition, such knowledge is irrelevant even to criminal prosecutions (as opposed to investigations) since, if suspects are identified through its uses, their DNA can be taken and their conventional STR profile directly compared to that already derived from the crime scene sample. The value of forensic genetic EVC inferencing is wholly investigative, in that it can be used to shape or support particular lines of inquiry, and as such, only criminal investigators or their surrogates will find it useful. It is difficult to argue that those involved in such legally sanctioned investigations do not have a right to know – or infer – this kind of information from recovered crime scene material, especially when other routine forms of forensic genetic knowledge prove unusable. However, this is not to say that the introduction of this kind of genetic technology – and the knowledge derivable from it – is entirely unproblematic.

Forensic DNA tests and databases are generally acknowledged to be intrusive interventions into the lives of citizens, even though the degree of intrusiveness may be contested. For Eric Juengst, the primary question which should frame our thinking about the range of legitimate uses of such technologies was 'What should society be allowed to learn about its citizens in the course of attempting to identify them?' (Juengst cited in Etzioni 2004, 210). Whilst this clearly is the basic question, any adequate answer to it has to consider carefully what agencies and actors are imagined to stand for 'society', the range of purposes to which such acts of identification are put, and the overall values to which these efforts are oriented. It may also be necessary to distinguish between the different categories of persons who may be subject to such identification practices, especially 'criminals', 'suspects and persons of interest', 'victims' and 'innocents'. Typically, it is argued that relevant authorities have a right to know the genetic identities of the first, whereas members of both the third and fourth categories are seen as needing protection from the risks posed by the use of such technologies in pursuit of justice. It is the second category of persons, 'suspects and persons of interest', that creates most deliberative difficulties concerning the application of forensic genetics.

Especially significant in this regard may be the risk to vulnerable minority social groups whose members may become the subject of investigative attention in cases of serious and high profile crimes where genetic profiling has identified suspect offenders as belonging to such groups. In addition, such investigative attention may feed and exacerbate existing social and criminal justice disadvantages already experienced by these group members. These arguments are still to be played out in a number of contemporary jurisdictions, but as might be expected, there are different ways in which jurisdictional authorities are seeking to govern the introduction of forensic genetic innovations into criminal justice systems. For example, in the United Kingdom there seem to be no legislative efforts to restrict the application of EVC or AIM technologies, whilst familial searching is governed by guidelines first agreed between the Association of Chief Police Officers and the Information Commissioner. However, other European jurisdictions have proceeded with more caution. Many states have enacted legislative restrictions on the use of genetic technologies that promise information about biogeographic ancestry or other phenotypical properties of persons, and the use of familial searching is not currently allowed in some states of the USA and in many European countries.

## The right to be known and the right to be forgotten

The previous section of this chapter has focused on the legitimate rights of specific social agencies to know the identities of those subject to criminal or civil procedure, as well as the obligations and costs that accompany those rights. This section considers two complementary claims that are sometimes asserted in contemporary modern societies. In the first instance, there are circumstances in which individuals may themselves assert (on their own behalf, or on behalf of others) a right to be known, seeming explicitly or implicitly to draw on notions of 'recognition' that derive from the work of Hegel. For Hegel, the identity of persons is an effect of the activities of others – actors and institutions – with whom they interact. Recognition of another person as an autonomous agent is a crucial instance of such activities since it is both an expression of value of one for another, and a fundamental feature of self-identity for the subject. In Norman's (1976) account, 'in order to see myself as being equally a person in just this same manner, I must not only recognise others as persons but also be recognised by them as a person. Thereby my own existence is given an objective validity' (Norman 1976: 47–8). This deeply embedded philosophical claim has been enacted in a variety of ways and in a variety of circumstances in modern societies. Contemporary notions of citizenship and the entitlements that accompany it are among the more obvious administrative realisations of this aspect of identity, and there is a large body of political and legal literature which reflects on the meaning and significance of the recognition of the self by legal and social institutions (e.g., Douzinas 2002; Honneth 1995; Szreter and Breckenridge 2012; Taylor 1994; Thompson 2006).

It is for these reasons that we accord some significance to the claim that there are circumstances in which it is reasonable for individuals to assert on their own and others' behalf a right to be (personally or categorically) known. Certainly modern states seem to acknowledge an obligation to meet this right through a series of measures. These include

birth records and death records, passports and a variety of other entitlement documents depending on the jurisdiction in question. On some
occasions, there will be bioinformatic features of such records, either
as component elements (as in the case of biometric passports), or as
underpinning evidence (as in the case of bodies identified through fin-
gerprints or DNA). Whilst many of these instances are elements within a
state control apparatus, the establishment and use of such technologies
are also shaped by the desire for recognition on the part of the subject
whose identity is being captured by them. It is for both of these reasons
that modern states have an obligation to record stable features of individuals' identities. Those whose identities have not been recorded in such
ways may well find themselves unable to benefit fully from many aspects
of contemporary life, including international travel, health provision
and a range of other forms of state assistance. In addition, even those
with recorded identities may seek to know to whom they are genetically
related, and a right to obtain that knowledge is increasingly embedded
in adoption, surrogacy and reproductive donation systems in many societies. Finally, the extensive investments in organisational infrastructures
and technological support for 'disaster victim identification' also test-
ify to a willingness to acknowledge the significance of individuals being
authoritatively 'known' by others, even after death.

Whilst there is no necessary connection between socio-legal 'recognition' and DNA as such, it is clear that confidence in the application of
genetics is increasingly critical for the resolution of contested claims over
identity, and therefore an increasingly trusted anchorage for the recognised identity of both living human subjects and human remains.

What then, about the other element in a possible pair of such (putative) rights – the 'right to be forgotten' (elsewhere known as the 'right
to deletion', the 'right to oblivion' or 'droit d'oubli'). Views of the existence of such a right are currently unsettled, at least as far as its current
instantiation in proposals concerning data protection rights of Internet
users are concerned. However, the notion of a right to be forgotten reso-
nates with a recognised feature of most modern criminal justice regimes
since these usually contain within them rehabilitative as well as punitive
imperatives. Most contemporary data protection legislation asserts that
individuals generally have a right to the deletion of information about
them when this information is no longer needed for legitimate purposes,
although special consideration is often given to the retention of information relating to criminal inquiries.

In the case of criminal matters, however, an additional argument is
sometimes made that the retention and dissemination of information
about offenders may also interfere with the state's ability to achieve the

legitimate goal of rehabilitating them, and then again, the informational rights of those convicted of criminal offences may be seen as very different from those who have only been suspected of involvement in such offences, have once been 'persons of interest' to the police or witnesses to a crime. Forensic genetic practices can interfere with this right when DNA databasing regimes allow the police to retain profiles from suspects or from the convicted for extended periods of time. It is for this reason that most DNA databasing legislation tends to have complex rules allowing for a differential retention of profiles from different categories and ages of persons for varying periods of time. Alongside these variations, there exist different rules for speculative searching according to the status of the person who has been sampled.[6] The most recent set of changes to the retention regime of the NDNAD of England and Wales has seen the establishment of the office of the 'Biometrics Commissioner', who will consider all requests by the police for the retention of DNA profiles from those who have not been convicted of a crime but are still the subject of 'legitimate' and grounded police suspicion as being a threat to individual safety or state security.

## Conclusion

Many different kinds of genetic information are mobilised in a number of diverse environments, including medical research, health care, advertising and popular culture. In each of these domains and others, claims for genetic informativity – that analysis of the human genome can provide domain-relevant information – are subject to differing criteria of evaluation and accountability. The kind of genomic information sought and produced by those using DNA profiling in forensic investigations varies according to the specific technologies used and on the more particular civil or criminal context in which such data are required, produced and negotiated. These contexts have administrative, legal and social dimensions that influence the production and interpretation of forensic genetic data, and as such their informative value and normative authority.

It is the view of some academic and legal authorities that a person has no reasonable expectation of privacy in their DNA profile if the sample from which the profile was developed was taken lawfully during the

---

[6] For reasons that we cannot fully understand, most contributors to the European debate about this topic prefer to characterise it as the problem of 'retention' whilst in the USA it is more often characterised as the problem of 'expungement'. It is the same problem, although it is perhaps worth noting that the early difficulties experienced with the illegal retention of profiles on the NDNAD by the (then) UK Forensic Science Service were a result of Police Service 'difficulties' in establishing the basis for robust expungement procedures.

course of a criminal investigation, and if the profile contains information without any medical or other personal meaning. Proponents of this argument usually cite its value to crime control imperatives, but also restrict the uses of such profiles to 'law enforcement' or to the 'investigation of crime and the prosecution of offenders', 'criminal justice' or 'police' uses. For others, such privacy rights are distributed according to the category of persons whose biological material has been sampled, alongside the recognition that individuals can move from one category to another, and that there may also be good reasons to treat adults who fall into any of these categories differently from children (see, for example, Levitt and Tomasini 2006).

In the first edition of this book, Henk ten Have (1997: 88) wrote: 'The fact that knowledge is available should not itself dictate its application. What is necessary is prior identification of the goals that we want to accomplish in using the knowledge, a careful balancing of the benefits and harms generated through the application of knowledge, and a delineation of the norms and values that should be respected.' In the course of this chapter we have tried to follow this advice by examining how a widening variety of forms of genetic knowledge are increasingly captured during the course of criminal and other legally authorised investigations. In each case the epistemic authority of genetic science is deployed as a powerful source of intelligence or evidence to support inquiries and judicial decision making. Globally, police investigators have been especially enthusiastic in their embrace of these possibilities. In turn, forensic geneticists have been eager to expand the repertoire of technologies available to the police by responding to recurrent investigative questions that are capable of being answered – at least in part – with new or modified genotyping practices. Even the most precautionary critics would not want to deny to legally recognised authorities the powers to use these technologies to establish the identity of criminal suspects, or those who have died following violence or natural disasters.

This mutually supportive enterprise, the goal of which has largely been to improve the effectiveness and robustness of criminal justice and the rule of law, has been both reinforced and disturbed by a variety of deliberations and commentaries in which other values, risks and desiderata have been considered alongside those of security and justice. Most usually cited amongst these other values and desiderata are the swarm of features that make up respect for human dignity, and it has been an orientation to this swarm that has shaped how questions of a 'right to know', a 'right to be known', and a 'right to be forgotten' bear on the ambitions and practice of forensic genetics. These features include consideration of the ways in which privacy rights, the protection of autonomous action, and safeguarding the liberties of human subjects all bear upon the use and dissemination of knowledge of individuals produced by the application of forensic genetics. In the course of this chapter we have tried to indicate the heterogeneity of technologies that are often included in the simple designation 'forensic DNA' or 'forensic genetics' along with some of the complexities that occur when different kinds of individuals – suspects, victims, offenders, persons of interest, relatives, volunteers, and others – either provide samples for analysis or are identified through the profiling of someone else's sample.

## References

Amorim, Antonio 2012. 'Opening the DNA black box: Demythologizing forensic genetics', *New Genetics and Society* 31(3): 259–70.

Bostanci, Adam 2011. 'Genetic ancestry testing as ethnic profiling', *Science as Culture* 20(1): 107–14.

Cho, Mildred K. and Pamela Sankar 2004. 'Forensic genetics and ethical, legal and social implications beyond the clinic', *Nature Genetics Supplement* 36: S8–S12.

Chow-White, Peter A. and Troy Duster 2011. 'Do health and forensic DNA databases increase racial disparities?' *PLoS Medicine* 8(10): e1001100.

Douzinas, Costas 2002. 'Identity, recognition, rights or what can Hegel teach us about human rights?' *Journal of Law and Society* 29: 379–405.

Duster, Troy 2003. *Backdoor to Eugenics*. 2nd edn, New York: Routledge.

Etzioni, Amitai 2004. 'DNA tests and databases in criminal justice. Individual rights and the common good', in David Lazer (ed.) *DNA and the Criminal Justice System. The technology of justice*. Cambridge, MA: The MIT Press, pp. 197–224.

Genewatch UK 2005. *The Police National DNA Database: Balancing crime detection, human rights and privacy*. Available at: www.genewatch.org/uploads/f03c6d66a9b354535738483c1c3d49e4/NationalDNADatabase.pdf (accessed 2 April 2014).

Goffman, Erving 1968. *Stigma: Notes on the management of spoiled identity*. London: Penguin Books.

Hindmarsh, Richard and Barbara Prainsack 2010. *Genetic Suspects: Global governance of forensic DNA profiling and databasing*. Cambridge University Press.

Honneth, A. 1995. *The Struggle for Recognition: The grammar of social conflicts*. Cambridge: Polity Press.

Kaye, D. H. 2010. *The Double Helix and the Law of Evidence*. Cambridge, MA: Harvard University Press.

Kayser, Manfred and Peter M. Schneider 2009. 'DNA-based prediction of human externally visible characteristics in forensics: Motivations, scientific challenges, and ethical considerations', *Forensic Science International: Genetics* 3: 154–61.

Lazer, David 2004. *DNA and the Criminal Justice System: The technology of justice*. Cambridge, MA: MIT Press.

Levitt, Mairi and F. Tomasini 2006. 'Bar-coded children: An exploration of issues around the inclusion of children on the England & Wales National DNA Database', *Genomics and Policy* 2: 41–56.

Lynch, M., S. Cole, R. McNally and K. Jordan 2008. *Truth Machine: The contentious history of DNA fingerprinting*. Chicago University Press.

M'charek, Amâde 2000. 'Technologies of population: Forensic DNA testing practices and the making of differences and similarities', *Configurations* 8(1): 121–58.

M'charek, A., V. Toom and B. Prainsack 2012. 'Bracketing off population does not advance ethical reflection on EVCs: A reply to Kayser and Schneider', *Forensic Science International: Genetics* 6(1): e16–e17.

Norman, R. 1976. *Hegel's Phenomenology: A philosophical introduction*. London: Sussex University Press.

Ossorio, Pilar and Troy Duster 2005. 'Race and genetics: Controversies in biomedical, behavioural and forensic sciences', *American Psychologist* 60(1): 115–28.

Pugliese, Joseph 2010. *Biometrics: Bodies, technologies, biopolitics*. London: Routledge.

Ruiz, Y., C. Phillips, A. Gomez-Tato, J. Alvarez-Dios, M. Scasares de Cal, R. Cruz, O. Maronas, J. Sochtig, M. Fondevila, M. J. Rodriguez-Cid, A. Carracedo and M. V. Lareu 2013. 'Further development of forensic eye colour predictive tests', *Forensic Science International: Genetics* 7(1): 28–40.

Sankar, Pamela 2010. 'Forensic DNA phenotyping: Reinforcing race in law enforcement', in Ian Whitmarsh and David S. Jones (eds.) *What's the Use of Race?* Cambridge, MA: MIT Press, pp. 49–62.

Skinner, David 2012. 'Mobile identities and fixed categories: Forensic DNA and the politics of racialized data', in K. Schramm, D. Skinner and R. Rottenburg (eds.) *Identity Politics and the New Genetics*. Oxford: Berghahn Books, pp. 53–78.

Spichenok, Olga, Zoran M. Budimlija, Adele A. Mitchell, Andreas Jenny, Lejla Kovacevic, Damir Marjanovic, Theresa Caragine, Mechthild Prinz and Elisa Wurmbach 2011. 'Prediction of eye and skin color in diverse populations using seven SNPs', *Forensic Science International: Genetics* 5: 472–8.

Szreter, Simon and Keith Breckenridge 2012. 'Recognition and registration: The infrastructure of personhood in world history', in Keith Breckenridge and Simon Szreter (eds.) *Registration and Recognition: Documenting the person in world history*. Oxford University Press, pp. 1–36.

Taylor, C. 1994. 'The politics of recognition', in Amy Gutmann (ed.) *Multiculturalism: Examining the politics of recognition*. Princeton University Press, pp. 25–73.

Ten Have, Henk 1997. 'Living with the future: Genetic information and human existence', in Ruth Chadwick, Mairi Levitt and Darren Shickle (eds.) *The Right to Know and the Right Not to Know*. Aldershot: Avebury, pp. 87–95.

Thompson, Simon 2006. *The Political Theory of Recognition*. Cambridge: Polity Press.

Toom, V. 2012. 'Bodies of science and law: Forensic DNA profiling, biological bodies, and biopower', *Journal of Law and Society* 39(1): 150–66.

Walsh, S., A. Lindenbergh, S. B. Zuniga, T. Sijen, P. de Knijff, M. Kayser and K. N. Ballantyne 2011. 'Developmental validation of the IrisPlex system: Determination of blue and brown iris colour for forensic intelligence', *Forensic Science International: Genetics* 5(5): 464–71.

Williams, R. and P. Johnson 2008. *Genetic Policing: The use of DNA in criminal investigations*. Cullompton: Willan Publishing.

# 6    Empowered by choice?

*Mairi Levitt*

At the heart of the right to know and the right not to know debate is the right to choose, which is predicated on the right to information, and other relevant resources, to enable a choice to be made. In many areas of every-day life choices have proliferated; in affluent countries there are more TV channels and types of eggs, ways of serving coffee or listening to music than ever before. Many of these choices may be trivial, but patients and parents are also increasingly bombarded with information and advice on more serious matters concerning health and child rearing. Patients and parents can obtain information to help make a choice of where to go for hospital treatment or which school they would like their child to attend. Hospital and school league tables and websites provide information on outcomes (e.g., survival rates after different types of surgery or examin-ation pass rates), staffing levels and other factors that might influence decisions (hospital car parking or school uniform policy). Even in soci-eties with universal health and education provision, it is acknowledged by providers that the more 'informed and articulate' have more choices, including the choice to go elsewhere into the private sector.

This chapter first discusses the choice agenda in health and the effects of choice on the chooser. Next, the possibility and desirability of chan-ging the focus from individual autonomy and ever-increasing choice is considered and discussed through the example of the genetic screening of embryos and children.

The assumption is frequently made that the individual will be empow-ered by choice, and more empowered when more choices are offered. In a study of an attempt to 'empower' the lives of elderly people living in long-stay hospital wards, empowerment was said to be about:

people's ability to control their lives and act as autonomous individuals. It is about people being able to define their own needs, rather than their needs being defined for them.

(Ahlquist 1997, p. 4)

Empowerment was a means to improve the quality of individuals' lives. In any society there is a relation between power and status on the one

85

hand and the choices available to people on the other. The impoverished are not only economically poor but will generally have fewer choices and control in all areas of their lives than the more affluent. Although increasing choice for all does not necessarily reduce these inequalities, the centrality of choice in education and health in the UK stresses an equal opportunities agenda.

Choice has always been available to some people. Some have had the resources to opt out of the NHS. Others have proved informed and articulate enough to access choices within the NHS that are not routinely available to others.

The Government believes that all patients should have the advantages of choices over their healthcare. The NHS should develop as a personalised service, open to everyone.

(Department of Health 2000)

The NHS Plan quoted above went on to stress the importance of a diversity of provision from which choices can be made to meet different needs. 'Equity and Excellence' was the title of the government white paper (Department of Health 2010). Decision making, it stated, is to be shared with patients who are to have information, choice and control. This is said to result in increased efficiency and higher standards in the health-care system. The subsequent consultation on the proposals had a 'vision of informed, empowered patients making personal choices' but acknowledged that there are 'major challenges in making sure that everyone can exercise choices that do not cause problems for them or the NHS (Department of Health 2010, point 7).

Choice alone, even in the absence of economic costs, does not ensure equality. In health care, and others areas such as education, the active, information-seeking, articulate parent or patient is both a problem, because their success in getting the best service impacts on others, and the model to emulate.

While it could be argued that what people really want is access to a good local hospital, rather than more choices, the assumption is that increased choice leads to greater satisfaction. Where there is more choice, fewer people are likely to get their first choice because the hospitals and facilities considered to be the best will tend to be oversubscribed. A report on the ethics of rationing in the NHS makes the case for 'nudging' patient choice:

Patients should be 'nudged' towards preferred uses of NHS services, through the provision of clear information and making it easy for patients to make the 'right' choices.

(Rumbold et al. 2012, p. 44)

Since the hospitals considered to be the best will be the most difficult to access, it seems likely that the existence, if not the reality, of choice will widen inequalities because those with the most social capital will find out the criteria to be given priority and endeavour to fulfil them, whatever they are.

In the commercial sector companies endeavour to persuade consumers to choose their products and be satisfied enough with their choice to purchase them again. Public providers hope that, in taking on responsibility for choice from the professionals, individuals will be both more satisfied and more engaged in the process.

There is extensive research into the effects of an ever-increasing range of choices on the chooser. While this is mainly in the field of consumer behaviour it has been applied to other fields, including choices in higher education (Arterian 2007) and health (Botti *et al.* 2009). Some key findings of these US studies are that:

- Being able to make choices has a beneficial effect on motivation and performance in research where participants are asked to complete tasks, including creative tasks, and at work where people have some control over their physical environment.
- There are class and cultural differences in the value accorded to being able to choose.
- Greatly increased choices in consumer goods can lead to confusion and indecision resulting in people being reluctant to choose at all (Chua and Iyengar 2006, p. 56).
- Being offered choice between undesirable options causes stress, anxiety and conflict in the chooser (Chua and Iyengar 2006, p. 54). In these circumstances those for whom a choice is made are more satisfied than those who choose for themselves.
- Those who explore every option before choosing ('maximisers') tend to have high expectations which are unlikely to be fulfilled and they suffer from dissatisfaction and stress (Schwartz 2004).

These studies begin to differentiate between choosers and subdivide them into groups according to personality traits, assessed by psychological tests, by culture and socio-economic status. The findings confirm that having choices is valued by those who are well educated, in a middle class or professional occupation and from a Western cultural background that valorises individualism rather than inter-dependence (Chua and Iyengar 2006). As Matravers argues, in Western societies to be an adult is to be an agent, with the ability to choose and liable to be held to account for the choices made (Matravers 2007, p. 4). Stephens, Markus and Townsend argue that choice is associated with agency but that agency is more central to the middle classes than it is to the working class, for whom conformity to the group is important to well-being (Stephens *et al.* 2007, p. 827).

### Choice and responsibility

In making a choice individuals become responsible for the outcome. It is their choice, whether good or bad. Of course not all choices can be lumped together and when it comes to choices that have a tragic consequence (e.g., the death of a newborn baby) parents who made the choice for themselves were found to cope less well with the outcome. An ethnographic study comparing parents with newborn children on life support in France and the USA found that decisions to switch off the machine were left to the physicians in France, whereas in USA parents had to make decisions themselves. The researchers concluded that 'when confronted by tragic choices individuals are likely to be better off if those choices are either physically or psychologically removed from them' (Botti *et al.* 2009, p. 349).

The authors do not use their findings to call for a return to paternalism but rather to argue that it is too simple to say offering choice is best when dealing with 'messy realities' and that the demand for participation will vary between parents (Botti *et al.* 2009, p. 350). Bearing the responsibility for choice was a burden for parents in those circumstances; they felt they were being asked to choose for their child to die, and to be able to follow expert advice provided support and made them feel better about the decision.

Similar findings were made in a qualitative study of UK women making decisions in pregnancy about antenatal screening (Ahmed *et al.* 2012). In the UK health professionals are required to provide the information necessary for patients to make 'autonomous, informed decisions' by providing the necessary value-neutral information and being non-directive (Ahmed *et al.* 2012, p. 2). While some have long argued that the ideology of genetic counselling does not, or cannot, be realised in practice (Clarke 1991; Mitchie *et al.* 1997) this study by Ahmed *et al.* found that women wanted advice to help them come to a decision about screening. The women interpreted 'advice' in different ways: as information alone, as guidance and support and as providing direction. Most understood that professionals did not want to give an opinion for ethical reasons, and the fear of being sued, but they would have valued their advice in order to help them come to their own decision (Ahmed *et al.* 2012, p. 6).

The problem with making choices in the real world is that outcomes are not predictable and so however much information is available it cannot answer the crucial question: will *my* baby be healthy? If I undergo one more course of IVF will *I* have a successful pregnancy? However small the risk, your baby may be the one in a thousand that has the condition; however many courses of IVF you have had there is a chance that the next one will be successful so how can you make the decision to stop? While the idealised situation is one in which 'the individual is free to select whatever action she or he desires...'(Paton 2007), in practice individuals live in particular social and cultural contexts that impinge on their decision making. Where IVF treatment is publicly funded, treatment will usually be limited; in England and Wales the recommendation is that three cycles should be offered for women who meet the criteria (National Institute for Clinical Excellence 2004). Women who can pay for private treatment have more choices. In Peddie *et al*.'s study of women who had undergone IVF without success, the psychological, emotional and social costs of prolonged and unsuccessful treatment were clear but the decision to end treatment was difficult. Two themes in the findings were unrealistic expectations of success and social and media pressure; the social obligation to keep trying new technology and the constant promises of new breakthroughs that might offer new hope (Peddie *et al*. 2005, p. 1946). In this example, women are being asked to choose between undesirable options: stopping treatment and so acknowledging that they will almost certainly never give birth, or continuing expensive treatment which affects their health with a diminishing chance of success after unsuccessful cycles.

The choice discourse is convenient for service providers and difficult for individuals to resist. However, as discussed, ever-increasing choices in consumer goods and health care do not ensure consumer or patient satisfaction or happiness. Rather, a 'proliferation of options seems to lead, inexorably, to the raising of expectations' (Schwartz 2004, p. 186). In a publicly funded health system, there will inevitably be dissatisfaction among those who find that the choice they made is not in fact available.

### Choosing as self-expression

The act of choosing is not just important because of the value attached to autonomy and the association of choice with freedom but because making choices is an expression of who we are (Iyengar 2010). We define who we are in relation to other people, so choosing is actually a social act that communicates to others what sort of persona we want to portray. As we choose we ask 'What kind of individual am I, and given who I am, what should I want, and given what I should want, what do I choose?' (Iyengar 2010, p. 272).

In this self-conscious model of the individual, we constantly monitor the reactions of others and modify our behaviour and choices accordingly. In the classic social constructivist account human beings construct their social world through interactions with others and then perceive it as objective reality which in turn constrains their actions. The ability to shape our environment could mean that human beings were overwhelmed by the constant choices that had to be made. As discussed earlier, the multiplication of choices can lead to confusion and anxiety, and the way of resolving this is to limit the need for decisions by establishing standards, routines and habits that reduce the need for choice (Schwartz 2004, p. 114).

In every society there are socially acceptable ways of doing things that remove the need for individuals to decide how to act in every situation; their actions become habitualised: 'Habitualization carries with it the important psychological gain that choices are narrowed ... This frees the individual from the burden of all those decisions' (Berger and Luckmann 1967, p. 71).

In many modern societies choices have multiplied in areas where there were once strong norms and sanctions for those who broke them, for example, sexuality, family life and gender roles.

### Removing choice

As 'choices' are burgeoning in both the public and private health sectors, is there an alternative to the stress on choice; could choices be restricted on ethical grounds that would be socially acceptable? The idea of simply removing choice has been discussed in relation to participation in medical research and to organ donation, both areas where informed consent must be obtained (Evans 2004; Harris 2003). The value attached to informed consent makes any suggestions of compulsion controversial. Evans (2004) argues that, in a publicly funded health-care system, there is a moral duty to take part in research in some circumstances. He limits this to cases where the patient has sought treatment for a condition and is eligible to be enrolled in research into treatment, the research is not expected to harm the patient and it may benefit others. In these circumstances enrolment should be automatic:

And because not everyone can be relied on to do their duty, in clinical research ... then responsibility for the decision must be given to others. You should be entered into the research automatically, and if you want to obtain treatment in these circumstances then you should no more have a veto over taking part in the research than you should have a veto over paying your income tax.

(Evans 2004, p. 202)

The argument is that those currently having treatment benefit from those who took part in medical research in the past and thus have an obligation to help others in the future.

In the case of organ donation many European countries have some form of opt-out system where the onus is on those who do not want to donate to make their wishes known. However, in practice, even in Spain, which has the highest rates of cadaveric donation, organs are not removed unless the family agrees (Navarro-Michel 2011, p. 160). Compulsion even in limited circumstances is controversial. After all, the emphasis on informed consent and the frameworks for ethical review of research involving human subjects followed the abuses carried out in the name of medical research in the 1930s and 40s. Abuses in human medical research have often involved subjects who are neither high status nor powerful. So, looking at the analogy Evans draws with income tax payment above, there are ways in which the elite may minimise their tax payments with the help of experts, while most UK employees have tax deducted by their employer. No doubt there would also be ways of avoiding compulsory enrolment in research for those with the resources to seek alternative treatment.

Imposing compulsion in an attempt to reach a desired end in health care – a wider cross-section of medical research subjects, more organs for transplant – might not be workable in a democracy. Would the media soon be reporting on tearful relatives whose loved ones' organs were taken against their wishes or on people refusing treatment because they did not want to be enrolled in medical research? But what about alternative ethical framings that are less individualistic? There have been criticisms of the value accorded to individual autonomy and a counter move in ethics to more communitarian values such as solidarity, reciprocity, dignity and prudence (Hayry 2003; Knoppers and Chadwick 2005). When discussing donations to biobanks, population genetic databases established for research purposes, the argument can be made for a solidarity-based approach rather than one based on individual autonomy (Prainsack and Buyx 2012). However, in other areas such as genetic testing, a solidarity approach seems less tenable because it would require people who are making choices about what is best for themselves or their children to focus on broader issues.

## Genetic tests, treatment and enhancement

For the individual, genetic tests are available for an ever-increasing range of traits that carry elevated risk of developing a disease or behavioural condition. Most people are probably unaware of the profusion of genetic tests but those who are pregnant, undergoing IVF or have a family history of a specific disorder will be offered a limited range of tests. While access to genetic testing will be restricted for publicly funded patients, and may vary according to their location, privately funded patients have more choices, which in turn puts pressure on the public health service to increase availability. Since 2009 UK clinics that offer fertility services have been licensed to test patients for specific genetic traits through pre-implantation genetic diagnosis (PGD), rather than having to apply on a case-by-case basis. Since 2010, traits that indicate lower penetrance and late onset conditions can be included, meaning that a percentage of those with the trait will never develop the condition and others will develop it only in adulthood. These include BRCA1 and BRCA2 muta-tions that carry an increased risk of breast and ovarian cancer and muta-tions associated with early onset Alzheimer's disease. For UK women with a breast cancer trait, their lifetime risk of developing breast cancer is raised from around 12 per cent to over half. The Human Fertilisation and Embryology Authority (HFEA) undertook a consultation entitled *Choices and Boundaries*, before introducing PGD for these conditions (HFEA 2006). A response from GeneWatch UK objected to the use of the term 'choice' rather than 'decision' in the title of the consultation, on the grounds that it 'tends to turn the process into one of marketing, not serious deliberation'(GeneWatch UK 2006). The particular imperative to emphasise choice in genetics is of course the shadow of eugenics in the sense of state-enforced controls over births. Wachbroit and Wasserman argue that this legacy of abuse is why those patients who are offered gen-etic tests and disease screening are seen to require specialist counsellors. The official role of genetic counsellors is non-directive; they are to offer individualistic, client-centred therapy that allows patients to make their own decisions (Wachbroit and Wasserman 1995, p. 238). As has been pointed out, the cumulative effect of individual choices can, like state-enforced controls, also lead to societal change. For instance, preferences for boys over girls have resulted in distorted sex ratios in parts of India and China (Hesketh 2011).

Regulation within a country may limit access to PGD, prenatal testing and childhood testing but direct-to-consumer testing operating in less regulated environments opens up availability. Is individual choice in this area empowering and, if so, who is empowered?

Savulescu supports a broadening of PGD to non-disease traits. In his view, parents should have information about non-disease traits through genetic testing, be able to freely choose which child to bear through PGD and be provided with 'non-coercive advice' on which child has the highest chance of having the best life (Savulescu 2001, pp. 424–5). Using the Internet and international market, consumers can currently purchase tests for themselves and their children either individually, as a package, or arrange an entire genome scan. They can investigate their genetic risk for all sorts of physical and mental disorders, including complex multifactorial disorders, look into their genetic ancestry, identify those genetically related to them or check out their child's 'inborn talent'. Companies based in the USA that offer hundreds of tests and even whole genome scans include 23andMe, deCODEme and SeqWright, all easily found by a web search engine. The California Department of Public Health wrote to thirteen companies based in the state requesting that they 'cease and desist' from offering testing to California residents (Magnus *et al.* 2009). The state of California requires companies offering such tests to be licensed and patients should not access tests without a physician's order (*ibid.*). The companies that replied made three arguments: that genetic information is a fundamental part of a person and individuals have a right to it; that the tests are not really genetic because they give information on genetic predisposition; and that people should have access to their own health information directly, without having to involve a physician (*ibid.*).

The company 23andMe markets DNA testing as 'a "one size fits all" perfect gift' that will allow the recipient to: 'Gain insight into your traits, from baldness to muscle performance. Discover risk factors for more than 200 health conditions with the assurance that the list grows each month.' These 'health conditions' include serious diseases like breast, stomach and lung cancer, Parkinson's disease and Alzheimer's disease, so it might not be a 'perfect gift' for all! For those testing newborn babies or toddlers who cannot yet spit, there is the opportunity to send for a special test kit that requires only a quarter teaspoon of saliva to be collected. No restrictions on parents testing their children are mentioned here.

Although the arguments evoke individual autonomy and the right to know, company websites may also appeal to solidarity and community in their marketing. The 23andMe website contains research findings and in a section entitled 'core values' has the following message to potential patients:

you're joining in a community of motivated individuals who can collectively impact research and basic human understanding. In today's connected information age, it's no longer just about me. Instead it is about how we can change our understanding of ourselves by joining together.

Another group of companies target their products specifically at parents of young children. Companies such as talent4me and My Gene Profile offer a raft of genetic tests claiming to reveal your child's 'inborn talents'. Parents are told that they will find out whether their child has a particular sporting talent or is musical so that they know how to best direct their child and avoid the frustration and failure that comes of encouraging participation in a type of sport in which he or she will not succeed. Parents can replace the hit-and-miss approach of giving their child all sorts of enrichment classes and instead take scientific direction, know where the child's talents lie and 'spend money wisely' (My Gene Profile).

Leaving aside the question of the validity and reliability of the tests and how many parents have actually used them, it is clear that the website material plays on parental insecurities and competitiveness. Your child can only succeed by having the edge over other people's children:

> These advertisements describe complex, confusing, and anxiety-producing genetic concepts for the consumer. Drawing on themes of 'choice,' 'hope,' 'fear,' and 'peace of mind,' these advertisements validate patients' worries about their genetic risks and appeal to their desire to assert control over potential outcomes.
>
> (Golhurst et al. 2002)

The advertisements are designed to create desires and demands in parents, increase the numbers using genetic testing and provide 'solutions' to problems that parents did not previously know they had (GeneWatch UK 2006). The view of genes conveyed in the brochure (English version) is that they are static things that can be read off to see whether or not a child has a strong 'leadership gene' or 'performance gene' so that parents can have scientific direction rather than a hit-and-miss approach to helping their children.

If parents took up the opportunity to access these tests to get the edge for their child, or prospective child, weighing up what to do with the results, whether using PGD or discerning a child's 'inborn talent', may not be straightforward. The more tests that can be performed the harder it will be to decide which the 'best' potential child is, or, which inborn talent to pursue. The embryo with the predisposition to aggression and criminal behaviour seems an obvious one to discard but if the increased risk is only in cases where the child is maltreated (Caspi et al. 2002) then perhaps this is better than a predisposition to alcoholism. If your child's inborn talent test reveals a talent for rugby football and susceptibility to alcohol addiction then perhaps the responsible parent would not encourage the child to play rugby because of the temptations of post-match alcohol consumption in later years!

While parents might struggle with information and choice overload the effect of free choice at the social level also has to be considered. Fukuyama argues that there will be in effect a 'genetic arms race' with parents forced to 'choose' to prevent their child being disadvantaged (Fukuyama 2002). Currently parents only have a choice from available embryos for specific traits but if many people chose, say, taller and more intelligent children (if such a thing became possible), then the average height and IQ would simply rise. As an enhancement becomes normal then it is no longer advantageous and so those who wanted their child to have the edge would need to seek another 'improvement'. As Hirsch wrote: 'If everyone stands on tiptoe, no one sees better' (Hirsch 1977, p. 5).

As research continues and more tests are developed there are also concerns that a right to know may become a routine requirement for parents to gain access to welfare services or insurance-based health-care systems. In a report on behavioural genetic tests, personalised information on behavioural predispositions was seen as valuable but:

> key concerns are that individuals remain free to choose whether or not they provide this information and suffer no discrimination or disadvantage from withholding their genetic information, and that any use of genetic information is equal and equitable – advances in behavioural genetics should not benefit one group in society more than another.
>
> (Dixon 2005, p. 15)

If the behaviour in question is illegal, stigmatised or imposes significant economic and social costs on society, these 'key concerns' that focus on individuals would have to compete with concerns about protecting the public. As the range of available tests continues to increase, what limits will there be to individual responsibility? Hearing of a child born with a condition for which there is routine prenatal testing, such as Down's, people might ask whether the mother 'took the test', but parents who choose to continue with the pregnancy are not necessarily condemned (although there is evidence in Britain of an increase in negative attitudes to welfare recipients in general and there may be an assumption that the disabled will be claimants) (Park et al. 2013, p. 30). However, in the case of tests for behavioural conditions the parents' decision could be seen as a public rather than a private matter. The child with a genetic trait associated with aggressive behaviour, addiction or impulsive behaviour might engage in behaviour that negatively affects others. While research indicates that these behaviours have multifactorial causes, evidence on genetic traits has already been presented in criminal courts, usually by the defence, and has in some cases resulted in reduced sentences (Calloway 2009; Farahany and Coleman 2006). Such evidence might also be used to argue that these individuals are particularly dangerous and likely to reoffend so should have a harsher sentence, particularly if they knew their genetic risk (Levitt 2013).

Parents, especially mothers, have choices to make that were unknown in previous generations and this undoubtedly increases anxiety. For some parents choosing PGD is empowering; they may be able to choose to implant an embryo free of a specific genetic disease or have a child who is a tissue match for a sibling (a so-called 'saviour sibling').[1] But when it comes to non-disease traits or mild conditions, are there any lines to draw or should all decisions on their children's genetic make-up be the responsibility of parents, however much further our knowledge and techniques develop? At the very least, if there is to be a free market then parents would need some way of managing the options available; perhaps expert choice advisers and packages of tests with computer-assisted decision-making programmes. Although parents are focused on their own children, it is conceivable that some will see a shared interest in coming together to resist testing, selection or enhancement in particular areas and/or to promote it in others.

## Choice

The picture that emerges is of the modern individual being bombarded with choices accompanied by more or less subtle messages about what the good parent or the responsible person should do. The right to know has become the responsibility to know. In the field of health care and especially genetics, what was considered to be part of nature that humans could not change is being opened up to choice. As discussed in this chapter, in specific circumstances choice can be a burden from which people would like to be relieved; it can lead to stress and confusion or if the available choices do not meet expectations, to disappointment and regret. Faced with a long and complicated menu at a restaurant, or another familiar set of choices, we can fall back on habit and have what we always have or opt for something new and unknown; the consequences are probably trivial. When it comes to choices made over our own or our children's health we are more likely to be in an unfamiliar situation where we have no experiences or habits to fall back on, yet our choices could have serious consequences. In this context choice and individual autonomy seem to be an insubstantial ethical framework that increases responsibilities but does not give us the means to choose well.

---

[1] There is also the possibility of parents wishing to select an embryo with what others would consider a disability. This was prohibited in 2008 in the UK by an amendment to the UK Human and Embryology Act (section 13, subsection 9). This amendment was probably a response to the highly publicised case in 2002 when a lesbian couple selected a sperm donor with hereditary deafness, and subsequently had a deaf child. However, they did not make use of PGD as their donor was a family friend.

## References

23andMe. Available at: www.23andme.com/ (accessed 22 November 2013).

Ahlquist, L. 1997. *Empowerment in Action. Practising empowerment.* Edinburgh: Age Concern Scotland.

Ahmed, S., Bryant, L. D., Zahra, Tizro Z. and Shickle D. 2012. 'Is advice incompatible with autonomous informed choice? Women's perceptions of advice in the context of antenatal screening: a qualitative study', *Health Expectations* doi: 10.1111/j.1369-7625.2012.00784.x

Arterian, H. R. 2007. 'Essays by American Law Deans. Legal education and the tyrannical "paradox of choice: why more is less"', *Toronto Law Review* 38: 495–505.

Berger, P. and Luckmann, T. 1967. *The Social Construction of Reality. A treatise in the sociology of knowledge.* Harmondsworth: Penguin.

Botti, S., Orfali, K. and Iyengar, S. S. 2009. 'Tragic choices: Autonomy and emotional response to medical decisions', *Journal of Consumer Research* 36(3): 337–52.

Calloway, E. 2009. 'Murderer with "aggression genes" gets sentence cut', *New Scientist* 22(27) 3 November 2009.

Caspi, A., McCLay, J., Moffitt, T. E., Mill, J. M., Judy, M., Craig, I. W., Taylor, A. and Poulton, R. 2002. 'Role of genotype in the cycle of violence in maltreated children', *Science* 297: 5582.

Chua, R. Y. J. and Iyengar, S. 2006. 'Empowerment through choice? A critical analysis of the effects of choice in organizations', *Research in Organizational Behavior* 27: 41–79.

Clarke, A. 1991. 'Is non-directive genetic counselling possible?', *Lancet* 338(8779): 998–1001.

Department of Health 2000. The NHS Plan: A plan for investment, a plan for reform. Available at: http://webarchive.nationalarchives.gov.uk/+/www.dh.gov.uk/en/publicationsandstatistics/publications/publicationspolicyandguidance/dh_4002960 (accessed 22 November 2013).

Department of Health 2010. Equity and Excellence: Liberating the NHS. Cm 7881. London: The Stationery Office. Available at: www.gov.uk/government/uploads/system/uploads/attachment_data/file/213823/dh_117794.pdf (accessed 22 November 2013).

Department of Health 2010. Consultation. Liberating the NHS: Greater choice and control. Available at: http://consultations.dh.gov.uk/choice/choice (accessed 22 November 2013).

Dixon, M. 2005. *Brave New Choices. Behavioural genetics and public policy.* London: IPPR.

Evans, H. M. 2004. 'Should patients be allowed to veto their participation in clinical research?' *Journal of Medical Ethics* 30: 195–203.

Farahany, N. A. and Coleman, J. E. Jr. 2006. 'Genetics and responsibility: To know the criminal from the crime', *Law and Contemporary Problems* 69:115–62.

Fukuyama, F. 2002. *Our Posthuman Future. Consequences of the biotechnological revolution.* London: Profile Books.

GeneWatch UK 2006. Submission to the HFEA consultation 'Choices and Boundaries' January 2006. Available at: www.genewatch.org/pub-507666 (accessed 22 November 2013).

Golhurst, S. E., Hull, S. C and Wilfond, B. S. 2002. 'Limitations of direct-to-consumer advertising for clinical genetic testing', *JAMA* 288(14): 1762–7.

Harris, J. 2003. 'Organ procurement: Dead interests, living needs', *Journal of Medical Ethics* 29: 130–4.

Hayry, M. 2003. 'European values in bioethics: Why, what, and how to be used?' *Theoretical Medicine* 24: 199–214.

Hesketh, T. 2011. 'The consequences of son preference and sex-selective abortion in China and other Asian countries', *Canadian Medical Association Journal (CMAJ)* 183(12): 1374–7.

Hirsch, F. 1977. *Social Limits to Growth*. London: Routledge & Kegan Paul.

The Human Fertilisation and Embryology Authority 2006. *Choices and Boundaries*. London: HFEA. Available at: www.hfea.gov.uk/docs/Choices_and_Boundaries.pdf (accessed 22 November 2013).

Iyengar, S. 2010. *The Art of Choosing*. New York: Twelve.

Knoppers, B. and Chadwick, R. 2005. 'Human genetic research: Emerging trends in ethics', *Nature Reviews Genetics* 6: 75–9.

Levitt, M. 2013. 'Genes, environment and responsibility for violent behaviour: "Whatever genes one has it is preferable that you are prevented from going around stabbing people"', *New Genetics and Society* 32(1): 4–17.

Magnus, D., Cho, M. K. and Cooke-Deegan, R. 2009. 'Direct to consumers genetic tests: Beyond medical regulation?' *Genome Medicine* 1: 17.

Matravers, M. 2007. *Responsibility and Justice*. Cambridge: Policy Press.

Mitchie, S., Bron, F., Bobrow, M. and Marteau, T. M. 1997. 'Non-directiveness in genetic counselling: An empirical study', *Am J Hum Genet* 60(1): 40–7.

My Gene Profile Testimonials. Available at: http://67.228.193.217/testimonials.html (accessed 22 November 2013).

National Institute for Clinical Excellence 2004. *Assessment and Treatment for People with Fertility Problems*. London: NICE.

Navarro-Michel, M. 2011. 'Transplanting the Spanish model of organ donation', in A.-M. Farrell, D. Price and M. Quigley (eds.) *Organ Shortage. Ethics law and pragmatism*. Cambridge University Press, pp. 151–70.

Park, A., Bryson, C., Clery, E., Curtice, J. and Phillips, M. (eds.) 2013. British Social Attitudes: the 30th Report. London: NatCen Social Research. Available at: www.bsa-30.natcen.ac.uk (accessed 16 April 2014).

Paton, K. 2007. 'Conceptualising "choice"; A review of the theoretical literature'. Working paper 5, Non-participation in HE Project Series. School of Education, University of Southampton.

Peddie, V. L., Teijlengen, E. van and Bhattacharya, S. 2005. 'A qualitative study of women's decision-making at the end of IVF treatment', *Human Reproduction* 20: 1944–51.

Prainsack, B. and Buyx, A. 2012. 'Solidarity in contemporary bioethics – Towards a new approach', *Bioethics* 26(7): 343–50.

Rumbold, B., Alakeson V. and Smith P. C. 2012. *Rationing Health Care*. London: Nuffield Trust. Available at: www.nuffieldtrust.org.uk/sites/files/nuffield/publication/rationing_health_care_240212.pdf (accessed 22 November 2013).

Savulescu, J. 2001. 'Procreative beneficence', *Bioethics* 15(5/6): 413–26.

Schwartz, B. 2004. *The Paradox of Choice. Why more is less*. New York: Harper Collins.

Stephens, N. M., Townsend, S. and Markus, H. R. 2007. 'Choice as an act of meaning: The case of social class', *Journal of Personality and Social Psychology* 93(5): 814–30.

Wachbroit, R. and Wasserman, D. 1995. 'Patient autonomy and value-neutrality in non-directive genetic counselling', *Stanford Law Review* 6(2):103–11; reprinted in H. Kuhse and P. Singer (eds.) 2006 *Bioethics An anthology*. 2nd edn, Oxford: Blackwell, pp. 237–45.

# 7    DIY genetics: the right to know your own genome

*Barbara Prainsack*

## Introduction

This chapter focuses on one specific area, namely the emergence of genetic and genomic tests offered online. These tests often require test takers to submit no more than their personal and credit card details and a DNA sample (typically a certain amount of saliva). The fact that many of these online services do not require that test takers go through their physician or any other medical professional has earned them the label 'direct-to-consumer' (DTC) or 'do-it-yourself' (DIY) genetics.[1] These labels, however, are confusing, as most online genetics companies offering health-relevant information do actually require the involvement of a health professional somewhere in the process (for example, test takers may need to order the test via their physician, but can access results directly online). Effy Vayena and I introduced the term 'beyond-the-clinic' (BTC) genomics as a label under which the various forms of interactions between service providers, users and medical professionals can be subsumed, and which also accommodates the increasing overlaps between online genetics and the clinic (Prainsack and Vayena 2013; see also Topol 2012; Vorhaus 2010).

It should be noted here that although some arguments presented in this chapter are applicable also to tests for genetic ancestry, the focus of the chapter is on tests that are explicitly health-relevant.

## What does it mean 'to know your own genome'?

### What is 'the genome'?

When asking whether a person has, or should have, the right to know her own genome, what do we mean by 'genome'? I suggest that we use an inclusive definition of the term 'genome' for this purpose: any data

---

[1] For reasons of simplicity, I will use the term 'genetic testing services' to refer to both services providing genome-wide analysis and those testing certain genes specifically.

Table 7.1: Selection of results from personal genome testing company 23andMe.

| Elevated Risk ❷ NAME | CONFIDENCE | YOUR RISK | AVG. RISK | COMPARED TO AVERAGE |
|---|---|---|---|---|
| Atrial Fibrillantion [sic] | | 20.5% | 15.9% | 1.29% = |
| Parkinson's Disease | | 2.4% | 1.6% | 1.50x ⋮ |
| Abdominal Aortic Aneurysms | | | | ↑ |
| Asthma | | | | ↑ |
| Brain Aneurysm | | | | ↑ |
| Keloid | | | | ↑ |
| Ovarian Cancer ♀ | | | | ↑ |
| Paget's Disease of Bone | | | | ↑ |
| Myeloproliferative Neoplasms | | | | ↑ |
| Preeclampsia ♀ | | | | ↑ |

| Decreased Risk ❷ NAME | CONFIDENCE | YOUR RISK | AVG. RISK | COMPARED TO AVERAGE |
|---|---|---|---|---|
| Type 2 Diabetes | | 14.0% | 2.07% | 0.68x = |
| Breast Cancer | | 10.0% | 13.5% | 0.74x = |
| Restless Legs Syndrome | | 3.1% | 4.2% | 0.75x ⋮ |
| Colorectal Cancer | | 3.0% | 4.0% | 0.75x ⋮ |
| Melanoma | | 1.3% | 1.7% | 0.75x ⋮ |

Source: author, with permission from 23andme.com.

representing a sequence of nucleotides in our genome – even if only within one specific gene or region – is considered genomic information in the context of my argument. These could be print-outs from sequencers or other tools, cleaned datasets or interpreted information (such as the disease risk calculations that online genetic testing services provide to their customers; see Table 7.1).

Non-human genomic information contained in a person's body is not included in the term 'genome' for this purpose, because the analysis of a person's microbiome raises different questions from the analysis of a person's human DNA. This is despite the growing use and utility of personal microbiome analysis for medical and other purposes.

*What does it mean to 'know' your genome?*

The question of what 'knowing' means in the context of a right to know one's own genome is more difficult to answer. Also here, I consider a wide definition of 'knowing' most helpful. I propose the distinction of

Table 7.2: Different forms of 'knowing (and sharing) one's own genome'.

| Instances of knowing (and sharing) one's genome | Who is affected? | Should there be a right to know? |
|---|---|---|
| 1. Genetic analysis within a clinical context | only tt[a] (or MZ[b] twin or multiple) | yes (pre-testing information and dialogue with others who are potentially affected should be encouraged by test providers) |
| 2. Genetic analysis carried out by a commercial provider and disclosed directly to the tt | only tt (or MZ twin or multiple) | yes (pre-testing information and dialogue with others who are potentially affected should be encouraged by test providers) |
| 3. Access to raw data | only tt (or MZ twin or multiple) | yes |
| 4. Download and store raw data and interpretation | only tt (or MZ twin or multiple) | yes |
| 5. Share with biological relative | tt, biological relatives | yes (but dialogue with others who are potentially affected should be encouraged before sharing) |
| 6. Share with other researchers | tt, biological relatives | yes |
| 7. Make it public | tt, biological relatives | yes (but dialogue with others who are potentially affected should be encouraged before sharing) |

[a] test taker(s).
[b] monozygotic.
Source: author.

seven instances of 'knowing', including some where knowing overlaps with putting knowledge to use. These seven instances are summarised in Table 7.2.

The first instance of 'knowing' one's genome is having it analysed in the clinic (see Table 7.2, 1). The typical answer to the question of whether people should have a right to have their genomes analysed in a clinical context has so far been affirmative, and this right has been practised as long as genetic analysis has existed – at least in wealthy countries where genetic testing has been used in the clinic. A typical requirement for patients to access genetic testing in the clinic is the presence of a medical indication, such as particular symptoms or other reasons to suspect genetic factors contributing to a particular disease or problem, a family history of diseases where genetic factors are known to play a significant role, or genetic testing in the reproductive context, such as pre-implantation genetic diagnosis, genetic carrier testing prior to procreation. Relevant caveats here are that not all of these scenarios are legal everywhere (e.g., pre-implantation genetic diagnosis remains prohibited in countries such as Austria), and that access to clinical analysis of genes or genomes for particular purposes depends on the specific legal and regulatory provisions pertaining to cost reimbursement in a given country, region or sometimes even institution. In sum, a right to know one's genome – understood as being able to have it analysed *in a clinical context* – has been acknowledged and practised for a long time, although it has not been universal and absolute.

A closely related, yet different instance of 'knowing' one's genome (Table 7.2, 2) would be to have it analysed by a commercial provider and without the involvement of a clinician. This means that test takers receive the analysed and interpreted data directly from the test provider, for example in the format of personalised disease risk calculations (such as those shown in Table 7.1). This instance thus reflects exactly the scenario of the 'pure' DTC model, where genetic information can be ordered, paid for and received by the test taker directly from the provider.

A further instance (Table 7.2, 3) pertains to accessing the raw data of one's genome, that is, the data from the device used for analysis (i.e. the sequencer, the SNP-genotyping device, etc.). 'Raw data' refers to the data before they are 'cleaned' (e.g., checked for mistakes), analysed and interpreted.

A number of further scenarios transcend the meaning of 'knowing' one's genome in the strict sense of the word. They extend to not only learning genomic information but also storing and sharing it: Scenario 4 in Table 7.2 pertains to users who download and store raw data and/or interpreted data and information, and thus move these data or information into their personal domain, rendering them more easily re-analysable and sharable. Scenarios 5 to7 pertain to sharing data or information with biological relatives (i.e. people for whom the information received by the test taker could be relevant as well), to sharing data with a wider group of researchers than those who carried out the analysis, and to putting data and/or information in the public domain.

*What does it mean to have a 'right' to know one's genome?*

The final question to explore before we can look at arguments in favour of, or against, a right to know one's genome is that of the meaning of 'rights' in this context. Should 'right' be understood as a negative right, that is, as a person's right *not to be prevented from* knowing her or his genome (in any or all the ways discussed above)? Or should it be seen as the positive right of a person *to obtain knowledge of her or his genome*, if necessary also at the cost of others?

The following section will discuss these questions for each of the different scenarios of 'knowing' one's genome distinguished above. A final section will then address the question of whether there should be a right *not* to know one's genome.

### Arguments in favour of the right to know your genome

Ruth Chadwick referred to 'at least four concepts in the right to know/right not to know debate: autonomy, confidentiality, privacy and solidarity' (Chadwick 1997: 13). Autonomy plays an obvious role here, as a person's articulation that she or he wants to know something is typically an expression of her or his autonomy. Chadwick points out that confidentiality and privacy play important roles in helping to draw the line between cases where third parties (e.g., biological relatives) may have a legitimate right to demand access to information about somebody else's genetic constitution, and cases where such access should not be granted.

In this chapter, I focus on the right of a person to know her or his *own* genome. I do not discuss the claim of other people to access that person's genomic information. Nevertheless, privacy and confidentiality remain indispensible concepts, because breaches of privacy and confidentiality are among the risks that need to be considered as potential unintended consequences of a person's right to know her or his *own* genome as well.

Ruth Chadwick saw the right to know one's own genetic constitution as relatively unproblematic 'because it is the least different from other areas of medicine and raises similar issues to claims of right to knowledge about one's medical condition, based on principles of autonomy and self-determination' (Chadwick 1997: 14). This reasoning is still applicable today. In contrast to 1997, however, when genetic analyses are carried out today, the test often discloses information beyond the question for which testing was initiated. For example, the parents of a child with learning disabilities could learn that the child is also at increased risk of breast cancer. The issue of such 'incidental findings' (Green *et al.* 2013) raises important questions about what kinds of such findings should be communicated to test takers, by whom, and who should make the decision. For the arguments developed in this chapter, this means that the decision to undergo testing has farther-reaching consequences than it did in the past, highlighting the need for adequate information and reflection preceding and accompanying the testing process.

Furthermore, genetic data today are embedded in digital infrastructures that regularly render data and information portable across the domains of different actors and institutions, so the scenarios inherent in 'knowing' one's genome have widened: we no longer receive information exclusively in the context of a conversation with our physician or genetic counsellor, perhaps accompanied by drawings or print-outs reminding us of some core figures and numbers. Nowadays – as Table 7.2 shows – we can also obtain genomic information in the form of raw data, in the form of interactive web-based visualisations of genetic risk calculations, and in some cases, entirely without the involvement of clinical experts. This opens up new options for test takers: we can run independent analyses on our raw data; we can make sense of the data with the help of online tools (e.g., http://evidence.personalgenomes.org/about); we can share our genetic and genomic information with others; or make it accessible for research (Lunshof *et al.* 2014). Inherent in these practices are a number of risks, such as the risk of a breach of privacy and confidentiality (e.g., unauthorised access to data stored online), the risk of causing distress to others by what we decide to do with our own genetic information (e.g., making it publicly available), or regretting our decisions when it is too late to prevent their consequences. Thus, the answer to our question of whether there should be a right to know one's own genome in each scenario listed in Table 7.2 should be guided by who would be affected by such a right.

In the first scenario – a person having her genome analysed in a clinical context – it is primarily the test taker who is affected by the consequences of this decision, assuming that all clinical safeguards are in place, and data and information are safely stored in the clinical realm and not given in bulk to the test taker. In this scenario, the risk of unauthorised access is very low. If the test taker has monozygotic siblings, however, or if the analysis discloses genetic information with significant clinical relevance for other biological relatives, then the question arises whether these relatives should be able to partake in the original testing decision. These relatives may want the test taker to refrain from having the test so that they can avoid receiving information that is, at least partially, applicable to them. I argue that the interest of test takers in having their genome analysed outweighs the interest of others in avoiding learning information against their will. An important reason for this is that if a person is referred to genetic testing in a clinical context, there is typically a health concern underlying this. Addressing this health concern must be considered more important than protecting other people from receiving unwanted information. Moreover, while for the person wanting to undergo genetic testing there is no other way to know her or his genome than having it analysed, for those not wanting to receive certain kinds of information, there are ways to prevent this. Even though these ways may not always be effective (e.g., if the test taker promises her or his twin or relative not to share the test results, but the test result can be inferred from the test taker's actions following the test), the interest of the person wanting to undergo clinical genetic testing to address a medically relevant question weighs more heavily than *any* interest of other parties. Thus, for scenario 1 (Table 7.2), I argue that there should indeed be a right to know one's own genome. This corresponds with current practice in countries that can afford genetic testing in the clinic.

But can we apply the same reasoning also to scenario 2, namely to a person's right to have her genome analysed by a commercial provider? In order to answer this question, we need to ask what the relevant difference between clinical genetic testing and commercial genetic testing is in terms of risks and benefits for the test taker and any other potentially affected parties. The main difference here is arguably the limited involvement of clinical experts in the context of commercial genetic testing. As mentioned above, while in some online testing procedures test takers need to order the test via their physicians and also receive results through them, in other instances clinicians are not involved in the process at all. In the latter scenario test takers thus rely on the information provided to them by the testing service (see Table 7.1). While many online genetics services place great emphasis on easy accessibility and comprehensiveness of information (i.e. they tell users how results are calculated, what markers are used for testing, and how genetic risks should be understood; see, for example, 23andme.com), most results of genetic tests are probabilistic.[2] Some authors (e.g., Howard and Borry 2012) are concerned that lay people struggle to understand probabilistic

---

[2] This is the case because at the time of writing this chapter, many tests do not involve the sequencing of entire genes but only look at small areas on the genome that have been found to correlate with certain health- or disease-related phenotypes (causal pathways are often unknown). Moreover, in the context of complex diseases – i.e. those that are caused by a complex interplay of genetic and non-genetic factors – any risk calculation based on genetic factors alone is necessarily probabilistic.

information without the help of a clinician. If we accepted this assumption, then this would mean that both test takers, and their biological relatives – if test takers shared test results with them – would be at greater risk if they received test results from commercial providers than if they received them within a clinical setting. Moreover, commercial testing services often disclose information that is not clinically actionable (e.g., genetic risks for diseases for which no effective preventive measures or treatments are available; see also Table 7.1), or even medically irrelevant; there is no consensus on whether access to this additional information is an advantage or an additional risk.

In conclusion, assuming again that an expression of a person's desire to have her or his genome analysed by a commercial provider – irrespective of whether or not there is a medical question motivating this desire – is typically an expression of that person's autonomy, the person should have a right to do as she or he wishes, unless there is a valid reason to prevent the person from doing so. Such valid reasons could be (i) the need to protect the person from herself or himself, or (ii) the need to protect others from unwanted information. With respect to scenario (i), there is no compelling evidence that customers of commercial genetic testing services are negatively affected by receiving test results without the involvement of a clinician (for an overview, see Saukko 2013). Moreover, some authors, including myself, have argued that in order to understand why people take such tests, we need to extend our concept of utility from clinical utility in the strict sense of the word to personal and social utility (Prainsack and Vayena 2013; Vayena et al. 2012). Such personal or social utility can include people benefiting from learning about the genetic factors contributing to health and disease; sharing potentially meaningful or relevant information with others, or 'only' finding their engagement with online platforms entertaining. Such wider utility of genomic information has only begun to be explored. At this point, however, no compelling arguments exist to justify the need to protect people seeking to have their genome analysed by a commercial provider from themselves because of the negative consequences that this knowledge would have for them, because any such negative consequences could very well be balanced by benefits. It is likely that the balance in practice will vary from person to person.

Another risk inherent in genetic testing outside the clinic comes from the fact that policies on data protection, privacy and data sharing outside the remit of clinical guidelines vary greatly (Kang et al. 2012). In the early days of online genome testing, concerns focused on databases in the commercial domain being hacked or leaked (e.g., Gurwitz and Bregman-Eschet 2009). Since then, our attention has shifted towards the business models of some of these services, which regularly include selling (anonymised) data to other commercial partners (see Prainsack, 2014). Because not all test takers read the small print of the terms of service, it can be assumed that many users 'consent' to their data being shared, and/or transferred to the ownership of the service, without their being aware of it. Is this, however, a sufficient reason to conclude that people wanting to undergo commercial testing need to be protected from themselves? This would be a rather drastic step to take, considering how many other practices we engage in on a daily basis without understating the possible consequences. What needs to be emphasised, however, is the need to raise awareness of the possibility of such unintended consequences and provide incentives to online genetic testing providers to be proactive in communicating their data protection and data sharing policies to potential users. One such unintended consequence may be the fact that by allowing commercial genetic testing companies to use our data, we are inadvertently creating value for them (see also Parry 2013; Prainsack, 2014).

With regard to family members not wanting test results to be shared with them, such concerns should be taken very seriously, because they are often not *a priori* outweighed by a medical reason for the test taker wanting to undergo testing. It would certainly be desirable for test takers to be encouraged to discuss – wherever reasonable and meaningful – with biological relatives and other family members what unintended consequences their test could generate, and how these could be avoided.

Based on the reasoning presented so far, our answer also to the question in scenario 3 (Table 7.2) – whether a person should have a right to access the raw data representing her or his own genome – would be affirmative. Again, the articulation of a person's desire to do this would be seen as an expression of her autonomy, and any other person's interest in preventing that person from doing so, either out of commercial interest or a biological relative seeking to protect herself from receiving unwanted information in the process, weighs less heavily than the test taker's interest in accessing her or his raw data. (Note that this applies to situations in which the analysis *has already been carried out*; the question whether or not a person should have her or his genome analysed in the first place is a different one, see above.) At present, people regularly waive the right to access their raw data when they consent to genome analysis, both in the clinical and in the commercial domains. (The waiver is often included in the consent; i.e. it would not be possible to participate without waiving any rights to accessing raw data.) This is a rather unfortunate scenario. Unless there are compelling reasons for an exception, people should have the right to access the raw data of their own genome. An important example for an exception would be significant costs for providing access to raw data in the case of publicly funded biobanks (see Prainsack and Buyx 2013).

Scenario 4 in Table 7.2 pertains to a test taker's right to download both raw data and the interpreted information (in any form provided by the testing service). This means that test takers would not only take home a print-out of their results, but they could store the results, and the raw data, on their own computer or elsewhere in their personal domains. This enables test takers to have their data re-analysed or reinterpreted by other experts, to run their own analyses (e.g., with the help of online tools that are freely available), or to integrate their genome data with other clinical and non-clinical datasets (e.g., by uploading them to personal or shared health data repositories). Current policies of genetic testing services, both clinical and commercial, vary greatly with respect to granting users access to raw data. Reasons for this range from commercial interests to paternalistic motivations. Regarding the latter, one rationale is that enabling test takers to store data in their own domains increases the risks of data loss or unauthorised access; even if employers or insurance companies would not dare (or care) to do this, vengeful ex-partners or angy neighbours could. Again, here, we can contend that people already store sensitive data in their personal domains, such as personal banking details and other personal information that could have detrimental effects on the owner when stolen. There is no convincing reason why genomic data should be treated differently from other sensitive data stored in the user's personal domain. Thus, granting people the right to download and store data and information obtained from the analysis of their own genome, whether in the clinic or outside, while at the same time encouraging them to consider any unintended consequences that this may have, seems the best solution (Lunshof *et al.* 2014). (That people have the right to access raw data does not, of course, preclude the possibility that they willingly waive this right, e.g. to help contain costs in the case of publicly funded biobanks.)

Scenarios 5–7 in Table 7.2 describe different practices of sharing genomic data: with biological relatives (scenario 5), with researchers other than those involved in the initial analysis (scenario 6), and with the general public, by, for example, making the data or information available online (scenario 7). What needs to be balanced in the scenario of sharing information with biological relatives – thus, with people to whom the test results could partially apply – are the interests of those who want to share this information with the interests of those who do not want to receive it. I have argued above that the interests of those who do not want to learn the test results of a biological relative are outweighed by the interests of the test taker – when it comes to the question of whether the person should be allowed to take the test in the first place. The question concerning us here is different: what we need to consider is whether or not person A – who has already taken the test – should have a right to share her or his results with a biological relative, person B. The answer to this, based on the lines of reasoning introduced above, should again be a positive one. Where B does not want to receive this information, however, A should be encouraged to respect B's decision. This is the case because B's interest in not being told A's test results explicitly outweighs A's interest in sharing them with B, even if B could clearly benefit from being told (e.g., if A learned that she or he was affected by a genetic disease that runs in families and there are measures for prevention or treatment available, so that B would benefit from taking the test her- or himself), or if A could benefit personally from telling B. In other words, *ethically*, in this instance, B's autonomous decision to avoid being given information (B's right not to know, see below) weighs heavier than A's right to share this information. There are reasons, however, why this ethical situation should not be translated into a right on the side of B: because it cannot be avoided in all cases that B can infer A's test results through actions that A may take in response to her or his test results, it is important that such an instance would not represent a breach of any 'right not to know' on the side of B. Thus, while a right not to know one's genome should exist vis-à-vis state authorities and their representatives (including the health-care system), such a right should not exist between individuals. (This does not mean, of course, that those wanting to share information about themselves should not be *encouraged* to respect others' desire not to know.)

The same line of reasoning applies to scenarios 6 and 7. Both biological and other relatives may have an interest in preventing test takers from sharing their data and/or results with other researchers or with the general public, which could, in the case of unauthorised reidentification, also impact negatively on the test takers' families or relatives. Those wanting to share their genome data in this manner should be encouraged to take concerns about unintended consequences for themselves and for others very seriously. Ultimately, however, a person's autonomous decision to share her or his own data in particular ways deserves greater protection than anybody else's interests, even those of identical twins or multiples (to whom their twin's personal genomic information typically applies in full). If we restricted the right of monozygotic twins and multiples to share their own genomic information due to the fact that this information also applies to somebody else, this would in effect discriminate against identical twins or multiples on the basis of biological characteristics. Anybody providing genome analysis to monozygotic siblings, and anybody receiving their genomic data or information, however, should ask the test taker to consider discussing this decision with her or his twin or multiple prior to testing or sharing.

In the final scenario (Table 7.2, 7), the sharing of one's genomic data or information with the general public, by, for example, depositing them in a public repository or even making data accessible online, those intending to do this should be encouraged (by the sites or organisations prompting such information) to consider potential negative financial or employment-related consequences in particular. Risk self-assessments that projects such as the Personal Genome Project at Harvard Medical School ask their volunteers to carry out before being able to register are examples for practical solutions to this challenge (see www.personal genomes.org).

In sum, for each of the seven scenarios discussed in Table 7.2, there are no compelling reasons to deny or limit people's right to 'know' (and share) their own genome, although in some instances, those analysing or processing genomic data and information should ensure that test takers consider possible unintended consequences for themselves or others.

Now that we have established that overall, a right to 'know' one's genome should exist, should we also claim that a person's right to know her or his genome should be understood as a positive right, requiring that resources are made available for her or him to undergo testing if these are not covered by the person's health insurance, and if the person is not able to pay for it out-of-pocket? I argue that the presence of a clear medical indication should be the separation line here. The analysis and interpretation, and, if applicable, the formulation of preventive or therapeutic strategies following from this, incurs considerable costs for society. In cases where there is an immediate medical reason, imposing these costs on health-care systems seems justified; in other instances, although people should be free to obtain, store and share data and information about their own genome, they should not be able to claim the costs for doing so from shared resources.

### The right not to know one's genome, and 'the right to be forgotten'

When discussing the right not to know in 1997, Ruth Chadwick pointed out that such discussions become pertinent when other people or institutions claim access to information that the individual does not know herself (Chadwick 1997: 17). Chadwick gave the example of identical twins, of whom one wanted to undergo a genetic test for something that the other twin did not want to know about. Another example could be an employer asking for information about an employee's genetic predisposition to developing complications resulting from handling certain materials. If the employee did not have this information and voiced the desire not to obtain it, should she or he be able to claim a right not to know? If so, this would most likely also prevent the employer from obtaining this information, because otherwise, the employee could infer the content of the information from actions that the employer takes (or not) as a result of learning the employee's test results (for example, denying a permanent contract, denying a promotion, or refusing to let the employee work in circumstances that are particularly risky for her or him).

Arguments in favour of a right not to know are sometimes based on the conclusion that arguments supporting a right to know are not sufficiently convincing. A frequent argument to the latter effect is that genetic information on complex traits, because of its probabilistic character, is not very useful to test takers. Chadwick dismissed any claims to a right not to know based on this reasoning because 'whether or not people do actually use information in particular ways cannot by itself determine whether they have a right to it' (Chadwick 1997: 17). I agree with this stance and argue that it should also be applied to arguments that genetic knowledge can be confusing or distressing for people. The fear that some people may get distressed when learning their genetic information should not be used to prevent those who decide to do so from obtaining such information. Thus, while there may be valid reasons in favour of a right not to know one's genetic information, they cannot be reasonably inferred from any absence of compelling arguments in favour of a right to know.

Valid concerns include considerations about individual autonomy (see Chadwick 1997: 19–20). Just as a person's articulation of wanting to know her or his genome is typically an expression of autonomy, such is the articulation of not wanting to know it. It is important to respect such autonomous decisions of individuals vis-à-vis authorities and those representing them. Thus, people should have a right not to know information about their genome, and be able to enforce it, in interaction with institutions such as their employers, insurers or the health-care system. They should not, however, have a right not to know towards other individuals who act *qua* individuals, not as representatives of institutions. The paradigmatic scenario where this would become relevant in practice would be people disclosing information about themselves that partially – or, in the case of monozygotic siblings, also fully – applies to others.[3] Establishing a right not to know information pertaining to one's genome that could be enforced vis-à-vis such individuals would in effect restrict one of the things that make us human, namely communication. Communication is both verbal and non-verbal, and the scenario that A unintentionally 'communicates' information to B against B's will cannot be avoided entirely. Also for this reason – to protect A from legal consequences in this situation – it is important *not* to establish a right not to know *intra* individuals.

## Conclusion

This chapter has addressed the question of whether or not there should be a right to know one's own genome. My point of departure has been the state of the debate as represented in the first edition of *The Right to Know and the Right Not to Know* (Chadwick *et al.* 1997). While the main lines of reasoning represented in this volume are largely still applicable today, an important difference now is that genomic data are embedded in multi-level, (relatively) easy access digital infrastructures. While this represents a range of new opportunities for test takers, it also brings along new challenges, such as issues related to data protection.

I have argued that for this purpose, a broad definition of the term genome, namely one that includes representations of any or all parts of a person's genome, would be the most fruitful. I have then distinguished between seven manifestations of 'knowing' your genome, some of which already include putting such information to use (e.g., by sharing it with others). For each case individually I have suggested that people should have a right to 'know' their genomes in this specific manner, although potential test takers should be encouraged to consider the unintended consequences that this could have for them, and for others. This should be done preferably in dialogue with other potentially affected individuals. Those analysing and processing genomic information – whether in the clinic or outside – should prompt test takers to do this.

With respect to a right not to know, I have concluded that individuals should have such a right vis-à-vis authorities. Such a right should not

---

[3] People should, of course, be able to prevent others from having their personal genome analysed and telling them against their will (i.e. B should be able to prevent A from analysing B's genome and telling B the results against B's will). Today, however, this is a moot point, because genetic testing services do not analyse results that were submitted by another person (unless samples were submitted by the parent or legal guardian of a child). If A managed to bypass the safeguards of testing service providers in this respect, then A would be breaking the law and could be held accountable by legal means.

exist, however, vis-à-vis other individuals when it comes to disclosing relevant information that also pertains to others when communicating *their own* genomic information.[4]

## Acknowledgements

I am grateful to Jeantine Lunshof and to Shiri Shkedi-Rafid for helpful comments on this manuscript, and to Mairi Levitt and Ruth Chadwick for being such wonderful editors.

## References

Chadwick, R. 1997. 'The philosophy of the right to know and the right not to know', in R. Chadwick, M. Levitt, and D. Shickle (eds.) *The Right to Know and the Right Not to Know*. Aldershot: Avebury, pp. 13–22.

Chadwick, R., Levitt, M. and Shickle, D. (eds.) 1997. *The Right to Know and the Right Not to Know*. Aldershot: Avebury.

Green, Robert C., Berg, Jonathan S., Grody, Wayne W., Kalia, Sarah S., Korf, Bruce R., Martin, Christa L., McGuire, Amy L., Nussbaum, Robert L., O'Daniel, Julianne M., Ormond, Kelly E., Rehm, Heidi L., Watson, Michael S., Williams, Marc S. and Biesecker, Leslie G. 2013. 'ACMG recommendations for reporting incidental findings in clinical exome and genome sequencing', *Genetics in Medicine* 15(7): 565–74.

Gurwitz, D. and Bregman-Eschet, Y. 2009. 'Personal genomics services: Whose genomes?', *European Journal of Human Genetics* 17(7): 883–9.

Howard, H. C. and Borry, P. 2012. 'Is there a doctor in the house? The presence of physicians in the direct-to-consumer genetic testing context', *Journal of Community Genetics* 3(2): 259–83.

Kang, J., Shilton, K., Estrin D., Burke K. and Hansen M. 2012. 'Self-surveillance privacy', *Iowa Law Review* 97: 809–47.

Lunshof, J. E., Church, G. M., and Prainsack, B. 2014. 'Raw personal data: providing access', *Science* 343: 373–4.

Parry, B. 2013. 'Knowing Mycellf TM: Personalized medicine and the economization of prospective knowledge about bodily fate', in P. Meusburger *et al.* (eds.) *Knowledge and the Economy*. Dordrecht: Springer, pp. 157–71.

Prainsack, B. 2014. 'Understanding participation: The "citizen science" of genetics', in B. Prainsack, S. Schicktanz and G. Werner-Felmayer (eds.), *Genetics as Social Practice*. Farnham: Ashgate, pp. 147–64.

Prainsack, B. and Buyx, A. 2013. 'A solidarity-based approach to the governance of research biobanks', *Medical Law Review* 21(1): 71–91.

---

[4] While elsewhere I have argued that solidarity should be an important principle in organising the generation, processing and sharing of genomic data (Prainsack and Buyx 2013), I consider solidarity less useful in the context of weighting the conflicting interests of biological relatives. We can assume that what motivates them to help each other, fight each other or take seriously each other's concerns are regularly bonds stronger than solidarity.

Prainsack, B. and Vayena, E. 2013 'Beyond the clinic: "Direct-to-consumer" genomic profiling services and pharmacogenomics', *Pharmacogenomics* 14(4): 403–12.

Saukko, P. 2013. 'State of play in direct-to-consumer genetic testing for lifestyle-related diseases: Market, marketing content, user experiences and regulation', *Proceedings of the Nutrition Society* 72(1): 53–60.

Topol, E. 2012. *The Creative Destruction of Medicine: How the digital revolution will create better health care*. New York: Basic Books.

Vayena, E., Gourma, E., Streuli, J., Hafe, E. and Prainsack, B. 2012. 'Early users of direct-to-consumer genomics in Switzerland', *Public Health Genomics* 15(96): 352–62.

Vorhaus, D. 2010. 'The past, present and future of DTC genetic testing regulation', *Genomics Law Report* (5 August 2010). Available at: www.genomicslawreport.com/index.php/2010/08/05/the-past-present-and-future-of-dtc-genetic-testing-regulation/ (accessed 19 July 2013).

# 8    Genomics, inconvenient truths and accountability

*Jeantine Lunshof and Ruth Chadwick*

Recently, genetics and genomics have become consumer products, moving beyond the research lab and outside the clinic into the daily life of modern citizens. Direct-to-consumer (DTC) marketed genetic tests are probably the best-known example, the 'products' being actually lab services, as Barbara Prainsack discusses in Chapter 7 of this volume. DNA-based genealogy tests to find out more about one's ancestry were among the first on the market.[1] Now that technology developments have led to the increasing availability of sophisticated but affordable tests, questions concerning genomics applications arise in a new context for individuals and families, and at a larger scale for communities and societies. While individual-centred, clinical and non-clinical use of genetic testing is booming, other areas of genetic research are also changing, as can be seen in, for example, human anthropology and population genetics. New insights and, in particular, new technologies in genomic science are leveraging the broad field of biomedicine and they imply changed patterns of accountability in research. Therefore, established normative frameworks that refer to classical (human) genetics require careful inspection and they may need to be adjusted in order to be applicable to the new knowledge from the genomic sciences.[2]

We aim to contribute to that revision by reviewing some classic cases that challenge our thinking about ethics and accountability in the sciences in various disciplines.

We will examine the interaction between science, ethics and accountability in the field of genomics research and present several cases that highlight unresolved issues that can arise in the context of genomics research at the community and population level. Research findings concerning

---

[1] Family Tree DNA is known as the first service provider on the market. See http://en.wikipedia.org/wiki/Family_Tree_DNA (accessed 29 October 2013).

[2] The genomic sciences include genetics. For reasons of readability we will further use 'genomics' in this text and use 'genetics' only if we specifically refer to this narrower field.

ancestry may heavily impact core concepts of identity, for individuals as well as for communities (Elliot and Brodwin 2002; Wolinsky 2006).

This does raise the question of whether groups – regardless of the decisions of individual group members – have the right to decline to learn the outcomes of scientific research. Such a right would be difficult to protect upon publication, and may at the extreme lead to calls for prohibiting the conduct of particular population-level studies that may convey unsolicited and unwanted insights.

We will analyse the accountability of scientists in the light of changing practices in the application of genomics research and the associated set of moral obligations. To that end, we first describe our view on the normative structure of accountability, in particular in the context of scientific research. Second, we present several examples of disputed or unwelcome findings in population genetics or ancestry studies from the past decades and, thirdly, we analyse the case of population-level research among the Native American Havasupai community, to illustrate the changing patterns of accountability in genomics research in a distinct population, over a long time. We will ask what, if any, specific conclusions can be drawn from this case, and what wider insights we can take from it about the responsible conduct of research and the different ways of sharing information.

## Science, ethics and accountability

What function does accountability have in the context of science today? And how does it relate to ethics?

In general, accountability has a crucial function in maintaining the standards of a discipline or a profession. Systems of accountability, with structures that codify the rules for both giving an account and holding to account, are in place in organizations of almost every profession (in the wide sense of the word), be it of lawyers, plumbers, physicians or car mechanics. In the academic world, rules for accountability can be found at all levels of the organization: the university itself, the institutes, the research groups and labs, as well as in education and within student organizations.

*Internal accountability*, that is the maintenance of standards within the profession itself, can be distinguished from *external accountability*, where professionals individually or collectively have to render account to public bodies or institutions or to specific other professions. The latter, external accountability at the interface of disciplines, professions and society is operationalized, for example, by funding bodies, science policy organizations and governmental research oversight bodies and also, obviously, by financial accountants.

Examples of internal accountability in the area of science include scientific review of research proposals and the process of peer review of publications. In many professions, certification of continuing education, professional licensing and disciplinary systems are internal measures for quality assurance that set benchmarks for accountability. This has led, however, to the rise of the *audit agenda* that, according to O'Neill, 'seeks to improve accountability by ever-more intensive monitoring, inspection and audit of performance' (O'Neill 2002, p. 131). The improvement of accountability entails an increase of trustworthiness, but this comes at the price of a decrease of trust, a result which can undermine the very raison d'être of the profession.

Ethics review bodies represent a specific system of accountability, as by definition they hold researchers to account for the fulfilment of moral obligations in the design and conduct of research. In biomedicine and in behavioural research, ethics review has become a ubiquitous phenomenon over the past decades. The system has been implemented in a variety of forms that often exist next to one another and thereby set standards that may be in tension or even contradictory, resulting in rather unclear accountability structures. Moreover, we should ask ourselves to what extent institutionalized ethics review has turned into an intrusive bureaucracy. This is another example of the 'audit culture' analysed by O'Neill, which was originally intended to improve accountability and secure trustworthiness (O'Neill 2002). In fact, however, although the audit culture was developed to restore trust, 'its spread actually creates the very distrust it is meant to address' (Power 1994, p. 10).

## Accountability in science

External and internal accountability as described above are mostly procedural, but also relate to the concept of the 'good' that science pursues (Chadwick 2005). However, added to that, there is a type of accountability intrinsic to the scientific endeavour itself. In science, apart from the procedures, there is the key issue of scientific *content*. Thorny issues in scientific accountability arise about the maintenance of standards that includes the research question and the scientific method, as well as the outcomes. There is a good that is internal to science and, according to Serageldin, it includes rationality, creativity, the search for truth, adherence to codes of behaviour and, as he calls it, a certain constructive subversiveness (Serageldin 2008). Scientists can be assumed to have the obligation of doing good science, they can be held to account for the way in which they conduct research and for the quality assurance of the outcomes according to the standards of the profession. The recent flood of published misconduct cases shows that the procedural control mechanisms do work, at least *ex post* (Investigation Committee Bell Labs 2002; Institute of Medicine 2012; Levelt, Noort and Drenth Committees 2012). But what are the standards for scientific content, and to whom are scientists accountable regarding the content of their work?

There is much discussion about method, in particular in the genomic sciences. Here, we want to look in particular at the object and the outcomes of research. Research findings and conclusions usually entail some truth claim. Also negative results of studies – where the hypothesis that the study set out to test turns out to be wrong – can be reported as a true conclusion about the absence of evidence. Such negative outcomes tend to be under-reported (Fanelli 2012). There can be, however, some very 'inconvenient truths' – from positive as well as negative outcomes – that may bring scientists into conflict not only with their sponsors and oversight bodies, but potentially also with their research subjects and their communities, or even society at large. The classic case of such an inconvenient truth is of course Galileo's heliocentrism, based on the earlier findings of Copernicus, the truth of which was confirmed by Galileo through systematic astronomical observations (Galilei 2001). Sticking to his conviction about the scientific fact of the planet Earth orbiting the sun, in front of the Inquisition and the head of the Roman Catholic Church, he ended up in lifelong house arrest.

On the other hand, deliberate denial of scientific truth for political or religious purposes is not confined to the past. Recent examples are the AIDS denial and the creationism controversy. The AIDS denial by president Mbeki of South Africa led to an estimated loss of more than 330,000 lives between 2000 and 2005 (Chigwedere *et al.* 2008). Mbeki denied that HIV was the cause of AIDS and blocked the provision of anti-retroviral drugs to the South African population. He rejected the firmly established consensus of the scientific community about the causative role of HIV, and referred to the so-called Duesberg hypothesis, claiming that the use of recreational drugs and of antiretroviral drugs are causes of AIDS (Duesberg *et al.* 2003). Another example, with great public and individual health impact, is the obstruction of the tobacco industry of the reporting of outcomes of studies on the risk of cancer – and other diseases – from environmental tobacco exposure (ETS, 'second-hand smoke') (Ong and Glantz 2000).

Serious conflicts arise when scientific findings, or particular interpretations of such findings, clash with public policy, as shown in the UK by the recent 'Nutt-gate' affair. David Nutt, a professor of neuropsychopharmacology, was the chairman of the UK Advisory Council on the

Misuse of Drugs (ACMD). In 2007 he published an article in *The Lancet* purporting to show that alcohol is the most harmful drug, before heroin and crack cocaine (Nutt *et al.* 2007). When he later compared the risk of harm from ecstasy to that of horse riding, he was sacked as chair of the ACMD (Nutt 2009). As Alan Johnson, the Home Secretary, stated, 'He was asked to go because he cannot be both a government adviser and a campaigner against government policy' (Guardian Online). In other words, it was denied that it was the scientific finding itself that was the problem. Further research confirmed the overriding harm caused by alcohol and in 2010 Nutt and his colleagues published a refined version of their article of 2007, reaching the same conclusions (Nutt *et al.* 2010).

A typical example of religiously motivated denial of corroborated scientific knowledge is 'creationism'. The anti-evolution 'Creation science' movement and its more recent subset of 'Intelligent Design' (ID) that are particularly active in the United States, reject the theory and findings of evolutionary biology. Originating in the 1920s, the argument about 'creation' or evolution has been ongoing for nearly a century. The current battle – that has resulted in a considerable number of law suits – is actually about education policy and the unsuitability of theories grounded in religious beliefs for the science and biology classroom[3] (Scott and Matzke 2007).

Questioning established knowledge and raising hypotheses as to its falsification are essential features of the scientific enterprise – and include questioning scientific method itself, a discussion that meanwhile has reached the general media (Ioannidis 2005; Lehrer 2010, p. 52). The requirement of reproducibility of results is a further key characteristic (Diamandis 2010). It necessitates sharing information, access to – the sources of – research data and unrestricted dissemination of findings. Scientific inquiry may shake long-held beliefs on any topic in any area, on seemingly small but very fundamental issues in science itself (Boogerd *et al.* 2011), as well as on the big questions in areas as remote as religion and cultural narrative. The latest developments in the biological sciences show that we are still sailing in uncharted waters and in particular the rise of synthetic biology presents us with what appear to be completely novel questions: we have moved from reading the genome to writing and editing genomes and are already 'remaking ourselves and our world' (Church and Regis 2012, p. 13). How far applications of molecular engineering, as, for example, genome editing or the use of synthetic

---

[3] On 3 December 2010 a settlement was reached with a family receiving $475,000 in the case of *Doe* et al. v. *Mount Vernon City School District Board of Education* et al.

DNA as a programmable material, challenge our conceptual and normative frameworks remains to be seen (Mali *et al*. 2013; Qi *et al*. 2013).

## Genomics, truth and accountability

Genetics and genomics regularly convey unwelcome messages and reveal
inconvenient truths. They can range from non-paternity issues in classical clinical genetics to revealing information about ancestry and geographical origin of communities that is perceived as highly disturbing
by the people in question. In both cases, the ethical, social and psychological implications are non-trivial.

What are the issues of professional and scientific accountability in this
context? What of truth and truthfulness? In the first case, the professions
of clinical geneticists and counsellors, well aware of the realities of family relationships and of hereditary disease susceptibility, have established
practical guidelines for dealing with such situations. Apart from that,
they are in the role of health-care providers – as physicians or other professionals – and it has been argued that the rules for truth-telling in the
patient–physician relationship allow for selective non-disclosure of information that, in the eyes of the physician, is assumed to be too disturbing
for patients. It is however questionable whether such a traditional 'therapeutic privilege' can be justified at all and maintained in current developments towards participatory healthcare, in particular also in the context
of DTC (genetic) testing services[4] (Prainsack 2011).

The second case, revealing information about ancestry and the origin
of populations, is far more complex. As argued, in the context of science and scientific research, there is no escape from the commitment to
the truth, or at least to truthfulness about the factual conclusions that
we draw, to the best of our knowledge, from the systematic analysis of
empirical findings.

In some cases, empirical evidence of ancestry – geographical, tri-
bal – is actively sought by communities or community leaders (Parfitt
2003; Thomas *et al*. 2000). In the case of the Lemba, the 'Black Jews of
Southern Africa', the search for genetic evidence has been tightly connected with the affirmation of religious identity with Judaism. While genetic studies are ongoing, a complex situation exists, as Jewish ancestry
can be highly relevant for the correct diagnosis of – otherwise rare – hereditary disorders (Ostrer and Skorecki 2013). As noted by Goodman in
his seminal text book:

---

[4] See, e.g.: Society for Participatory Medicine at: www.participatorymedicine.org (accessed
29 October 2013).

If one is afflicted with a hereditary disease characteristically observed in Jews, in most cases, that individual must be a Jew genetically. According to the Halacha (Jewish Law), however, one is a Jew if one's mother is Jewish or if one converts to Judaism according to the requirements of the Law.[5]

(Goodman 1979, p. 3)

While the Lemba sought for genetic evidence of ancestry and identity, other people did not want this type of knowledge to be imposed upon them and conclusions from studies turned out to be detrimental to the group and to individuals. For example, in the case of the Maori of New Zealand, population-based studies into particular genetic traits that were interpreted by the researchers as confirming hypotheses concerning ancestry and migration as well as causally connected with present-day culture and behaviour, led to increased stigmatization and tension in society (Evans 2012; Perbal 2013).

In both cases, the Lemba and the Maori, the genome analysis and interpretation may have been correct according to the objective criteria for biological research.

However, considerable harm to the people involved and a loss of trust in science and scientists may result under certain circumstances from taking the objectivist approach (Boghossian 2007). We will describe the genomics research among the people of the Havasupai tribe who live in the Grand Canyon in Arizona as an example of the major impact of a neglected clash of cultures.

### Genomics research in human populations: the case of the Havasupai

The story of the Havasupai people about their participation in genetic research (which ended in April 2010 with return of the samples and a settlement for damages) has received much attention (Callaway 2010; Couzin-Frankel 2010; Editorial 2010; Harmon 2010; Vorhaus 2010). The report of a formal investigation initiated by Arizona State University (ASU) was published in 2003 (Hart and Sobraske 2003). The principal investigator of the project, Therese Markow, responded to the publication in a letter in *The New York Times*[6] (Markow 2010, p. A24).

---

[5] With thanks to Rabbi T. R. Bard, Boston/Newton, MA, for the text book reference and discussion.

[6] In August 2013 the results were published of a study among institutional review board (IRB) chairs and researchers at National Institutes of Health (NIH)-funded institutions. This small, qualitative study showed that the Havasupai case did not have a large impact on the practice of these respondents (Garrison and Cho 2013).

The focus of the discussion has been almost entirely on the informed consent or rather, the alleged lack of consent. That allegation, however, seems hard to substantiate, as the Havasupai gave so-called broad consent that was not limited to the study of one particular trait in this particular study. In the following, we will examine the case from a different viewpoint, highlighting the complex interaction of agents, acts, obligations, rights and the relationships of accountability.

As a brief description of the case, the people of the Native American tribe of the Havasupai live in a remote part of the Grand Canyon in Arizona, USA. The tribe is numerically small, with (in 2010) about 650 members. In 1990, a request from the tribe members for help in finding the cause of the very high incidence of type 2 diabetes (55% of Havasupai women and 38% of Havasupai men were affected in 1991 (Dalton 2004)) led to the initiation of a medical genetics research project. At that time, an extensive genealogical data set already existed that had been collected in the course of anthropological research over several decades, providing an ideal source of background data for the analysis of genetic variation. The researchers – John Martin, the anthropologist who had studied the Havasupai for many years, and Therese Markow, a geneticist – obtained funding from ASU and the National Alliance for Research on Schizophrenia and Depression (NARSAD) for a study of genetic variants among the Havasupai. The study participants signed a broad consent, for the study of 'the causes of behavioural/medical disorders', although the initial request from the tribe members was only about finding a cause of the high incidence of diabetes. The collected samples and data were used in a multitude of studies, by the initial researchers as well as by others with whom data were shared over the years (Hart and Sobraske 2003, pp.63–137). One early publication reported on human leukocyte antigen (HLA) polymorphism among the Havasupai. In theory this could have shed a light on the diabetes incidence, as previously found among the Native American Pima tribe, but the results were inconclusive (Markow et al. 1993). The researchers reported on their efforts towards diabetes control in a brief contribution in The Lancet (Zuerlein et al. 1991). A further early publication by Markow and Martin focused on the effects of inbreeding on so-called developmental stability (Markow and Martin 1993). Only many years later, in 2003, the Havasupai community became aware by accident of the ways in which their samples and data had been used over the years. Meanwhile there had been publications on, among other topics, inbreeding and population migration. The latter research findings contradict the Havasupai's own beliefs about their origin and geographical ancestry. In 2004, a lawsuit was filed, claiming over $50 million in damages for 'severe harm, extreme distress, and emotional trauma' (Editorial 2010). In April 2010, ASU agreed in a settlement to pay $700,000 to 41 members of the Havasupai tribe.

In August 2013, the chain of events, from the original project in 1990 to the publicity surrounding the settlement in 2010, was recounted by Ricki Lewis in a blog post (Lewis 2013) that elicited many comments, including several responses by Teresa Markow. A key issue was the clarification about the actual scope of the research and the lack of publications from the project, taking into account the frequent reference in the media to schizophrenia studies performed on the Havasupai or their data. According to Markow, with the techniques available at the time of the study, no sufficient and appropriate variants could be found to perform any association studies at all, neither for diabetes nor for other disorders. In the end, only clinical and educational help to reduce the burden of diabetes could be provided to the Havasupai, as reported by the team (Zuerlein et al. 1991). Yet, there is much contradictory information on the actual course of the research and many questions remain open in spite of recent in-depth analysis (Van Assche et al. 2013).

### Beyond consent: moral matters for indigenous people

The case of the research among the Havasupai raises many questions. As already indicated, much attention has been paid to the apparent problems with the original informed consent from 1990. The broad scope of it, in spite of the fairly narrow and concrete medical question concerning the Havasupai, the failed communication about the consent implications, and the fact that for data sharing as well as for later new studies by the ASU group no reconsent was sought, suggest a lack of appropriate attention to detail in the conduct of research, to say the least. Strategies for improving the consent process in this type of research have been proposed (Boyer et al. 2011; Jacobs et al. 2010; Mello and Wolf 2010). In general, the question of whether or not reconsent for later and/or other research is necessary is an important matter of ongoing debate. But the case raises other questions as well, showing some morally relevant matters that by their very nature are beyond consent. First, the use of specific terminology by the researchers in their publications – a seemingly minor issue, but with serious consequences. 'Inbreeding' originates from the context of livestock breeding as a means to promote desirable, and to eliminate not-desired, traits in animals, and was applied from the mid-19th century onwards by the eugenics movement propagating the 'improvement' of humans (Galton 1865). As the title of the early article by Markow and Martin (1993) shows, the authors unfortunately chose the technical term 'inbreeding' to describe the actual consanguinity among the Havasupai people. After mentioning developmental instability 'in inbred and outbred invertebrates and vertebrates', the authors continue to describe the rationale of their research question: 'reports on the influence of inbreeding ... in humans have not been consistent. We have identified a population, the Havasupai Indians of northern Arizona, which is uniquely suited to address this question' (Markow and Martin 1993, p. 389). Arguably few populations would not feel offended.

Apart from that, referring to inbreeding, a Havasupai spokesperson is quoted as saying: 'We say, if you do that, a close relative of yours will die' (Harmon 2010), which suggests that there may be additional confusion concerning inbreeding and incest.

Careful explanation and use of the scientifically correct term of 'consanguinity' might have prevented at least part of the humiliation as perceived by the tribe members.

Second, the more fundamental issue concerns the acceptability for individuals and communities of empirical evidence that contradicts traditional beliefs and sacred knowledge. By its very nature, this is beyond what can be a matter of consent. The application of genomics very often touches upon descent, paternity, ancestry and related issues. This applies not only to classical hereditary disorders, but with the development of genomic medicine this is the case for an increasing spectrum of health and disease traits. As a consequence, certain traditional narratives and long-held beliefs may appear in a different light. For a community this may result in considerable so-called 'dignitary' harm that, however, is highly subjective and situation-specific and may be an unavoidable effect of scientific inquiry.[7]

Further considerations are that communities and populations may not accept the Western world model of science at all, or that a research agenda may be perceived – rightly or wrongly – as part of a political agenda. This may happen in the field of genomics research, as the history of the Human Genome Diversity Project (HGDP)[8] has shown, but it can in principle occur in any area of science (Cavalli-Sforza 2005). Current criticism from representatives of indigenous peoples' organizations is directed towards the Genographic Project. The Genographic Ethical Framework Document states that:

Principal Investigators are required to be (and are) sensitive to the fact that knowledge generated by the project may give rise to narrative accounts that function as an alternative to some traditional accounts of the origin of the cosmos (including

---

[7] On dignitary harm and the example of the Havasupai, see the in-depth analysis by Van Assche, Gutwirth and Sterckx (2013).

[8] See www.hagsc.org/hgdp/ (accessed 21 October 2013).

people). All project participants understand that scientific narratives do not have priority over other types of narrative – and that Indigenous communities will determine the extent (if any) to which such narratives might complement their existing world views.

(The Genographic Project 2013)

While this seems to be a sufficient warning in mainstream research practice, it is deemed inadequate and inappropriate by representatives of indigenous peoples' groups (Harry and Kanehe 2005). We have not addressed these issues here in detail, but these concerns are substantial and, obviously, cannot be resolved through traditional mainstream models of consent. Through the joint efforts of global organizations of indigenous peoples new approaches have been developed, notably by the Free, Prior and Informed Consent Initiative (FPIC), with a broad scope encompassing rights to land and natural resources and preservation of cultural identity.[9]

## Science, inconvenient truths and accountability: some conclusions

We set out to investigate the intricate relationship between science, ethics and accountability against the background of developments in the genomic sciences.

We looked at the various forms of accountability and the way in which they function in the scientific environment and arrived at the question about accountability for scientific content – to whom are scientists accountable with respect to the content and outcomes of their work? Highly inconvenient truths may result from meticulous empirical observation and rigorous theoretical analysis. What to do, if carefully derived, robust research findings clash with the deep convictions and key components of people's traditional knowledge – in particular if it concerns vulnerable populations? Can people be expected to consent to the confrontation with 'enlightenment'? Respect for persons and populations requires respect for choosing to adhere to tradition and narrative.

Scientists should adhere to the values of science that, according to Ismail Serageldin, presuppose 'freedom to enquire, to challenge, to think, and to envision the unimagined' and they may thereby reveal some inconvenient truths (Serageldin 2008).

---

[9] See www.culturalsurvival.org/consent (accessed 21 October 2013).

## Acknowledgements

This chapter draws on material that was first published as Editorial: Genetic and genomic research – changing patterns of accountability, in *Accountability in Research* 2011, 18(3): 121–31. It is reprinted by permission of Taylor & Francis (www.tandfonline.com). Jeantine Lunshof has received funding from the People Programme (Marie Curie Actions) of the European Union's Seventh Framework Programme (FP7/2007–2013) under REA grant agreement n° 298698.

## References

Boghossian, P. 2007. *Fear of Knowledge. Against relativism and constructivism*. Oxford/New York: Oxford University Press.

Boogerd, F. C., Ma, H., Bruggeman, F. J., van Heeswijk, W. C., García-Contreras, R., Molenaar, D., Krab, K. and Westerhoff, H. V. 2011. 'AmtB-mediated $NH_3$ transport in prokaryotes must be active and as a consequence regulation of transport by GlnK is mandatory to limit futile cycling of $NH^+_4/NH_3$', *FEBS Letters* 585(1): 23–8.

Boyer, B. B., Dillard, D., Woodahl, E. L., Whitener, R., Thummel, K. E. and Burke, W. 2011. 'Ethical issues in developing pharmacogenetic research partnerships with American indigenous communities', *Clinical Pharmacology & Therapeutics* 89(3): 343–5.

Callaway, E. 2010. 'Native American settlement highlights DNA dilemma', *New Scientist* 2757, 27 April 2010.

Cavalli-Sforza, L. L. 2005. 'The Human Genome Diversity Project: Past, present and future', *Nature Review Genetics* 6: 333–40.

Chadwick, R. 2005. 'Professional ethics and the "good" of science', *Interdisciplinary Science Reviews* 30(3): 247–56.

Chigwedere, P., Seage, III, G. R., Gruskin, S., Lee, T.-H. and Essex, M. 2008. 'Estimating the lost benefits of antiretroviral drug use in South Africa', *Journal of Acquired Immune Deficiency Syndrome* 49(4): 410–15.

Church, G. M. and Regis, E. 2012. *Regenesis: How synthetic biology will reinvent nature and ourselves*. New York: Basic Books.

Couzin-Frankel, J. 2010. 'DNA returned to tribe, raising questions about consent', *Science* 328: 558.

Dalton, R. 2004. 'When two tribes go to war', *Nature* 430: 500–2.

Diamandis, E. P. 2010. 'Cancer biomarkers: Can we turn recent failures into successes?' *Journal of the National Cancer Institute* 102: 1462–7.

Duesberg, P., Koehnlein, C. and Rasnick, D. 2003. 'The chemical bases of the various AIDS epidemics: recreational drugs, anti-viral chemotherapy and malnutrition', *Journal of Biosciences* 28(4): 383–412.

Editorial 2010. 'Culture clash on consent', *Nature Neuroscience* 13(7): 777.

Elliot, C. and Brodwin, P. 2002. 'Identity and genetic ancestry tracing', *BMJ* 325: 1469–71.

Evans, D. 2012. 'Whakapapa, genealogy and genetics', *Bioethics* 26(4): 182–90.

Fanelli, D. 2012. 'Negative results are disappearing from most disciplines and countries', *Scientometrics* 90: 891–904.

Galilei, G. 2001. *Dialogue Concerning the Two Chief World Systems, Ptolemaic & Copernican*. Translated by S. Drake, Foreword by A. Einstein, Introduction by J. L. Heilbron. New York: Modern Library.

Galton, F. 1865. 'Hereditary talent and character', *Macmillan's Magazine* 12: 157–66; 318–27.

Garrison, N. A. and Cho, M. K. 2013. 'Awareness and acceptable practices: IRB and researcher reflections on the Havasupai lawsuit', *AJOB Primary Research* 4(4): 55–63.

Goodman, R. M. 1979. *Genetic Disorders among the Jewish People*. Baltimore, MD: John Hopkins University Press.

Guardian Online, 'David Nutt's sacking causes mass revolt against Alan Johnson,' Monday 2 November 2008. Deborah Summers, Sam Jones and Robert Booth. Available online at: www.theguardian.com/politics/2009/nov/02/david-nutt-alan-johnson-drugs.

Harmon, A. 2010. 'Indian tribe wins fight to limit research of its DNA', *New York Times*, 21 April 2010.

Harry, D. and Kanehe, L. M. 2005. 'Genetic research: Collecting blood to preserve culture?' *Cultural Survival Quarterly* 29(4). Available at: www.culturalsurvival.org/publications/cultural-survival-quarterly/none/genetic-research-collecting-blood-preserve-culture (accessed 21 October 2013).

Hart, S. and Sobraske, K. A. 2003. 'Investigative report concerning the medical genetics project at Havasupai'. Available at: www3.alcatellucent.com/wps/DocumentStreamerServlet?LMSG_CABINET=Docs_and_Resource_Ctr&LMSG_CONTENT_FILE=Corp_Governance_Docs/researchreview.pdf&lu_lang_code=en_WW (accessed 29 October 2013).

Institute of Medicine 2012. *'Evolution of Translational OMICS. Lessons learned and the path forward'*. Washington DC: The National Academies Press.

Investigation Committee Bell Labs 2002. *Report of the Investigation Committee on the Possibility of Scientific Misconduct in the Work of Hendrik Schön and Co-authors*. Available at: www3.alcatel-lucent.com/wps/portal/ (accessed 3 November 2013).

Ioannidis, J. P. 2005. 'Why most published research findings are false', *PLoS Medicine* August 2(8): e124.

Jacobs, B., Roffenbender, J., Collmann, J., Cherry, K., Bitsói, L. M. L., Bassett, K. and Evans Jr., C. H. 2010. 'Bridging the divide between genomic science and indigenous peoples', *Journal of Law, Medicine & Ethics* 38(3): 684–96.

Lehrer, J. 2010. 'The truth wears off – Is there something wrong with the scientific method?' *The New Yorker*, 13 December 2010.

Levelt, Noort and Drenth Committees 2012. *Flawed Science: The fraudulent research practices of social psychologist Diederik Stapel*. Available at: www.commissielevelt.nl/ (accessed 3 November 2013).

Lewis, R. 2013. 'Is the Havasupai Indian case a fairy tale?' *PLOS Blogs, DNA Science blog*, 15 August 2013. Available at: http://blogs.plos.org/dnascience/2013/08/15/is-the-havasupai-indian-case-a-fairy-tale/ (accessed 21 October 2013).

Mali, P., Yang, L., Esvelt, K. M., Aach, J., Guell, M., DiCarlo, J. E., Norville, J. E. and Church, G. M. 2013. 'RNA-guided human genome engineering via Cas9', *Science* 339: 823–6.

Markow, T. A. and Martin, J. F. 1993. 'Inbreeding and developmental stability in a small human population', *Annals of Human Biology* 20(4): 389–94.

Markow, T., Hedrick, P. W., Zuerlein, K., Danilovs, J., Martin, J., Vyvial, T. and Armstrong, C. 1993. 'HLA polymorphism in the Havasupai: Evidence for balancing selection', *American Journal of Human Genetics* 53: 943–52.

Markow, T. A. 2010. 'Dispute over use of DNA'. Letter. *New York Times* (New York edition), 3 May 2010.

Mello, M. M. and Wolf, L. E. 2010. 'The Havasupai Indian tribe case – Lessons for research involving stored biological samples', *New England Journal of Medicine* 363(3): 204–7.

Nutt, D., King, L. A., Saulsbury, W. and Blakemore, C. 2007. 'Development of a rational scale to assess harm of drugs and potential misuse', *The Lancet* 369: 1047–53.

Nutt, D. 2009. 'Government *vs* science over drug and alcohol policy', *The Lancet* 374: 1731–2.

Nutt, D. J., King, L. A. and Phillips, L. D. 2010. 'Drug harm in the UK: A multicriteria decision analysis', *The Lancet* 376: 1558–65.

O'Neill, O. 2002. *Autonomy and Trust in Bioethics*. Cambridge: Cambridge University Press.

Ong, E. K. and Glantz, S. A. 2000. 'Tobacco's industry efforts subverting International Agency for Research on Cancer's second-hand smoke study', *The Lancet* 355: 1253–9.

Ostrer, H. and Skorecki, K. 2013. 'The population genetics of the Jewish people', *Human Genetics* 132: 119–27.

Parfitt, T. 2003. 'Constructing black Jews: Genetic tests and the Lemba – the "Black Jews" of South Africa', *Developing World Bioethics* 3(2): 112–18.

Perbal, L. 2013. 'The 'Warrior Gene' and the Maori people: The responsibility of the geneticists', *Bioethics* 27(7): 382–7.

Power, M. 1994. *The Audit Explosion*. London: Demos.

Prainsack, B. 2011. 'Voting with their mice: Personal genome testing and the "participatory turn" in disease research', *Accountability in Research* 18: 132–47.

Qi, H., Ghodousi, M., Du, Y., Grun, C., Bae, H., Yin, P. and Khademhosseini, A. 2013. 'DNA-directed self-assembly of shape-controlled hydrogels', *Nature Communications* 4: 2275 (doi: 10.1038/ncomms3275).

Scott, E. C. and Matzke, N. J. 2007. 'Biological design in science classrooms', *Proceedings of the National Academy of Sciences of the USA* 104; Suppl. 1: 8669–76.

Serageldin, I. 2008. 'Science in Muslim countries', *Science* 321: 745.

The Genographic Project 2013. 'The Genographic Ethical Framework Document'. Available at: https://genographic.nationalgeographic.com/wp-content/uploads/2012/07/Geno2.0_Ethical-Framework.pdf (accessed 21 October 2013).

Thomas, M. G., Parfitt, T., Weiss, D. A., Skorecki, K., Wilson, J. F., Le Roux, M., Bradman, N. and Goldstein, D. B. 2000. 'Y chromosomes traveling south: The Cohen modal haplotype and the origins of the Lemba – the "Black Jews of Southern Africa"', *American Journal of Human Genetics* 66: 674–86.

Van Assche, K., Gutwirth, S. and Sterckx, S. 2013. 'Protecting dignitary interests of biobank research participants: Lessons from Havasupai Tribe v Arizona Board of Regents', *Law, Innovation and Technology* 5(1): 54–84.

Vorhaus, D. 2010. 'The Havasupai Indians and the challenge of informed consent for genomic research', *Genomics Law Report*, 21 April 2010. Available at: www.genomicslawreport.com/index.php/2010/04/21/the-havasupai-indians-and-the-challenge-of-informed-consent-for-genomic-research/ (accessed 21 October 2013).

Wolinsky, H. 2006. 'Genetic genealogy goes global', *EMBO Reports* 7(11): 1072–4.

Zuerlein, K., Martin, J. F., Vaughan, L. and Markow, T. A. 1991. 'NIDDM: Basic research plus education', *The Lancet* 338: 1271.

*Part III*

# Emerging issues

## 9 The right to know and the right not to know in the era of neoliberal biopolitics and bioeconomy

*Henk ten Have*

### Introduction

With advancing knowledge and information the right to know and the right not to know are becoming increasingly problematic. Whether or not we have these rights is debatable as it seems we are more and more absorbed in processes that make it unavoidable to know. It is even argued that there is a duty to know, so that whether we like it or not, we are dictated by knowledge to decide how we wish to apply it. I have earlier attributed the association between availability and application to the phenomenon of geneticization (Ten Have 1997). This is the socio-cultural process of interpreting and explaining human beings using the terminology and concepts of genetics, so that not only health and disease but all human behavior and social interactions are viewed through the prism of biomolecular technology (Ten Have 2012b). Geneticization has since then only amplified its outreach and impact. Many human behaviors have been associated and 'explained' by the existence of a specific gene. The well-known discussion on the 'warrior gene' attributed to the Maori in New Zealand is no exception. The occurrence of this gene was used in a murder case in 2010 to argue for diminished responsibility, and it influenced the jury's decision ('not murder') (Hagerty 2010). The discovery of the gambling gene (1996) and adultery gene (2010) have opened up interesting perspectives for the notion of responsibility. There is even a search for a genetic origin of human rights (Keane 2010). Medicine in particular is affected by geneticization. Genes are increasingly considered as the origin of health and disease. There is only a limited role for psychological, social and environmental factors since the ultimate causal factors are genetic. The concept of health is also changing (Torres 2006). With the possibility of detecting mutations in the genome that might in the future produce serious diseases, one is only considered healthy if the genome is healthy. As soon as a mutation is discovered one is no longer healthy but 'unhealthy.' The implication is that as genetic technologies are multiplying the number of healthy people will decline, and ultimately, most people will be unhealthy. Health will become exceptional and rare with the progress of genetics. In fact, with this logic, the genetic framework will become inescapable (Stempsey 2006). If our genetic constitution determines our identity (genetic essentialism) and if our genetic constitution is causing diseases (genetic reductionism), we *are* our diseases. But also, if genes are constitutive of diseases, in fact all diseases are genetic diseases. A right to know or not to know in this framework is futile.

### Possible obstacles

The inevitable rise of a genetic framework for human existence will produce a genetic civilization strategy aimed at a particular governance of human conduct. As I argued earlier, there are two obstacles to the implementation of such a strategy (Ten Have 1997). First, there is an increasing need to be selective. The exponential production of data is self-defeating when distinctions are not made between what is relevant and what is not. Being inundated with data is paralyzing to any action. The only response is continuing collection but this makes information useless unless there are meta-level selection mechanisms. The drive is to collect information about every citizen in a population, enabling the National Security Agency (NSA) to assemble Internet data on 75 percent of the US population. To make photocopies of all slow mail distributed in the country (160 billion pieces last year; Nixon 2013), mimics the genetic drive to engage in whole genome sequencing of every person. Such genome sequencing is applauded by some bioethicists (Grady 2013). The question of purpose is no longer asked, it is assumed that more knowledge is obviously always better, just as in the consumer market more products seem to generate more choices. The second obstacle to increasing geneticization is the normativity of medicine (and science, as I will add now). Medicine is guided by specific values and norms. It is not a neutral activity, at least as long as it is primarily regarded as a profession rather than a business. This normative perspective seems to be on the wane, particularly in the USA, as medicine comes to be regarded as a commercial enterprise and care services as its businesses. Therefore both obstacles are on the way to being removed and the future appears open to the unlimited application of genetic technologies.

The above conclusion might be misleading. After reviewing the past decades of bioethical reflection, Walters (2012) does not detect any obvious misuse or catastrophic misapplications of the new genetics. This, however, does not imply that the whole setting is unchanged. Metaphorically speaking, one does not ignore the gradual clouding and decrease in vision due to a cataract in order to happily avoid retinal ablation. What I would like to show in this chapter is first, that genetics is not alone in the driving seat; it is a very visible component of a wider framework which is often not analyzed, let alone criticized in mainstream bioethical discourse. The emphasis on personal autonomy and individual responsibility is in fact a feature of a dominant ideology that is merely reflected in discussions about genetic knowledge and technology. In other words, geneticization is a vector of a more encompassing ideology. Arguing that this ideology is currently under critique in various areas of science will be the purpose of the second part of this chapter. Contemporary discussions about privacy, public access, patenting and data sharing indicate that efforts to delineate the public domain are at the heart of defining and demarcating the specific normative nature of science and medicine. Its purpose is to ensure that genetic data will not be managed as mere commodities.

## Global context

Today globalization is a major source of bioethical problems. While there are different interpretations of globalization, the common core of these interpretations has been identified as 'the operation of a dominant market-driven logic' (Kirby 2006, p. 80), shifting policies away from maximization of public welfare to the promotion of enterprise, innovation and profitability. This logic changed the nature of state regulation, 'prioritizing the well-being of market actors over the well-being of citizens' (Kirby 2006, p. 94). Rules and regulations protecting society and the environment are weakened in order to promote global market expansion. A new social hierarchy emerged worldwide placing the integrated at the top (those who are essential to the maintenance of the economic system), the precarious in the middle (those who are not essential to the system and thus disposable) and the excluded at the bottom (the permanently unemployed) (Cox 2002). More than exploitation, precariousness and exclusion are characteristics of this new social order of globalization. Due to increasing risks and lower resilience, people all around the world but especially in developing countries have diminishing abilities to cope with threats and challenges.

The impact of globalization has significant consequences for bioethics. Since its emergence in the 1970s it has focused on empowering individuals. The main challenge was the impact of science and technology, and the main moral question was how the rational, individual decision maker would be able to select benefits and avoid harms. The concern was primarily with the ethical issues raised by new scientific knowledge and technological interventions: reproductive medicine, transplantation and organ donation, intensive care treatment and, of course, the new genetics.

However, when confronted with globalization and facing the challenges of poverty, inequality, environmental degradation, hunger, pandemics and organ trafficking such a discourse is no longer sufficient. The main challenge for bioethics today is the impact of the neoliberal market ideology worldwide. The usual discourse must therefore be complemented with a broader framework, for example as provided in the Universal Declaration on Bioethics and Human Rights, presenting a wider range of ethical principles going beyond the individual perspective, including solidarity, care, social responsibility and respect for human vulnerability. It can therefore be argued that bioethics has now entered a new phase, i.e. global bioethics (Ten Have and Gordijn, 2014). On this new stage, global bioethics needs to go beyond the focus on human beings as autonomous individuals; it must emphasize the interconnectedness of humans, and the inter-relations between human beings and the environment. This means building bridges between the present and the future, science and values, nature and culture, and human beings and nature, exactly as argued by Potter (Ten Have 2012a).

## Neoliberal biopolitics

The turn to global bioethics implies a critical analysis of the dominant ideology of neoliberalism. The range of present-day problems such as environmental degradation, persistent poverty, violence, growing inequalities, brain drain, exploitation, marginalization and discrimination are not so much the result of globalization as they are of a particular kind of globalization. This kind of globalization emphasizes that only free markets can foster individual liberty and human well-being. In this ideology, public utilities, social welfare provisions and public institutions should all be privatized. Every domain of human life should be open for market transactions so that individual citizens are free to choose what they want. Genetic tests and preventive as well as therapeutic interventions are consumables. Healthcare is a business that will flourish in a climate of competitiveness and efficiency. Medical research can thrive if it operates in a global market. This ideology proclaims that only the market model is able to provide individuals with a range of choices concerning drugs and interventions, broader than ever before (Braedley and Luxton 2010; Harvey 2005).

Neoliberal ideology is often uncritically reiterated in the bioethical discourse. Its focus is on the autonomous individual rather than on the citizen who is connected to others and is part of a larger community.

The same is true for the moral debate concerning genetic technologies. Discussing the ethical implications generally tends to highlight the impact of genetics at the level of individuals. The principle of respect for autonomy is often the starting point for considering these implications. Emphasis is on the proper management of information by individual citizens, on informed consent, privacy regulations, and the right to know and the right not to know. The citizen is regarded as a consumer who has to choose on the basis of his or her perceived self-interest among the many possibilities that are offered by modern genetics. Life is a 'business plan' that requires constant accumulation of genomic data and careful management by its owner (Sunder Rajan 2006, p. 144). The moral debate is therefore not theoretical but focused on the practical applications. What will be the impact of this new finding or test for the individual with a particular condition or disease? The potential use of new knowledge drives the attention of the media, as for many other innovative products on the public market. New discoveries and research findings in the bio-molecular life sciences are rapidly presented and discussed in public forum. The moral debate is characterized by the immediate interest of translating the public's fascination with new data, devices and discoveries into practical applications for the public consumer market.

The awareness that the context of the bioethics assessment of genetics and new technologies in general has significantly changed carries fundamental consequences. First, it articulates the fact that mainstream bioethics itself is impregnated with the market ethic of neoliberalism. Bioethical discourse can only have a really critical stance if it liberates itself from the dependency on the neoliberal discourse. Second, the process of geneticization is a manifestation of the logics of neoliberalism in the area of genetics. It is like the process of medicalization as analyzed in the 1970s. It is an exemplar of more general, encompassing processes that have been summarized since Michael Foucault under the label of 'biopolitics' (Lemke 2011). This specific form of exercising power has transformed human beings into autonomous subjects with control over body, life, death, health and disease. But while some forms of individualization were allowed, other forms were denied. The same movement that empowered individuals and liberated them from some forms of oppression resulted in other forms of domination. This is also the Janus face of medicalization: at the same time as it provides certain benefits, it also subjects patients to forms of discipline.

However, medicine is not simply 'medicalizing.' Instead of using domination and control, the field of medical power has been reformulated. The locus of medical power is no longer the individual physician but is instead located in large, pervasive structures encompassing physicians and patients alike. Medical power is also no longer exclusionary but has become inclusive; challenges from alternative healthcare, bioethics, the hospice movement or patient organizations are rapidly incorporated into 'orthodox' medical practice. The new field of medical power, therefore, is not so much dependent on domination and control as it is on monitoring and surveillance. The governance of individualization requires self-regulation, stimulation, nudging and incentives. Because the application of technologies depends on the individual choice of rational consumers, it is increasingly difficult and no longer relevant to address the social context of decision making. If health is the product of (responsible) choice, and human enhancement technologies can even further improve individual health, why should one bother about social and economic determinants of health (Birch 2008)?

Today it is recognized that biopolitics cannot be separated from the economization of life. The rational consumer is not independent but fundamentally guided by the market processes. Since protection and safety provided by the state are deliberately decreased, individuals must rely on self-management and various forms of self-care. We are autonomous managers of ourselves; disease and death are the result of investment decisions in our biocapital (Lemke 2011). This does not imply an increase of self-determination but is rather a new type of social control; only certain decisions about the body are regarded as rational and responsible (Memmi 2003). Biopolitics has become equivalent to bioeconomics. Biotechnical innovations and the life sciences represent a new form of neoliberal economy, embodying the high-risk, free-market frontier spirit of innovation that is characteristic of American genomics compared to biotechnology in India (Sunder Rajan 2006). The drive towards personalized medicine, for example, brings together the medical risks of patients and the financial risks of pharmaceutical companies. Sunder Rajan (2006, p. 112) calls this a form of 'speculative capitalism,' not based on concrete products, but on hopes and expectations, just as in finance futures and derivatives have replaced sales and profits. Genomics has especially developed into a venture science. This is the reason why the emergence of biotechnology has been connected to the rise of neoliberalism (Cooper 2008). Creation and speculation, rather than production and generation are the main features of such techno-scientific capitalism. Biotechnology will only be funded if its promissory visions are credible (independent of whether they are true or not). Biotech companies have to sell 'their visions of future products as much as or more than selling the products themselves' (Sunder Rajan 2006, pp. 129–30). Credibility is obtained when the future accounts for the present. It is only through propagating visions of the future that the conditions of possibility of the present can be created.

## Delineating and expanding the public domain

### Patenting

The decision of the US Supreme Court in June 2013 that human genes are not patentable marks an important step in redefining the public domain. By affirming the boundary between products of nature and human inventions, the court invalidated Myriad Genetics' patents on breast cancer genes. This decision, as recent commentators put it, will 'foster scientific discovery by protecting and expanding the public domain' (Kesselheim *et al.* 2013, p. 6). The important implication is that the balance between commercial interests and public health is going in the direction of the latter. Health is more important than profits. The common arguments that patents are needed to protect property rights and innovation have been substantially undermined. At least in this particular case, the evidence suggests that the business practices of Myriad Genetics had in fact reduced access to testing and reduced product development (Kesselheim *et al.* 2006). As a result of the court's decision it will be more difficult for companies to claim a monopoly on genetic diagnostic testing. There are also two important ethical notions involved. One is fairness. Like many other discoveries and innovations, the initial breakthroughs took place in the public domain. Without the pioneering research of Mary-Claire King at the University of California the BRCA genes could not have been isolated (Davies and White, 1995). This illustrates an important point that is sometimes lost in the neoliberal reimaging of science, one that is aptly expressed by Stiglitz: 'Most of the key innovations ... were not motivated by pecuniary gain. They were motivated by the quest for knowledge' (Stiglitz 2013, p. 4). It does not seem fair that the benefits of this research are then appropriated for the commercial interests of private parties. Similar unfairness is the result of the patenting regime; it is creating monopoly-like power with a lack of competition which especially drives up the pricing of medication. The result is that access to new drugs decreases for many people, in particular those in resource-poor countries (Blasi 2012; Correa 2004). The patenting system thus contributes to global injustices. The other notion involved is the common heritage of humankind. The Universal Declaration on the Human Genome and Human Rights, adopted by UNESCO in 1997, used this notion to argue that the human genome is the heritage of humanity and 'shall not give rise to financial gains' (UNESCO 1997). This position is now endorsed by the Supreme Court. This notion emphasizes that scientific ideas should be freely exchanged and therefore that access to knowledge should not be restricted. This will be an important change in US science policy, while in the European Union the patenting of DNA and the human genome has been prohibited since 1998 (in the USA the Myriad patents were granted in 1998 and will expire in 2015).

### Data sharing

Another area where the public domain is currently being redefined is in data sharing. Initiatives have been taken to publicly release all patient-level data from clinical trials. These public repositories will facilitate further analysis and examination so that claims about efficacy, effectiveness and safety can be independently scrutinized. It has been known for a long time that negative information is hardly ever published, and that published clinical evidence is often selective, biased or incomplete. The sharing of data at an early stage can therefore be beneficial for patients. The ethical point is that public benefit is regarded as justifying the overriding of data protection (and sometimes industry secrets). But it also demonstrates that scientific activity is a communal and cooperative enterprise. It should be an open and collective effort to corroborate the best evidence available to make sure that approved therapies are really beneficial. The expectation is that pharmaceutical companies will soon start sharing detailed clinical trial data. This surely signals that the culture of science is changing (Krumholz *et al*. 2013). Recently many research funding organizations such as National Institutes of Health (NIH) and National Science Foundation (NSF) in the USA have established data sharing policies. However, scientists in general are reluctant to share data. Some disciplines are positive exceptions. In astronomy, for example, scientists have built archives of shared digital images of the universe. Genomics research is also based on the principles of open access and sharing. These principles have been strongly enforced due to the competition in the Human Genome Project between public and private researchers and the possibility that private company Celera would patent the human genome. Genomic research therefore has developed, at an early stage, data-sharing policies, requesting that all data be publicly released and accessible. Particularly with the emergence of global collaborative research networks it is imperative to share data and samples. The assurances of freely available knowledge are the basis for projects such as the International HapMap Project and the 1000 Genomes Project (Kaye 2012). But even in this academic area, 47 percent of interviewed academic geneticists reported that they had been denied access to published information, data and materials by colleagues (Campbell *et al.* 2002). The current trend to data sharing is a paradigm shift because it prioritizes openness and transparency. Thomas Merton has recognized this as essential for science for two reasons: it is crucial for the integrity of science since it allows independent verification, replication and peer review of evidence, and it is crucial for the training of the next generation of scientists (Ten Have 2007). It is no longer debated whether data should be shared, the debate is now how to share data. Sharing has now become the norm.

*Open access*

Another recent development is the increase of open-access publishing. This movement is re-emphasizing the traditional value of free circulation of scientific knowledge. Unrestricted access to publications is essential for the progress of science (Willinsky 2006). Researchers do not write publications for money, and the Internet now provides many more opportunities for circulating knowledge. It is clear that current business models will not easily be overturned, with publishers shifting the financial burden from readers to authors, increasing the costs of research projects that now need to include budgets for publications, and with the increase of predatory publishers who hope to benefit from the author-pays model (Beall 2012; 2013). However, since free access is essential for global, democratized science enabling everybody, including patients, to learn the results of the latest research, the scientific community is taking various initiatives, for example the creation of institutional repositories at universities.

## Open science

The three developments discussed, namely the rejection of gene patenting as well as the moves towards data sharing and open access, indicate that after decennia of neoliberal ideology contemporary science is attempting to redefine its territory. Perhaps in response to the series of scandals concerning scientific misconduct and conflicts of interests, a new *ethos* of science is emerging, emphasizing that science should be developed for the sake of specific values such as knowledge and health, not for profits. It is a human activity that may be promoted or stimulated with economic support but that may not itself be a commercial activity, risking otherwise the loss of its specific identity and its normative basis. The lesson of the last decade is that science has too often been compromised by commercial interests and external influences. This has seriously affected its credibility and jeopardized society's trust and support. Demarcating and expanding the public domain will allow science to remain an independent and collaborative endeavor. This will create optimum conditions in which the right to know for everybody can be effectuated. However, the new ethos of science is producing growing tensions with the notion of privacy. Science is profiling itself as an expression of human creativity, not for private gain but for public benefit, and thus different from commercial enterprises. It strives to establish non-economic 'markets' or rather *agora* for the free exchange of ideas and knowledge. The question is how can a more open science that is maximizing the right to know be reconciled with the conservation of the right not to know?

## Protecting privacy

The right not to know is important in protecting the intimate sphere of the individual person. It defines a zone of inaccessibility that demands the respect of other people for one's personal autonomy and integrity. This explains why privacy is important. One argument is that everybody has the need to preserve his or her subjectivity. In social interactions we are 'persons', i.e. masking and playing roles in order to sustain these interactions. We need to have the ability to retreat into a private sphere in order to maintain our integrity. If we can no longer demarcate our subjectivity in this private sphere, we have no personality left. Another argument is that private information is necessary to establish and intensify personal relationships. The individual decision to share information with someone transforms this person into an *intimus*. If everybody knows everything about us, we will no longer be able to engage in personal relationships. A third argument is that private information can only be properly understood in the narrative context of the whole life of the individual. This is also the reason to keep it private since out of context it is easily misinterpreted and may lead to a false and one-sided image of that individual. This is particularly relevant for genetic information; we do not want to be labeled as a carrier or someone with susceptibility for a specific disease. We need to independently define ourselves and not be submitted to others' projections and labeling: 'without a degree of privacy we are in danger of being judged out of context' (Herring and Foster 2012, p. 23). All arguments to protect privacy share a common assumption that privacy is a social value. Concerns about the private sphere can only emerge because people live together and are inter-related in the first place. Furthermore, individual existence only has its specific qualities as long as other people respect its unique character. Even if privacy protection is focused on the individual person, its value is derived from the social character of human beings.

It is important to articulate the reasons to protect privacy because nowadays it is widely felt that privacy is rapidly becoming an illusion. Recently, cases came to light showing that privacy is not well respected. The publication of the HeLa genome sequence and the subsequent negotiations with the family of Henrietta Lacks demonstrate that not only had the cell line been created without the consent of Henrietta in 1951, but that in 2013 genome data are simply regarded as public information. Researchers could not even imagine the private concerns of family members (Callaway 2013; Zimmer 2013). The summer of 2013 also made it clear that in principle all communication is accessible for security services. The private sphere is evaporating under the continuous surveillance of the contemporary state, and personal information is retrievable and usable for the sake of 'security' without public accountability and outside proper legal frameworks (Ellsberg 2013). The practical impossibility of privacy protection was illustrated earlier the same year in a publication showing that the identity of 50 individuals who participated anonymously in genetic studies could be discovered by cross-referencing their samples with publicly available information (Gymrek *et al.* 2013). The scholarly literature now abounds with warnings about 'genome leaking', 'DNA theft' and 'genome hacking' (Brenner 2013; Hayden 2013a; Joh 2011).

The current precariousness of privacy has serious repercussions for the efforts to expand the public domain. In my view there are two different discussions. One concerns the public domain as an area to promote knowledge and health, the other as a commercial market. In the first area we are confronted with legitimate attempts of geneticists to share data, for example the recent initiative to set up a global alliance for data sharing (Hayden 2013b). International cooperation may not only determine standards for storing and assessing the accuracy of genetic sequences, but also for access and sharing. It may also overcome the current deficiencies through techniques of de-identifying and making data anonymous (Knoppers, Zawati and Kirby 2012). However, the challenges are not only technical. They also require rethinking procedures for consent, as well as modalities of access to biobanks and biorepositories, so that the right not to know can be preserved. In this area of discussion the general assumption seems to be that privacy protection is facing practical difficulties and may never be fully guaranteed. It is an ethical consideration that needs to be pursued as much as possible, otherwise the public will lose trust in medical and genetic research. This is the view of the recent report of the Presidential Commission for the Study of Bioethical Issues (Gutmann and Wagner 2013). It advocates three levels of protection: individual consent, institutional control of access and professional standards to prevent misuse. The conditions necessary to implement the right not to know must therefore be further strengthened and articulated in enhanced policies.

In the other area of the debate the assumptions are different. It is argued that whole genome sequencing is unavoidable, and that direct-to-consumer testing is already widely available, and so personalized medicine as a commercial enterprise is already there. In this context people who donate genetic materials should know that their privacy cannot be guaranteed. So much personal information is currently exchanged through social media and the Internet that privacy is dead anyway. The general expectations of the public regarding privacy are also changing (Rodriguez et al. 2013). Surveys show that the majority of research participants are in favor of public data release (McGuire et al. 2011). These views are consistent with neoliberal ideology: it is up to the individual to decide whether, when and how privacy is protected. No harm has been done to anyone identified. Whether there is any harm is determined by the rational consumer/provider. The right not to know in this view is ultimately privatized but has at the same time become futile since the individual can no longer control how personal information is used once it is released. The arguments in this view are in fact proceeding from geneticization of privacy; it has become a set of genes that expresses the identity of the person. Privacy is like a commodity that can be used, exchanged and transacted. It reiterates the genetic conception of the self. I remember the story told by American biologist Lee Silver during a conference in Portugal in the 1990s; since he himself had healthy genes, he was looking for a spouse with healthy genes too. When he met an interesting candidate, the first thing they did was exchange genetic profiles.

The debate on privacy demonstrates that it does matter whether privacy is regarded from an individual or social perspective. In the neoliberal view of science and healthcare as business, privacy is a commodity controlled by each individual, especially now that it is reduced to the genetic make-up of the individual. With the new technologies of sequencing and online testing more information is easily obtainable, but the boundary between personal and public knowledge is disappearing. Just as information about shopping habits or Internet browsing preferences are shared for the benefit of the market, genetic information is no longer purely private information. This is not because it is relevant for relatives but rather because it is necessary to free exchange which is the hallmark of the free market and necessary for the expansion of the business of science. This view then, paradoxically, emphasizes privacy as an individual value while at the same time submits it to the controls of the neoliberal market. In the ideal consumer society every client is open and transparent so that transactions are not restricted.

The inadequacy of this approach is demonstrated in the survey mentioned above; white participants are less restrictive concerning data sharing than participants from minority groups (McGuire *et al.* 2011, p. 954). Privacy has already been articulated for a long time through concerns about access to information by third parties: governmental agencies, insurers and employers. Privacy immediately raises the specter of genetic discrimination and stigmatization. From this perspective, privacy is primarily a social value. Human beings are not merely characterized by biological life, marked by illnesses identifiable with genetic technology, but perhaps even more by political life, engaged in common efforts of societies and communities. The distinction between biological and political life, however, is continuously challenged by new technologies that reduce collective perspectives to individual ones, and eliminate the demarcation between private and public. The ideal of 'personalized medicine' is criticized because of this exact tendency. By dividing the large population into small sub-populations defined by specific genetic profiles, health interventions can be tailored for individuals. The benefits of 'better' therapy for some individuals imply the progressive exclusion of many others. Many individuals and populations will become 'orphaned' (Savard 2013, p. 200).

### The role of bioethics

The implications of the concept of geneticization on bioethics are being increasingly studied (Keane 2010; Nowotny and Testa 2010; Rouvroy 2008; Weiner and Martin 2008). Using the concept requires a critical analysis of the current ethical discourse in genetics. The principle of respect for autonomy plays a crucial role in this discourse. Patients are not passive 'docile bodies' under the control of medical power but articulate consumers and autonomous decision makers. However, this emphasis on autonomy tends to overlook the fact that social arrangements frequently predetermine the range of choices available to individuals in a particular society. Autonomous choices always take place within specific social and cultural settings and are therefore determined by the constraints of this context. Patients' choices regarding the use of genetics are predetermined by the constraints of the healthcare system but more importantly by the 'geneticized' environment. This context is 'consonant with the contemporary neoliberal emphases on individual responsibility, self-governance and a prudential approach to controlling and transforming one's future' (Clarke *et al.* 2009, p. 33). Many of these neoliberal values are emphasized by bioethics.

The concept of geneticization redirects philosophical scrutiny and refocuses moral discussion. It particularly draws attention to social–ethical issues, which tend to be neglected or disregarded because of the current domination of the moral principle of respect for individual autonomy. This is also true for the debate on the right to know and not to know; it is often concerned with analyzing the individual possibilities and applications rather than the social context in which these rights are articulated and exercised. The notion of geneticization allows bioethical analysis to criticize the oversimplifications in current approaches to genetics, and to rethink common concepts of 'disease', 'health', 'body' and 'information'. The genetic discourse of today is itself the manifestation of the major values of a neoliberal society and culture, but it is shaping them into an objective, scientific form, presenting 'neutral' options that can satisfy the preferences and desires of informed and rational consumers. Bioethics should not be seduced by genetics as a scientific endeavor but should first of all critically focus on the neoliberal ideology in which genetics is used to meet the expectations, hopes and desires of individual consumers with their perennial quest to overcome aging, suffering, disability and finiteness. In this ideology genetics is often used as the primary driver to commodify and commercialize human life and human bodies.

The contemporary trend towards open science and the aim to expand the public domain are efforts to demarcate science (and healthcare) from the dominant reign of neoliberalism. The right to know in this approach is extended to anyone, regardless of economic and social interests. Expansion of the public domain is impacting on the right not to know, especially if privacy is regarded as a merely individual concern. But when rejection of gene patenting and emphasis on data sharing and open access are considered as expressions of the desire to preserve a context of commonality for the search of knowledge, a different view of privacy will emerge. Personal information in this view is not merely relevant for the individuals concerned but is necessary for the creation and care of interpersonal relationships and bonds within communities and societies. It is therefore necessary to utilize sophisticated information technology to ensure that the right not to know can be exercised. It also requires the continuous involvement of participants in research projects and donors of biomaterials in ongoing scientific activities, updating and renewing consent processes. From this viewpoint, concerns for the public domain and for protection of privacy are both the expression of the idea of moral community. They show the influence of new approaches within the emerging field of global bioethics, articulating new principles such as protecting future generations, intergenerational justice, benefit sharing and social responsibility. The new discourse on the global moral community is motivated by the concept of the 'common heritage of humankind' (Joyner 1986; Ten Have 2011, 2013). Introduced into international law in the late 1960s to regulate common material resources, such as the ocean bed and outer space, the concept was expanded in the 1970s to include culture and cultural heritage. It led to a global civilization project that seeks to create a new global community representing humanity as a whole, enabling the identification of world citizens, and evoking a sense of global solidarity and responsibility. A significant new step was the application of the concept in global bioethics, first in the field of genetics in the late 1990s, followed in the 2000s by the adoption of a global framework of ethical principles by almost all countries in the world (Ten Have and Jean 2009).

The emergence of this broader ethical framework can be an important antidote to the neoliberal market approaches in science and healthcare. Bioethics can liberate itself from this dominant ideology and be reborn as critical discourse that represents a global geography of moral values that enables humanity itself to be regarded as a moral community. It implies that citizens of high-income countries will no longer be indifferent to double standard clinical research practices or unequal healthcare settings in low-income countries since the same moral values and standards will apply within the global community. It also implies that current efforts in science to reclaim the public domain and at the same time protect privacy should be supported by bioethical analysis since it affirms that scientific research is primarily committed to benefit humanity rather than to generate profits for an already privileged section of the population.

### References

Beall, Jeffrey 2012. 'Predatory publishers are corrupting open access', *Nature* 489: 179.

Beall, Jeffrey, Beall's list of predatory publishers 2013. Available at: http://scholarlyoa.com/2012/12/06/bealls-list-of-predatory-publishers-2013/ (accessed September 13, 2013).

Birch, Kean 2008. 'Neoliberalising bioethics: Bias, enhancement and *economistic* ethics', *Genomics, Society and Policy* 4: 1–10.

Blasi, Alexandra E. 2012. 'An ethical dilemma. Patents & profits v. access & affordability', *Journal of Legal Medicine* 33: 115–28.

Braedley, Susan and Meg Luxton (eds.) 2010. *Neoliberalism and Everyday Life*. Montreal and Kingston: McGill-Queen's University Press.

Brenner, Steven E. 2013. 'Be prepared for the big genome leak', *Nature* 498: 139.

Callaway, Ewen 2013. 'Deal done over HeLa cell line', *Nature* 500: 132–3.

Campbell, Eric G., Brian R. Clarridge, Manjusha Gokhale, Lauren Birenbaum, Stephen Hilgartner, Neil A. Holtzman and David Blumenthal 2002. 'Data withholding in academic genetics. Evidence from a national survey', *JAMA* 287: 473–80.

Clarke A. E., J. Shim, S. Shostak and A. Nelson 2009. 'Biomedicalisation of health and identity', in P. Atkinson, P. Glasner and M. Lock (eds.) *Handbook of Genetics and Society; Mapping the new genomic era*. London/New York: Routledge, pp. 21–40.

Cooper, Melinda 2008. *Life as Surplus. Biotechnology and capitalism in the neoliberal era*. Seattle, WA and London: University of Washington Press.

Correa, Carlos Maria 2004. 'Ownership of knowledge – The role of patents in pharmaceutical R&D', *Bulletin of the World Health Organization* 82: 784–90.

Cox, Robert W. 2002. *The Political Economy of a Plural World: Critical reflections on power, morals and civilization*. London: Routledge.

Davies, Kevin and Michael White 1995. *Breakthrough. The quest to isolate the gene for hereditary breast cancer*. London: Macmillan.

Ellsberg, Daniel 2013. 'Edward Snowden: Saving us from the United Stasi of America', *The Guardian*, June 10, 2013. Available at: www.theguardian. com/commentisfree/2013/jun/10/edward-snowden-united-stasi-américa (accessed September 11, 2013).

Grady, Christine 2013. 'Reflections on two decades of bioethics: Where we have been and where we are going', *American Journal of Bioethics* 13: 8–10.

Gutmann, Amy and James W. Wagner 2013. 'Found your DNA on the web: Reconciling privacy and progress', *Hastings Center Report* 43: 15–18.

Gymrek, M., A. L. McGuire, D. Gloan, E. Halperin and Y. Erlich 2013. 'Identifying personal genomes by surname inference', *Science* 339: 321–4.

Hagerty, B. B. 2010. 'Can your genes make you murder?' Available at: www.npr. org/templates/story/story.php?storyId=128043329 (accessed September 11, 2013).

Harvey, David 2005. *A Brief History of Neoliberalism*. Oxford/New York: Oxford University Press.

Hayden, Erika Check 2013a. 'The genome hacker', *Nature* 497: 173–4.

Hayden, Erika Check 2013b. 'Geneticists push for global data-sharing', *Nature* 498: 16.

Herring, Jonathan and Charles Foster 2012. '"Please don't tell me." The right not to know', *Cambridge Quarterly of Healthcare Ethics* 21: 20–9.

Joh, Elizabeth E. 2011. 'DNA theft: Your genetic information at risk', *Nature Review Genetics* 12: doi:10.1038/nrg3113.

Joyner, Christopher C. 1986. 'Legal implications of the concept of the common heritage of mankind', *International and Comparative Law Quarterly* 35: 190–9.

Kaye, Jane 2012. 'The tension between data sharing and the protection of privacy in genomics research', *Annual Review of Genomics and Human Genetics* 12: 415–31.

Keane D. 2010. 'Survival of the fairest? Evolution and the geneticization of rights', *Oxford Journal of Legal Studies* 30: 467–94.

Kesselheim, Aaron S., Robert M. Cook-Deegan, David E. Winickoff and Michelle M. Mello 2013. 'Gene patenting – The Supreme Court finally speaks', *New England Journal of Medicine*: DOI:10.1056/NEJMhle1308199.

Kirby, Peadar 2006. *Vulnerability and Violence. The impact of globalisation.* London/ Ann Arbor, MI: Pluto Press.

Knoppers, Bartha Maria, Ma'n H. Zawati and Emily S. Kirby 2012. 'Sampling populations of humans across the world: ELSI issues', *Annual Review of Genomics and Human Genetics* 13: 395–413.

Krumholz, Harlan M., Joseph S. Ross, Cary P. Gross, Ezekiel J. Emanuel, Beth Hodshon, Jessica D. Ritchie, Jeffrey B. Low and Richard Lehman 2013. 'A historic moment for open science: The Yale University Open Access Project and Medtronic', *Annals of Internal Medicine* 158(12): 910–12.

Lemke, Thomas 2011. *Biopolitics. An advanced introduction.* New York and London: New York University Press.

McGuire, Amy L., Jill M. Oliver, Melody J. Slashinski, Jennifer L. Graves, Tao Wang, P. Adam Kelly, William Fisher, Ching C. Lau, John Goss, Mehmet Okcu, Diane Treadwell-Deering, Alica M. Goldman, Jeffrey L. Noebels and Susan G. Hilsenbeck 2011. 'To share or not to share: A randomized trial of consent for data sharing in genome research', *Genetic Medicine* 13(11): 948–55.

Memmi, Dominique 2003. 'Governing through speech: The new state administration of bodies', *Social Research* 70(2): 645–58.

Nixon, Ron 2013. 'US postal service logging all mail for law enforcement', *New York Times* July 3, 2013. Available at: www.nytimes.com/2013/07/04/us/ monitoring-of-snail-mail.html?pagewanted=all&_r=0 (accessed September 9, 2013).

Nowotny, Helga and Giuseppe Testa 2010. *Naked Genes. Reinventing the human in the molecular age.* Cambridge, MA London, England: The MIT Press.

Rodriguez, Laura L., Lisa D. Brooks, Judith H. Greenberg and Eric D. Green 2013. 'The complexities of genomic identifiability', *Science* 339: 275–6.

Rouvroy, A. 2008. *Human Genes and Neoliberal Governance: A Foucauldian critique.* New York: Routledge-Cavendish.

Savard, Jacqueline 2013. 'Personalised medicine: A critique on the future of health care', *Bioethical Inquiry* 10: 197–203.

Stempsey, William F. 2006. 'The geneticization of diagnostics', *Medicine, Health Care and Philosophy* 9: 193–200.

Stiglitz, Joseph E. 2013. 'How intellectual property reinforces inequality', *New York Times* July 14, 2013. Available at: http://opinionator.blogs.nytimes. com/2013/07/14/how-intellectual-property-reinforces-inequality/?_r=0 (accessed September 10, 2013).

Sunder Rajan, Kaushik 2006. *Biocapital. The constitution of postgenomic life.* Durham and London: Duke University Press.

Ten Have, Henk 1997. 'Living with the future: Genetic information and human existence', in Ruth Chadwick, Mairi Levitt and Darren Shickle (eds.) *The Right to Know and the Right Not to Know.* Avebury: Aldershot, pp. 87–95.

Ten Have, Henk 2007. 'The need and desirability of an (Hippocratic) Oath or Pledge for scientists', in J. Engelbrecht and J. J. F. Schroots (eds.) *New*

*Perspectives in Academia.* ALLEA Biennial Yearbook 2006. Amsterdam: KNAW, pp. 19–30.

Ten Have, Henk 2011. 'Global bioethics and communitarianism', *Theoretical Medicine and Bioethics* 32: 315–26.

Ten Have, Henk 2012a. 'Potter's notion of bioethics', *Kennedy Institute of Bioethics* 22(1): 59–82.

Ten Have, Henk 2012b. 'Geneticization: Concept', in *Encyclopedia of Life Sciences (eLS 2012).* Chichester: John Wiley & Sons, Ltd. Available at: www.els.net/ (accessed April 8, 2014).

Ten Have, Henk 2013. 'Global bioethics: Transnational experiences and impacts on Islamic bioethics', *Zygon: Journal of Religion and Science* 48(3): 600–17.

Ten Have, Henk and Bert Gordijn 2014. 'Global bioethics', in Henk ten Have and Bert Gordijn (eds.) *Compendium and Atlas of Global Bioethics.* Berlin: Springer Publishers, pp. 3–18.

Ten Have, Henk A. M. J. and Michèle S. Jean (eds.) 2009. *The UNESCO Universal Declaration on Bioethics and Human Rights. Background, principles and application.* Paris: UNESCO Publishing.

Torres, J. M. 2006 'Genetic tools, Kuhnian theoretical shift and the geneticization process', *Medicine, Health Care and Philosophy* 9: 3–12.

UNESCO 1997. *Universal Declaration on the Human Genome and Human Rights.* Paris: UNESCO. Available at: http://portal.unesco.org/en/ev.php-URL_ID=13177&URL_DO=DO_TOPIC&URL_SECTION=201.html (accessed September 10, 2013).

Walters, Leroy 2012. 'Genetics and bioethics: How our thinking has changed since 1969', *Theoretical Medicine and Bioethics* 33: 83–95.

Weiner, K. and P. Martin 2008. 'A genetic future for coronary heart disease?' *Sociology of Health & Illness* 30: 380–95.

Willinsky, John 2006. *The Access Principle: The case for open access to research and scholarship.* Cambridge, MA: Massachusetts Institute of Technology. Available at: http://arizona.openrepository.com/arizona/bitstream/10150/106529/1/jwapbook.pdf?utm_source=dlvr.it&utm_medium=twitter (accessed September 13, 2013).

Zimmer, Carl 2013. 'A family consents to a medical gift, 62 years later', *New York Times,* August 7, 2013. Available at: www.nytimes.com/2013/08/08/science/after-decades-of-research-henrietta-lacks-family-is-asked-for-consent.html?ref=nationalinstitutesofhealth&_r=0 (accessed September 11, 2013).

# 10    The parental love argument against 'designing' babies: the harm in knowing that one has been selected or enhanced

*Anca Gheaus*

In this chapter, I argue that children who were selected for particular traits or genetically enhanced might feel, for this reason, less securely, spontaneously and fairly loved by their parents, which would constitute significant harm. 'Parents' refers, throughout this chapter, to the people who perform the social function of rearing children, rather than to procreators. I rely on an understanding of adequate parental love which includes several characteristics: parents should not make children feel they are loved conditionally, for features such as intelligence, looks or temperament; they should not burden children with parental expectations concerning particular achievements of the child; and parental love is often expressed in spontaneous enjoyment and discovery of children's features. This understanding of parental love provides a reason to question the legitimacy of parental use of selection and enhancement and to explain why parents should not engage on a quest for the 'best child'.

## Introduction

Is there anything morally objectionable about parents trying, with the help of genetic technology, to ensure that their children will have features that are usually regarded as advantageous, such as good looks, exceptional cognitive abilities or sunny temperaments? Given that parents cannot but shape their children in a variety of ways – through deciding on diets, socialisation, education, use of free time and so on – what, if anything, speaks against a parental decision to select or to enhance their future children in medically and morally irrelevant ways?

There are many worries about the creation of 'designer babies' (Buchanan 2011). Several apply independently of whose decision it is to select or enhance, and they concern: the risks involved in the use of genetic technology (Buchanan *et al.* 2000: 191–6); the diminished autonomy of the resulting children (Habermas 2003; Harris 2007: 137–42) and failure to respect the children's right to an open future (Buchanan *et al.* 2000:170–6); the misdirection of scarce resources into trivial or misguided goals (Rajczi 2008); and the likely futility of using genetic technology to manipulate features which are valued for the competitive advantage they can confer (Buchanan *et al.* 2000: 182–7). If enough children were to become, through genetic technology, more attractive, intelligent and socially pleasant, then the very standards of beauty, intelligence and social appeal would change.

Other objections focus, specifically, on the limits of the authority that *parents* may exercise in relation to their children. First, there is an egalitarian concern about the permissibility of buying advantage, especially competitive advantage, for one's children (Buchanan *et al.* 2000: 187–91; Daniels 2001). A second worry stems from the special impact of the parent–child relationship on children's (future) autonomy: genetic engineering for medically and morally irrelevant features imposes on children the parents' particular conception of the good (Clayton 2006: 104).

I propose an explanation of the wrong of parental 'design' that elaborates on the latter kind of criticism, unpacking the meaning of parental imposition in this context. I base my account on a morally informed conception of parental love that requires parents to value their children independently from the children's non-moral characteristics. Adequate parents, in this account, are accepting, can enjoy their children spontaneously and refrain from putting burdens of expectations, beyond very minimal ones, on their children. This *desiderata* is often expressed in everyday moral reasoning in the thought that parental love should be unconditional. Here I defend this claim about parental love by reference to the values of a secure and fair attachment between children and parents.

This is not to deny that, while 'designing' involves a sort of harm to children, it *can* also bestow benefits – some of which may be morally important. An all-encompassing evaluation of particular enhancements will have to reflect various considerations, only one of which is discussed here (Buchanan 2011: 175–6). Depending on how much weight one gives to the ideal of parental love advocated here, relative to other interests of children, parents may or may not turn out to have a moral right to create 'designer babies'.

In a nutshell, I hold that it is wrong to burden individuals with very particular parental expectations, since this unduly limits their psychological freedom to lead their lives without the guilt of disappointing their parents. I suggest that children who know they have been subjected to genetic engineering will be likely to carry an illegitimate burden of parental expectation; this situation could be avoided only if parents concealed from their children the fact of their genetic engineering. However, it is implausible that parents have a moral right to lie to their children in this particular situation; lying is inimical to love and intimacy, and in this case it can easily be avoided by refraining to engage in genetic engineering in the first place. Therefore, good parents have a *pro tanto* reason not to use genetic engineering to ensure medically and morally irrelevant features of their children.

### The traditional argument against parental design

The spirit of my argument is captured by many people's belief that good parents should not use genetic technology to 'design' non-medical features of their future children, such as looks, intelligence and personality. Several recent documents on the ethics of new biotechnologies reflect this belief. In 2003, The Human Fertilisation and Embryology Authority (HFEA) released a document, based on wide public consultation, which recommended outlawing gender selection and, in general, opposed non-therapeutic uses of genetic technology. The report argued that 'children selected for their sex alone may be in some way psychologically damaged by the knowledge that they have been selected in this way as embryos'. More specifically, the worry is that 'such children would be treated prejudicially by their parents and that parents would try to mould them to fulfill their (the parents') expectations' (quoted in Harris 2007: 156). In the United States, the President's Council on Bioethics raised a similar concern, suggesting that the use of genetic technology in order to shape one's future child is incompatible with the kind of parental love essential to good parenting – and thus implying that 'designer' children would suffer some sort of psychological harm:

The attitude of parents toward their child may be quietly shifted from unconditional acceptance to critical scrutiny: the very first act of parenting now becomes not the unreserved welcoming of an arriving child, but the judging of his or her fitness, while still an embryo, to become their child, all by the standards of contemporary genetic screening.

(President's Council on Bioethics 2003: 54–5)

The worry is that, by setting conditions on the child they will have, parents make, at least to some extent, their welcoming of their child conditional. In other words, the attitude encouraged by genetic design is incompatible with the ideal of parental love, which should not be dependent on morally indifferent features of the beloved:

the idea of parenthood should take for granted: that each child is ours to love and care for, from the start, unconditionally, and regardless of any special merit of theirs or special wishes of ours.

(President's Council on Bioethics 2003: 71)

Some philosophers, too, have worried that selection or enhancement might either entail or at least indicate something morally objectionable about the parents themselves: a lack in parental virtue (McDougall 2005; McDougall 2007). Adequate parenting, according to this view, must find the right balance between extremes of control and restraint which ensures enough guidance to children without failing to accept them as they are (Fox 2008). Since I rely on an ideal of adequate parental love which is accepting and not overly controlling and burdening, there is an obvious connection between my argument and discussions of selection and enhancement in terms of virtue ethics. However, my concern is not with parental character but with the possible harm to the children; hence I shall not couch my arguments in the language of virtue ethics.

I reformulate the above worries by taking the child's perspective, to show that their validity does not depend on the plausibility of virtue ethics. I assume children have a powerful interest in adequate parental love. Unlike some of the above criticism, I do not hold that parents who enhance their babies *necessarily* fail to love them for this reason; but, rather, that children who know their parents decided to enhance them *are likely to feel*, for this reason, burdened with unfair parental expectations. One does not need to rely on an ideal of parental love that is entirely unconditional – it is enough to claim that such love should not be conditional on morally irrelevant features such as looks, intellectual abilities and temperament. An additional assumption is that, in the context of the very intense and asymmetric relationships between parents and children, love is not always perfectly transparent. It is possible for a parent to feel love for her child and, while acting on it, make the child feel unduly burdened by parental expectations, and, for these reasons, experience parental love less securely and fairly.

The scope of the present argument is restricted to non-moral, and also to non-medical uses of genetic technology; the distinction between medical and non-medical uses of genetic technology, sometimes referred to as therapy versus enhancement, is far from straightforward. Yet, I assume that disease and disability entail serious harm. Much of this harm might indeed be, as proponents of the disability movement have argued, socially generated. While we collectively might have a duty to eliminate the socially generated harm, any particular parent who lives in a society she cannot change, has weighty reasons to try to protect her (future) children from disease and disability. This provides a strong reason to prevent disease and disability. Because there are very weighty reasons to prevent harm, it is unlikely that children will perceive their parents' genetic therapy as unloving in any way.

Parents can (in theory) use genetic technology to decide on features of their future children either by selecting from a number of already existing embryos those that have the most 'promising' genes (henceforth, 'selection'), or by prenatal gene therapy (henceforth 'enhancement'). Because selecting determines which children will exist while enhancement affects already existing embryos, the arguments of this paper will apply differently to cases of enhancement and cases of selection. The reason for this differentiation has to do with the non-identity problem. The two different types of design lead to two different worlds. A world with selection is a world which contains different individuals than a world without selection; hence, it cannot be claimed that there is any individual who would have been better off without selection. However, if one subscribes to a non-comparative conception of harm (Shiffrin 1999), one can see why a child whose important interests are frustrated can be said to suffer harm even if the act that caused the harm was necessary for bringing that child into existence. By contrast, enhancement is objectionable because it harms children that would have existed anyway.

In the next section I argue that there is a *prima facie* reason to worry that using selection or enhancement will be harmful to children. In the fourth section I briefly look at possible consequences of enhancement and selection for people other than the selected or enhanced children themselves and at the implications of my arguments for parents' environmental choices.

## The child's interest in unconditional parental love

Parental love that is conditional on morally irrelevant features of the child hurts the child's interests in a love that is accepting, spontaneous and fair – that is, free from illegitimate psychological burdens. These interests are likely to have different degrees of importance, and, for the sake of this argument, the most important is the interest in fairness. Also, these interests need not amount to the existence of a *right* in the kind of parental love that I defend in order to indicate that selection and enhancement are morally problematic. But if these interests exist, children have grounds for complaint when parental love is conditional on morally irrelevant features of the child. The language of needs, or interests, rather than rights, is an obvious choice in discussing the morality of reproductive choices in general. Interests and rights are closely related concepts, since, according to one prominent theory, rights protect very powerful interests. So, framing the issue in terms of interests will allow for more fine-tuned guidance, even if not all interests can ground children's rights or parental duties. Everyday discussions about moral issues involving people who are in close personal relationships are often formulated in terms of needs or interests. Because interests carry normative implications, and because there are likely to be more interests than rights, a moral analysis in terms of interests is capable of identifying a wider range of moral reasons than an analysis that appeals exclusively to rights. Moreover, an ideal of identifying, negotiating and satisfying interests seems a better guide to evaluation and action involving people who are engaged in intimate and long-lasting relationships with each other, than appeals to rights. This is the main insight into what came to be known as a feminist 'ethics of care', defined by a choice of moral language that places needs and interests at its core (Gilligan 1982; Noddings 1984; Ruddick 1989). This is not to say that, if conflicts cannot be settled in ways that satisfy all parties, appeals to rights are out of place in intimate relationships. But as long as individuals love each other – that is, as long as they do not see their interests as mutually independent or only contingently dependent on the other person's interests (Kittay 1999) – the harming of one party's interests is a serious ground for moral criticisms even if no rights have been infringed upon. Since I assume that adequate parents love their children, their harming of their child's interests is morally problematic whether or not this amounts to a violation of the child's rights.

Alongside interests in physical preservation and development, one of the fundamental interests of children is that of forming a secure, personalised and fair attachment to their parents. I stipulate that, in order to create such an attachment, parental love has to be unconditional on morally irrelevant features of the child. Love that is unconditional in this way responds to the child's interest because it facilitates a secure, personalised and fair attachment. First, it makes children feel accepted and valued beyond the individual features they have. Adequate parental love is, at the very least, *perceived* as unconditional because it is not given for the sake of particular characteristics such as intelligence, memory, physical features, happy temperament, creativity or special talents. Children feel securely loved when they are convinced that their parents would continue to accept and value them if they decided to dramatically change their looks, if they turned out to be less intelligent, creative or skilful than expected, if they discovered a different sexual or gender identity for themselves, and so on. By contrast, the worry that one is being loved for any or a combination of such characteristics erodes one's sense of being securely loved. When one worries that one might be loved because one is blond, tall, smart and cheerful, one actually worries that he or she is not really being loved. Especially for small children, a *secure* feeling that one is accepted and valued for who one is (and becomes) is particularly important for one's development as a confident, well adjusted, resilient and hopeful human being (Liao 2006).

Second, unconditional love can foster a sense of personalised attachment to the parent, because such love is more conducive to parental attitudes that encourage the children to discover who they are; moreover, loving one's children unconditionally seems to require an ability to take pleasure in discovering who the child is.

Finally, in order to feel adequately loved by their parents, children should not be burdened with excessive responsibility for their parents' happiness. Good enough parental love is unconditional also in the sense that parents' happiness does not depend on any particular, or outstanding, form of success of their children. It also implies that parents should not make children feel responsible for the various sacrifices adequate parents often make for their well-being. This is not to deny that adequate parents should strive to equip their children with the necessary knowledge, habits and intellectual and social skills to lead good lives. The parental duty to foster their children's development involves encouraging certain features and discouraging others, and often making decisions that will affect profoundly the children's development. But parental duty does not mean that parents may push their children into either high levels of achievement (like reading and writing extremely early) or special kinds of achievements (like playing the piano). When children seem to develop their own desire to learn how to read at three or to play the piano for most of their free time, thus giving clear hints about what a good life might come to mean for them, parents might be under a duty to facilitate, and even gently steer their children to *explore* this path. However, in order to pursue good lives successfully, children need, alongside nurturing and education, the 'permission' of their parents to be and do whatever makes them happy. They need to not feel guilty for being or trying to become something that their parents would not have chosen themselves. In other words, they need to feel 'free' to lead the kind of life they choose within the limits of what is permissible – free, that is, from any guilt that they are making their parents unhappy. If this need is frustrated by parents, children are likely to feel less loved than they would if their parents did not burden them with perfectionist expectations. This is, obviously, an empirical, psychological claim. Transactional analysis, amongst other schools of psychological therapy, works with the assumption that many people limit their own development, or force on themselves choices that do not make them happy due to more or less conscious feelings of responsibility and guilt towards their parents' plans for them. As evidence at the level of common knowledge, it is true that people sometimes wish their parents had encouraged them more to develop talents they think they would have liked to develop. But it is uncommon, if at all plausible, to complain that one's parents have not *forced* you into some kind of special achievement.

With this speculative, but hopefully not implausible, sketch of how children need to be loved by their parents, the concerns expressed by the President's Council on Bioethics appear justified:

> Selecting for desired traits inevitably plants specific hopes and expectations as to how their child might excel. More than any child does now, the 'better' child may bear the burden of living up to the standards he was 'designed' to meet. The oppressive weight of his parents' expectations – resting in this case on what they believe to be undeniable biological facts – may impinge upon the child's freedom to make his own way in the world.
>
> (President's Council on Bioethics 2003: 55)

An ideal of parental love like the one I uphold here is more modest than the 'unconditional love' frequently referred to in literature (Davis 2008; Fox 2008). Unconditional love would require parents to accept, value and maybe even enjoy children who are developing in morally unacceptable ways, or children who failed to learn enough about reciprocity and cooperation to develop *any* mutuality in relationships, or children so deeply distressed or depressed that looking after them well requires exceptional resourcefulness. I am agnostic on the possibility and desirability of a parental love so unconditional that the parent values and accepts their children in spite of the children's serious moral shortcomings. I make the more modest claim that adequate parents will not give reasons to their children to feel that their parents' love is conditional on features such as looks, intellectual abilities and even temperament. Such features certainly include most, if not all, of those that are usually considered in the context of selection and enhancement: higher intelligence, better memory, perfect pitch, calmer temperament, sunnier disposition, greater ambition (President's Council on Bioethics 2003: 37).

A child's knowledge that her parents have selected or enhanced her is likely to impact on her secure sense of being loved for who she is. The suspicion that her – selected or enhanced – features are partly determining her parents' love is very likely to creep in. Equally important is the question of whether selected or enhanced children would feel overly responsible for their parents' happiness. Arguably, children who know they are very gifted in whatever way because their parents wanted them to be certain kinds of people or to successfully pursue particular activities, will feel the burden of parental expectations and, with it, a diminished freedom from 'existential' responsibility to be whatever they wish to be or do whatever they wish to do. Because children are so emotionally attached to their parents, and dependent on their parents' approval, parental desires tend to have an impact on children which is easily underestimated. Finally, the spontaneous discovery and enjoyment of the selected or enhanced features of the child would be, if not prevented, at least diminished.

Enhanced and selected children will be affected in slightly different ways. Enhanced children might feel that they were not deemed to be good enough without the enhancement, while selected children will know they would not have been born, had they lacked the feature for which they had been selected. It is not clear which of the two situations is worse from the point of view of the child's interest in forming a secure, personalised and fair attachment with her parents. Yet, children from both groups will be likely to perceive the parental choice as a conditional valuing of them and feel the burden of their parents' expectations.

Allen Buchanan formulates the following worry: 'the issue is whether genetically designing children is or is not likely to lead to parents regarding their offspring as manufactured items' (Buchanan 2009: 146). I suggest a slight shift in the perspective from which this worry was raised, by saying that it is important whether children themselves would be likely to feel they are, in their parents' eyes, 'manufactured items'. Parents' and children's perceptions need not coincide. I assume that the main problem with regarding someone as a manufactured item, and with feeling like someone's manufactured item, is that, *qua* item, one's role is to fulfil somebody else's interests or desires. Others have pressed the Kantian complaint that selection and enhancement may lead to treating children as mere means and not as ends in themselves (Watt 2004). Here I raise the objection that, to the extent that one perceives oneself *qua* another's manufactured item, one is unlikely to feel loved in the secure, personalised and fair way outlined above. The two claims are clearly connected: to love somebody involves having an interest that her own needs, or interests, are being met. Thus, to the extent that selection and enhancement induce in children the worry that they are their parents' manufactured items, they are seriously detrimental to adequate parental love.

The claim is not that parents who select or enhance will necessarily fail to *feel*, but rather that they will fail to *express* unconditional love for their children. One can imagine that some parents who select or enhance their children would come to love their children in fully accepting, spontaneous and non-controlling ways, that is, independently of the enhanced features. Yet, by selection or enhancement, they have already sent the message that they wanted a particular kind of child, thus inducing the serious suspicion (to whoever knows that selection or enhancement took place) that, in some way, their love is determined by those features. They are also likely to have sent the message that they want the child to be a certain kind of person, leading a certain kind of life. While such an expectation is legitimate as long as it refers to features all children need for a good life – which means a few, thinly defined characteristics – it is much more problematic with respect to very specific features – as are those that we are more likely to ever attempt to produce by genetic technology.

For this reason, children themselves will be likely to feel less unconditionally loved and that in the loving relationships between children and parents it will be more difficult to sustain the standards of acceptance, freedom from 'existential' responsibility and spontaneous enjoyment outlined above. But it is not unreasonable to also suppose that parents' ability to love *is* favoured by a non-controlling attitude. Adequate parental love is incompatible with an excessively controlling attitude (i.e. parents may legitimately use only the amount of control needed to ensure proper, but not necessarily exceptional, development in children). Fox (2008) elaborates on the argument that using genetic technology would indicate a shortcoming of parental love by burdening the resulting children with expectations and with parents' own projects.

A child who knows it has been designed will, for that reason, occasionally feel that the parent's love is conditional. The past fact of designing cannot be erased, and the message it sent is still there, inscribed into the child's body and personality.

One may object to this argument by saying that parents who use enhancement could, and should, conceal this from their children. It is true that parents often lie to their children in order to protect them; the moral status of this practice is controversial even when the lie is about something trivially connected to the child's life, or when it concerns a regretted parental mistake. Lying to children about the use of enhancement seems particularly problematic, since enhancements are done intentionally and they affect children's identity directly. It is difficult to see how a principled endorsement of lying to one's children about deliberate parental choices regarding the children's features can be morally acceptable.

John Davis has attempted to rebut the argument against selection from unconditional love, saying that, in fact, unconditional love require parents to ensure the best genes for their children. His argument is based on an analogy with making a good endowment for one's future child: Given the choice, which good parent would not choose for her child a good endowment, all other things being equal – for instance, if this did not cause social injustice by upsetting fair distributions? But the analogy is misleading because it presupposes that, like a good endowment, particularly 'good' genes are necessarily good for you, regardless of how they came about. The question, however, is precisely whether having particularly 'good' genes, which you know have been selected for you by your parents, is better than merely being free from 'bad' genes. I have argued that the very fact that parents have chosen these genes for you – or, in the case of selection, they have chosen you for these genes – can make your life worse by making you feel unduly burdened with parental expectations, or even insecure with respect to your parents' love. In the everyday relationship between parents and children, the particularly 'good' genes play a role that endowments do not *necessarily* play: they condition and direct the expression of parental love and entail expectations that are not obviously legitimate because they can be exceedingly burdensome. Endowments can, of course, also come with such expectations. Unlike genes, many endowments can be declined. Yet, to the extent to which it is psychologically costly for children to decline them, endowments come with burdening expectations and are objectionable for the same reasons that make selected genes objectionable.

### Harm to third parties?

To evaluate parental use of selection and enhancement one should also consider the effect on parties other than the parents who 'design' their children. I suggest that selection or enhancement for non-medical reasons, if widespread, could harm people's general ability to sustain loving relationships with their children by adversely affecting the ideal of accepting and unburdening parental love.

Making selection and/or enhancement legally available for those ready to pay for it would introduce (or, rather, amplify) conflicts between fairness and care for one's own child. Some of the enhanceable features are positional goods. If many, or most, children of well-off parents would have genetic advantages bought for them, those who do not will inevitably be disadvantaged. As a consequence, parents who do not, although they could afford to, use selection and enhancement to gain competitive advantage for their children might be perceived as less loving (by the media, by other parents, possibly by their own children). Widespread use of selection and enhancement for non-medical reasons by affluent parents, in combination with knowledge of this use, would put social pressure on all affluent parents to conform.

Ironically, then, some of the non-selected or non-enhanced children, as well as selected and enhanced ones, might feel less secure about their parents' love. The more widespread parental selection and enhancement are, the stronger the expectation that affluent parents use genetic technology to buy competitive advantage for their children. It seems reasonable then to see selection and enhancement as undesirable because of the risk of corrupting the social ideal of parental love. Unfortunately, in some social environments in countries such as the USA the social ideal of parental love already includes excessive ambition, expressed in relentless parental pursuits to give their children competitive advantage (Fox 2008).

This objection is not unique to selection and enhancement. Children have always been intentionally shaped by their parents in a variety of ways – through socialisation, education, choice of partner and, indeed, through the use of medical services (Mameli 2007). I do not claim that there is an important moral distinction between genetic and environmental enhancement. Criticism of parental use of genetic technology for 'designing' babies is grounded in the same reasons as criticism of parents' concerted efforts to shape, by environmental means, their children's characteristics beyond the usual range of normal functioning (Agar 2004).

Hence, my argument entails that parents' environmental choices should also be limited if their children are to feel adequately loved: secure and unburdening love is not compatible with parents' insistence, and utmost efforts to ensure, that the child becomes very good at, for example, mathematics, or sports, or piano-playing. Equally, it is not compatible with parental insistence and efforts to ensure that the child leads a particular lifestyle (as regards religion, family, profession or diet, for example). As I have argued, making one's child feel responsible for her parents' happiness is incompatible with adequate parental love. Therefore, both genetic and environmental shaping of a child, when justified as a way of promoting parents' well-being, enabling them to satisfy deep-seated desires about how their children turn out, is morally objectionable.

Two premises play an important role in the argument of this chapter: first, that 'designer babies' would be very likely to feel that their parents' love for them is at least partly conditional on the 'enhanced' features and burdening them with parental expectations; and second, that the need to feel adequately loved by one's parents is important for all children. These are largely empirical claims (although defining 'adequate parental love' includes normative elements). It is the role of public conversation (and of social scientists), rather than that of philosophers, to assess these premises. Jurgen Habermas (2003: 52–3) has claimed that, in order to decide whether enhancement by genetic means would be harmful to the 'designed' children, we should be able to say what it is like to be a genetically enhanced person. Public discussion can help us to imagine what it must be like, for example by analogy to people whose parents attempted enhancement by *non*-genetic means of features such as looks, intellectual abilities and skills or temperament. Examples could be those whose parents put significant amounts of money, energy and persuasion into making sure their child's school or social performance was above average when this did not seem to coincide with a desire of the child herself to perform particularly well.

Further, explorations of widespread beliefs and personal testimonies might help assess the importance of feeling loved unconditionally by one's parents relative to the importance of enjoying features (such as memory, or mild temper, or a high IQ) that could be enhanced. This would be a way to determine if, all things considered, genetic enhancement or selection are harmful to children.

## Conclusion

I have argued that using genetic technology to design non-moral and non-medical features of one's child is objectionable because the 'designer babies' will have reasons to doubt their parents' unconditional love; parental love might be perceived as conditional on characteristics on which love in general, and parental love in particular, should not depend. Selected or enhanced children would be likely to be burdened with inappropriate parental expectations and possibly miss out on some of the spontaneity of their parents' enjoyment of them, which is an important facet of parental love. Because I assume that one of the most important interests of children is to experience secure, spontaneous and fair parental love, this amounts to harm.

## Acknowledgements

While writing the last version of this chapter I have benefited from a De Velling Willis Fellowship at the University of Sheffield. I am grateful to Matthew Clayton, Speranta Dumitru, Iseult Honohan, Ingrid Robeyns, Anders Schinkel and Daniel Weinstock for interesting discussions on earlier drafts.

## References

Agar, N. 2004. *Liberal Eugenics: In defence of human enhancement*. Victoria: Blackwell.

Buchanan, A., Brock D. W., Daniels N. and Wikler D. 2000. *From Chance to Choice. Genetics and justice*. Cambridge: Cambridge University Press.

Buchanan, A. 2009. 'Human nature and enhancement', *Bioethics* 23(3): 141–50.

Buchanan, A. 2011. *Beyond Humanity? The ethics of biomedical enhancement*. Oxford: Oxford University Press.

Clayton, M. 2006. *Justice and Legitimacy in Upbringing*. Oxford: Oxford University Press.

Daniels, N. 2001. 'It isn't just the sex...', *American Journal of Bioethics* 1(1): 10–11.

Davis, J. 2008. 'Selecting potential children and unconditional parental love', *Bioethics* 22(5): 258–68.

Fox, D. 2008. 'Parental attention deficit disorder', *Journal of Applied Philosophy* 25(3): 246–61.

Gilligan, C. 1982. *In a Different Voice: Psychological theory and women's development*. Cambridge, MA: Harvard University Press.

Habermas, J. 2003. *The Future of Human Nature*. Cambridge: Polity Press.

Harris, J. 2007. *Enhancing Evolution. The ethical case for making better people*. Princeton, NJ: Princeton University Press.

Kittay, E. 1999. *Love's Labour. Essays on women, equality and dependency*. New York: Routledge.

Liao, M. 2006. 'The right of children to be loved', *Journal of Political Philosophy*, 14(4): 420–40.

McDougall, R. 2005. 'Acting parentally: An argument against sex selection', *Journal of Medical Ethics* 31: 601–5.

McDougall, R. 2007. 'Parental virtue: A new way of thinking about the morality of reproductive actions', *Bioethics* 21(4): 181–90.

Mameli, M. 2007. 'Reproductive cloning, genetic engineering and the autonomy of the child: the moral agent and the open future', *Journal of Medical Ethics* 33: 87–93.

Noddings, N. 1984. *Caring: A feminine approach to ethics and moral education*. Berkeley, CA: University of California Press.

President's Council on Bioethics 2003. *Beyond Therapy. Biotechnology and the Pursuit of Happiness*. Available at: https://bioethicsarchive.georgetown.edu/pcbe/reports/beyondtherapy/index.html (accessed 8 April 2014).

Rajczi, A. 2008. 'One danger of biomedical enhancements', *Bioethics* 22(6): 328–36.

Ruddick, S. 1989. *Maternal Thinking. Towards a politics of peace*. Boston, MA: Beacon Press.

Shiffrin S. 1999. 'Wrongful life, procreative responsibility and the significance of harm', *Legal Theory* 5: 117–48.

Watt, H. 2004. 'Preimplantation genetic diagnosis: Choosing the "good enough" child', *Health Care Analysis* 12(1): 51–60.

# 11 The press and the public interest

*Joachim Allgaier*

Journalistic mass media are an important and for some people the only source of information about biomedical and scientific developments. How the media treat these topics hence frames the public debate about the ethical and legal issues regarding medical applications and technologies. However, the inter-relationships and inter-dependence of scientists and researchers, journalists and the public are more complex and require deeper investigation. What may appear as objective reporting of facts is often more subjective and hence prone to socio-cultural and political framings of the debates. In this chapter an overview is provided on how research on science and technology in the media and public opinion can contribute to a better understanding of public debates about biotechnology.

Genetics and biotechnology started to become a controversial topic in public debates and media coverage from the 1990s onwards. Accordingly, a lot of research on news coverage and public opinion related to biotechnology has been done during the emergence and controversy phase of this technology (e.g. Gaskell and Bauer 2001; Bauer and Gaskell 2002). Genetic manipulation and biotechnology became a topic of mass interest in the mid-1990s in Europe, after genetically modified soy beans were introduced in Europe and the birth of the first cloned mammal, Dolly the sheep (see, e.g., Holliman 2004) was announced in February 1997 (Hampel 2012). It was also around that time that the debate around biotechnology settled into the distinction between agri-food (green) and bio-medical (red) biotechnology. This distinction had consequences for how the different technologies were portrayed in the mass media and also for how they were perceived by the public (Bauer 2005).

Biotechnology has changed dramatically since its invention. What started as a method decades ago has turned into various applied technologies. Applications range from the industrial production of enzymes, to the manipulation of plants and crops, from genetic screening to genetic and stem-cell therapies, genetic fingerprinting and cloned animals

165

(Hampel 2012). Accordingly, the foci of coverage regarding gene research and biotechnology have also changed over the years. While earlier studies examined media coverage and public opinion towards genetic manipulation per se, later studies have focused on particular areas of application and coverage in particular media and communication channels.

However, it is important to note here that mass media do not report neutrally about new technologies. They rather form a sort of public arena in which particular aspects of new research and research applications can be discussed and various actors are taking part in the debates. In the context of the mass media, journalists so far have played a particular role as gatekeepers, whereas the audience has remained rather passive. Particularly in the natural sciences it is often assumed that the media, meaning mainly journalists, create the public image of science and research, technologies and their effects. The role of the media and its influence on decision makers and public opinion is also insinuated in the field of biological and biotechnological research and medical genetics (Ruhrmann 2012). The scientific establishment has not always been content with the way the topics of biotechnology and genetics have been covered by the mass media. In the UK, a specific science media centre has been established as a remedy for inaccurate and distorted coverage about biotechnology and to convey more precise and accurate coverage about genetics, biotechnology and other research in the media (Callaway 2013). However, other actors, such as environmental non-governmental organizations or churches and other religious groups, are also doing professional public relations work in order to influence media coverage and public opinion with the long-term goal of changing public policies.

It must also be stressed that research on journalistic news media is not sufficient if one wants to understand public images of and public opinion about biotechnology and applications of genetic research. Moreover, it is also important to get an understanding of how this kind of research and the applications that are stemming from it are represented in popular culture (Turney 1998; Maio 2006) and entertainment media (Condit 2001; Görke and Ruhrmann 2003). For instance, it is often believed that images of biotechnology and genetics in soap operas, comic books, blockbuster movies such as *Jurassic Park* (Ten Eyck 2005), and novels such as Ken Follet's *The Third Twin* can also have an impact on what citizens think and how they feel about genetics and biotechnology. It has been documented that classic novels such as Mary Shelley's *Frankenstein* or Aldous Huxley's *Brave New World* have served as cultural reference points from the early days of genetics up to the present day (Turney 1998). So far the research on genetics and biotechnology in the media has mainly focused on conventional news media (and particularly on journalistic print media), but the study of genetics and biotechnology in popular and entertainment media is still a neglected research area where more work remains to be done for a better understanding of the issue (see, e.g., Dijck 1998; Condit 1999).

Furthermore, media infrastructure has changed dramatically in the recent two decades and has moved away from the one-way communication model of the traditional mass media to more dialogic communication models of contemporary online media (Brossard 2012). This means that the filter function that the journalistic mass media had loses weight in the era of dialogic social online media and, moreover, it is not the mass media alone that sets public agendas any more (Hampel 2012). The role of media consumers has also changed. Individuals are increasingly turning to online environments to find information about science and to follow specific scientific developments. They can search actively for issues and topics relevant to their personal interests. Compared to the passive consumption of traditional mass media content this assigns citizens a more active role for consuming information about science. In addition, many Internet users do not only use the web receptively but they are also creating and disseminating user-generated content themselves, with all kinds of different agendas and worldviews in the background. It is therefore crucial for scientists, scientific institutions and science communicators to think about how science can and should be communicated in online environments, how to engage with citizens online, and how destructive images of biotechnology and the life sciences can be countered in social media (Brossard 2013).

## Media coverage of biotechnology and genetics

From the 1970s onwards there was a constant rise of mass media coverage of biotechnology and genetics (Nisbet and Lewenstein 2002; Hampel 2012). By the end of the 1990s coverage of biotechnology was strongly science-centred: about two-thirds of the topics related to biotechnology discussed in the media were scientific topics. The discussion of political and ethical questions remained in the background during that time. Various studies also emphasized that scientists were the main actors and sources who appeared at that time in the coverage (see, e.g., Petersen 2001; Anderson 2002; Hampel 2012). An international comparison of coverage of biotechnology in opinion-leading newspapers by Kohring, Görke and Ruhrmann (1999) found that there was a common tendency in the coverage to underline the potential utility of medical applications and that the coverage of potential risks was more or less neglected.

Petersen (2001) added that stories of hope and promise appear regularly in printed news media coverage about (medical) genetics, and that geneticists were often depicted as warriors and heroes.

It also turned out that coverage of biotechnology on television differed from coverage of biotechnology in the press because in popular science programmes on television only topics that can be visualized adequately had news value. Television journalists often considered many topics about medical biotechnology and molecular medicine as too complex for a mass audience to visualize and understand (Ruhrmann 2012). That is one reason why there is generally more print media coverage on biotechnological topics and also why scientific information concerning biotechnology is often disseminated in textual form (Bromme and Kienhues 2012).

All in all, the coverage of medical genetics has been favourable (Condit 2001). However, in the second half of the 1990s, debates focusing on risk, ethics and liability emerged to a noteworthy extent (e.g. Nisbet and Lewenstein 2002; Hampel 2012), related for instance to topics such as cloning (Haran et al. 2007) and green biotechnology (Gaskell et al. 2003). The consideration of negative social, economic and ethical elements has increased over time. However, medical (red) biotechnology was still generally reported with a positive slant and associated with progress and had less controversial coverage than that for green biotechnology concerning agricultural crops and genetically modified food (e.g., Condit 2001). Research on stem cells emerged as a controversial topic at the end of the 1990s and continued to be controversial, particularly when embryonic materials are needed for the research (e.g., Ten Eyck and Williment 2003). Still, the reporting on medical biotechnology had its focus mostly on the benefits and utility of medical applications for society, while potential risks of these emergent biomedical technologies were often not mentioned or sidelined in media reports (Ruhrmann 2012). The way in which genetic research was covered was often personalized and based on specific events, but human-interest angles and emotions are also important news factors for journalists (Schäfer 2007; Ruhrmann 2012). Important 'trigger events' for coverage were, for instance, the announcement of the first cloned sheep by British scientist Ian Wilmut (Weingart, Salzmann and Wörmann 2008), the completion of the Human Genome Project (Nerlich, Dingwall and Clarke 2002) or the scandal around the South Korean stem-cell researcher Hwang Woo-Suk when it emerged that many of his data on somatic cell nuclear transfer were fabricated (Kitzinger 2008). The patterns of reporting are complex and hard to anticipate, and they reveal different courses depending on the kind of technology and value sensitivity (Weingart,

Salzmann and Wörmann 2008). Here it is important to note that many of the events that 'triggered' news coverage were staged for the public or particularly the mass media on behalf of scientific institutions (Schäfer 2007). Orchestration and professional public relations work on the part of science has been documented in various cases and science communication researchers are taking this as evidence that genetics research and the life sciences in general are also in the process of becoming increasingly 'medialized' (Rödder 2009).

Various topics emerged over the years, such as DNA testing to diagnose or anticipate hereditary diseases, the discussion about reproductive versus therapeutic cloning particularly after the Hwang scandal, gene therapy, privacy and the opposition to employers', governments' and insurers' use of personal genetic data. Topics such as xenotransplantation or synthetic biology have generated little mass media coverage so far (Hampel 2012). However, Schäfer (2007) and others reported that negative evaluations of these topics in the media were still rare and that most of them could be found in coverage concerning stem-cell research and the use of embryonic materials.

It has also been found that national cultural contexts can have an effect on how red biotechnology topics have been covered. For instance, Reis (2008) compared newspaper coverage of stem-cell research in the USA and Brazil between January 2001 and March 2005. While coverage of political, ethical and religious aspects was the centre of attention (86 per cent) in the USA, only 44 per cent of the articles in Brazilian newspapers were concerned with such aspects. In contrast, much of the Brazilian coverage contained the rhetoric of medical breakthroughs and a dominant discursive media frame was about scientific progress. During this time the political and ethical debate about stem cells raged in the United States, while in Brazil various successful research results in the stem-cell area were achieved.

It has also been suggested that the results of (medical) genetics and biotechnical research have often been 'hyped' in the news media and represented inaccurately, and that exaggerated claims have been made in the media (Geller, Bernhardt and Holtzman 2002). An investigation of daily newspaper reporting of gene discoveries and associated technologies in Canada, the United States, Great Britain and Australia (Bubela and Caulfield 2004; Caulfield 2004), however, found that the print media coverage was 'surprisingly' accurate and that it often conveyed a message that was mainly created by the scientific community itself. The researchers also found an overemphasis on the benefits of genetic discoveries and an under-representation of risks in newspaper articles, but also in the scientific articles that they examined.

Coverage about green biotechnology generally focuses more on risks than the coverage of (potential) medical applications of biotechnology (Hampel 2012). This trend has been confirmed by various studies. For instance, a study by Marks *et al.* (2007) that investigated mass-media coverage of medical and agricultural biotechnology over a 12-year period in the United Kingdom and the United States found that diverse biotechnologies have been framed differently: medical applications have been framed more positively in the coverage, agricultural biotechnology more negatively (see also Ten Eyck and Williment 2003; Bauer 2005). The authors concluded that this way of framing topics can result in different public perceptions of biotechnology, with negative or ambivalent views for agricultural and positive views for medical applications (Marks *et al.* 2007). Various studies have confirmed this notion. For instance, a case study from Switzerland (Bonfadelli, Dahinden and Leonarz 2007) investigated media coverage of genetics in Swiss newspapers and conducted surveys and focus groups on the public perception of biotechnology. They found that a dominant media frame for medical (red) biotechnology was based on the idea of (scientific and societal) progress and that this frame put red biotechnology in a positive light and linked it with advantages for health and society. Green biotechnology, in contrast, had been framed in more ambivalent, sceptical and even outright negative terms and it was often also called to public account in the media. The results from the focus groups showed a clear difference between attitudes towards medical versus green applications of biotechnology. While medical applications were evaluated in a continuum between ambivalent and positive, agricultural applications were mostly rejected. Survey data also confirmed that Swiss citizens judged the different applications of biotechnology in different ways. Red biotechnology was evaluated far more positively than green biotechnology. While red biotechnology was seen as being useful and morally acceptable, green biotechnology was not seen as useful, without practical benefits, risky and morally unacceptable. An interesting result of this study is that 40 per cent of those in favour of biotechnology stated that media coverage had influenced them to view biotechnology even more favourably, while 44 per cent of those who opposed biotechnology shifted towards viewing it even more negatively. The authors assert that both groups seemed to view the media as having reinforced their attitude. They concluded: "the intense public controversy did not result in an anti-science shift, but, instead, led to increasing awareness and public understanding of biotechnology as a complex scientific topic" (Bonfadelli, Dahinden and Leonarz 2007: 123).

However, the precise connection between public opinion and mass media portrayals of genetics is not yet fully understood. Ten Eyck (2005), for instance, compared survey data collected in the United States with media coverage of genetics and biotechnology in two newspapers in the United States. He found that a one-dimensional media effect is not occurring and that slants in the media do not predict public opinion. Ten Eyck rejected the assumption that there are causal links between media discourses and public opinion, because audiences use various interpretative filters and may not only be influenced by journalistic media, but by online content, entertainment media, popular culture and other accounts as well. However, at the same time, he wrote that it is also not possible to argue that no such relationship between the media and public opinion exists (Ten Eyck 2005).

It is therefore generally assumed that various factors influence the attitudes of citizens to medical genetics. Some factors that are often mentioned in this context are, for instance, the educational level and knowledge about science, political orientation and religiosity. Here various studies have found a link between religious beliefs and attitudes towards emerging technologies in general, to things genetic and the manipulation of life in general (see Allum *et al.* 2013). However, the connections between these factors are complex and not straightforward. For instance, in a study about public attitudes towards stem-cell research in the United States, Ho, Brossard and Scheufele (2008) found an interaction between political ideologies on the one hand and religious convictions and the relationship between knowledge of and attitudes towards stem-cell research on the other hand. In obtaining more knowledge about stem-cell research people with a politically conservative world view and people with strong religious convictions oppose stem-cell research more strongly. People with a liberal political attitude, in contrast, rather support stem-cell research with the more knowledge they gain about it.

Based on this and other studies Allum *et al.* (2013), using statistical analyses of survey data, examined the idea that strong religious commitment might act as a 'perceptual filter' through which citizens acquire and use scientific knowledge in the formation of attitudes towards medical genetics in the British context. They found that citizens' religious beliefs, to some extent, mirror the concerns of religious institutions about genetics and genetic testing of unborn babies in particular. Also, people who hold creationist beliefs are less optimistic about the future developments of medical genetics. However, there is no clear relationship with religious beliefs when it comes to the personal willingness to take genetic tests. Allum *et al.* (2013) found evidence that religion can act as a 'perceptual filter' for attitudes towards genetic testing, but not for general optimism about medical genetics. Religious people that are highly knowledgeable about science tend to have more negative attitudes toward genetic testing than those who say that they are less scientifically literate. These findings support the idea that people's predispositions can affect the way in which information is processed and adapted and attitudes are formed. In general scientifically literate people are more supportive towards genetics, but this is not necessarily the case for religious people. Even though there is also support among religious citizens for genetic research, strongly religious people who are knowledgeable about science do not show more support for genetic testing and research. A potential practical implication of this finding is that trying to enhance public understanding of the science of genetics in a group of strongly religious people is likely to fail in precisely the group that is most likely to object to medical genetics (Allum *et al.* 2013).

### Public opinion and attitudes towards genetics biotechnology

In general laypeople do not use scientific knowledge for the same reasons as scientific experts. Often they are looking for orientation and solutions for concrete everyday problems in order to reach reasonable decisions (e.g., Bromme and Kienhues 2012). Therefore the public interest and expectation on science is that it provides secure knowledge, solutions for problems and also new ways of treatment and therapies for severe diseases and disorders. It is likely that many citizens' interest in genetics and biotechnological research, therefore, focuses on health-related aspects, be they innovative new therapies or ways of avoiding personal health problems. Journalists generally anticipate readers' interests and that might be a reason why science news in general has become increasingly 'biomedicalized' (Bauer 1998). Although reports about genetics in the mass media should not be seen as an accurate reflection of what members of the public are actually thinking about it, they can still constitute key social issues that affect public policy and decision makers (Condit 2001).

Various studies and surveys have tried to shed light on what members of the public think about genetics and biotechnology. It has been found that the various applications of biotechnology are perceived and evaluated very differently. Somewhat bluntly put, the message is that red biotechnology is accepted by the majority of the population in Europe and the USA, but a large proportion of the population rejects or is much less enthusiastic about green biotechnology (Hampel 2012). For instance, in 2002 it was found in a representative survey in Germany that the population has a positive attitude towards medical biotechnology. Sixty-four per cent thought that advances in biotechnological research will lead to great medical progress; and 62 per cent said they were willing to use pharmaceuticals that are the result of genetic modifications (Wieland 2012). All in all, various surveys showed that the German public has a differentiated view towards various fields of biotechnical applications. Health added the value of legitimation to red biotechnology. There is strong affirmation for diagnosing hereditary diseases and the use of biotechnology for the production of innovative pharmaceuticals, but a large proportion of the population oppose the genetic modification of crops and speak out against genetically modified organisms in their food. This picture is similar all over Europe, but in Germany, biotechnological applications for human beings sparked particularly lively debates and faced strong opposition since they are regarded as particularly problematic in ethical terms. This debate has its roots in the country's history of eugenics and unethical research on human subjects in Nazi Germany (Jasanoff 2005). This historical legacy has contributed to the trouble stem-cell researchers have had in general in Germany and to the opposition to embryonic stem-cell research in particular (Fundación BBVA 2008).

Considerable public controversy was also created by research using embryonic stem cells in the United States. Here many people's attitudes were strongly related to their religious worldview and moral principles. However, public support for medical research that uses stem cells from human embryos has grown since 2002 in the United States (National Science Board 2012). Since 2004, a majority of the public (63 per cent) has supported stem-cell research. There is even more support (71 per cent) for stem-cell research that uses stem cells from sources that do not involve human embryos. Americans strongly oppose cloning when there is no medical purpose mentioned. In 2010, eight out of ten Americans rejected the idea of cloning or genetically altering humans. However, support for cloning technology for medical research and treatment has been growing with 55 per cent in favour and 40 per cent opposed (National Science Board 2012). In this context it is worth noting that the number of Americans who said they comprehend the difference between reproductive and therapeutic cloning in 2008 was lower than in previous surveys and also that the self-assessed understanding of stem-cell research declined between 2008 and 2010 (National Science Board 2012). Another issue for Americans is the use of genetic information. A survey conducted in 2007 (Genetics and Public Policy Center 2007) found that the majority of Americans 'enthusiastically' supported genetic testing for research and health care. However, concern was expressed by a large majority (92 per cent) who feared that results of such tests could be used in harmful ways. A majority stated that they would trust doctors and genetic researchers to have access to genetic test results. But, there is serious concern and distrust about discrimination that could result if insurers and employers get hold of and use results from citizens' genetic tests.

In Britain, green biotechnologies have also received much less public support compared to red biotechnology (Gaskell *et al.* 2003). However, according to the Wellcome Trust Monitor survey (2009), the UK public was overwhelmingly positive about medical advances through genetic research: in 2009, 86 per cent said they were either somewhat or very optimistic. In the second survey wave in 2012 enthusiasm was still high: 79 per cent of young people and 80 per cent of adults stated that they were optimistic that in the next twenty years developments in genetic research would improve health care. At the same time, the level of self-assessed understanding of the relevant science varies. Citizens often think that it is the role of scientists and researchers to know and decide about genetic research and a majority of citizens (57 per cent) said that they did not personally want to be involved in public consultations about medical research. While 60 per cent of adults said that they had a 'good' or 'very good' understanding of the term 'DNA', only 11 per cent said their understanding of the term 'human genome' was good. In the cases of 'genetic modification' (34 per cent) and 'stem cells' (31 per cent) about a third of questioned adults said their understanding of the term was very good or good.

Particularly helpful for the understanding of public opinions about biotechnology in Europe are the regularly conducted Eurobarometer surveys (European Commission 2013) on public attitudes towards biotechnology that the European Commission has coordinated since 1991. For instance, a key result of the fourth Eurobarometer survey carried out in November 1999 suggested that Europeans clearly distinguished between different applications of biotechnology. They were supportive of biomedical applications of biotechnology (e.g., genetic testing and the production of pharmaceuticals), but have increasingly become opposed to genetically modified food and the cloning of animals (Gaskell *et al.* 2000). Another interesting finding of this survey is that the cloning of human cells and tissues for medical purposes received moderate support, but the cloning of animals for medical purposes was widely rejected. However, even the most favoured applications (genetic testing and medicines) were also troubling, even to those who expressed support (Gaskell *et al.* 2000).

The Eurobarometer 2002 survey on Europeans and biotechnology further documented support for biotechnology and showed that 43 per cent of Europeans were optimistic that biotechnology would improve their way of life, 17 per cent were pessimistic, 12 per cent said it would make no difference. Optimism in biotechnology had increased and Europeans continued to distinguish between supported medical applications and rejected agricultural and food applications. In this survey it is the exploitation of genetic information that was a source of concern for many Europeans. Access to genetic information by government agencies and by commercial insurance was largely regarded as unacceptable.

Three years later the Eurobarometer 2005 survey showed that European citizens were increasingly optimistic about biotechnology, more informed and more trusting of the biotechnology system. This has to do with the trust in the state and the legislation that is supposed to regulate genetic research. There was still widespread support for medical applications and opposition to agricultural biotechnologies in all but a few countries. Gene therapy was perceived as useful to society and also morally acceptable. There was also support for embryonic stem-cell research across Europe, but citizens tend to be more supportive of non-embryonic sources of stem cells. Citizens in this case felt it important that stem-cell research was tightly regulated (Gaskell *et al.* 2006).

Regulation of new technologies was also an issue in the following Eurobarometer 2010 survey. Europeans expected appropriate regulation and opposed the reliance on market forces. While in the United States the regulation of research on embryonic stem cells was still a public controversy, 63 per cent of Europeans now supported human embryonic stem-cell research and there was a similar level of support for gene therapy. Europeans did not only solidly support medical applications, they were also approving of non-therapeutic applications. Fifty-six per cent of European citizens approved of research for enhancing human performance without medical indication. However, approval was contingent and dependent on adequate regulation by the state. The contrast in the public reception of red and green biotechnology was greater than ever: opponents of green biotechnology outnumbered supporters by 3 to 1 and there is no country where there was a majority of supporters of agricultural and food biotechnologies (Gaskell *et al.* 2011).

## Outlook

In order to understand public debates about legal and ethical issues associated with particular technologies it is crucial to take into account how these technologies have been covered by the mass media. It is likely that the way the mass media cover particular scientific and biomedical topics and related technologies has an influence on what the public knows and thinks about them. It seems that the European and American public – despite some ethical and political controversies – have largely embraced and welcome medical applications of biotechnology. In general this seems to correspond with favourable news coverage about red biotechnologies. However, this is a rather general and superficial picture of the relationship between public opinion and media coverage of genetics and biotechnology. As mentioned at the beginning of the chapter, it is important that future research on this relationship takes into account the impact of entertainment media and popular culture. Further research is also needed on the move from traditional one-way mass media reception to the more active roles of recipients in online environments and if and how this move changes the attitudes of citizens towards medical genetics and red biotechnology.

Another departure point for further research is that the term red biotechnology is too comprehensive and does not allow for differentiation between particular medical applications. Therefore we will hopefully see more studies that investigate how particular biomedical applications of biotechnology are treated in the media and are perceived by the public. Here it is also probable that it becomes more difficult to determine what actually counts as a medical application of biotechnology. The health science research community already discusses what they call a 'third revolution' – the convergence of life sciences, physical sciences and engineering – in health science research (MIT 2011).

Given the favourable coverage that medical biotechnologies seem to have received so far it might also be the case that some people are disappointed if the anticipated breakthroughs and promised new treatments do not materialize – a possible consequence of very positive news coverage. At least one recent article in the UK broadsheet *The Observer* has asked 'Stem cells: What happened to the radical breakthroughs?' (Roach 2013).

### References

Allum, N., Sibley, E., Sturgis, P. and Stoneman, P. 2013. 'Religious beliefs, knowledge about science and attitudes towards medical genetics', *Public Understanding of Science*, published online before print 9 July 2013: doi: 10.1177/0963662513492485.

Anderson, A. 2002. 'In search of the Holy Grail: Media discourse and the new human genetics', *New Genetics and Society* 21(3): 327–37.

Bauer, M. 1998. 'The medicalization of science news – from the "rocket-scalpel" to the "gene-meteorite" complex', *Social Science Information* 37(4): 731–51.

Bauer, M. W. 2005. 'Distinguishing red and green biotechnology: Cultivation effects of the elite press', *International Journal of Public Opinion Research* 17(1): 63–89.

Bauer, M. W. and Gaskell, G. (eds.) 2002. *Biotechnology – The making of a global controversy*. Cambridge: Cambridge University Press.

Bonfadelli, H., Dahinden, U. and Leonarz, M. 2007. 'Mass media and public perceptions of red and green biotechnology: a case study from Switzerland', in Brossard, D., Shanahan, J. and Nesbitt T. C. (eds.) *The Media, the Public and Agricultural Biotechnology*. Cambridge, MA: CABI, pp. 97–125.

Bromme, R. and Kienhues, D. 2012. 'Rezeption von wissenschaft – mit besonderem fokus auf bio- und gentechnologie und konfligierender evidenz', in Weitze *et al.* (eds.), pp. 303–48.

Brossard, D. 2012. 'A Brave New World: Challenges and opportunities for communicating about biotechnology in new information environments', in Weitze *et al.* (eds.), pp. 427–45.

Brossard, D. 2013. 'New media landscapes and the science information consumer', *PNAS* 110, supplement 3: 14096–101.

Bubela, T. M. and Caulfield, T. 2004. 'Do the print media "hype" genetic research? A comparison of newspaper stories and peer-reviewed research papers', *CMAJ* 170(9): 1399–1407.

Callaway, E. 2013. 'Science media: Centre of attention', *Nature* 499: 142–4.

Caulfield, T. 2004. 'Biotechnology and the popular press: Hype and the selling of science', *Trends in Biotechnology* 22(7): 337–9.

Condit, C. M. 1999. *The Meaning of the Gene*. Madison. WI: University of Wisconsin Press.

Condit, C. 2001. 'What is "public opinion" about genetics?' *Nature Reviews Genetics* 2: 811–15.

Dijck, J. V. 1998. *Imagenation: Popular images of genetics*. New York: New York University Press.

European Commission 2013. Eurobarometer surveys. Available at: http://ec.europa.eu/public_opinion/index_en.htm (accessed 15 November 2013).

Fundación BBVA 2008. *BBVA Foundation International Study on Attitudes to Stem Cell Research and Hybrid Embryos*. Bilbao: BBVA Foundation.

Gaskell, G., Allum, N., Bauer, M., Durant, J., Allansdottir, A., Bonfadelli, H., Boy, D., Cheveigné, S. de, Fjaestad, B., Gutteling, J. M., Hampel, J., Jelsøe, E., Jesuino, J. C., Kohring, M., Kronberger, N., Midden, C., Nielsen, T. H., Przestalski, A., Rusanen, T., Sakellaris, G., Torgersen, H., Twardowski, T. and Wagner, W. 2000. 'Biotechnology and the European public', *Nature Biotechnology* 18: 935–8.

Gaskell, G., Allum, N., Bauer, M., Jackson, J., Howard, S. and Lindsey, N. 2003. 'Climate change for biotechnology? UK public opinion 1991–2002', *AgBioForum* 6: 55–6.

Gaskell, G. and Bauer, M. W. (eds.) 2001. *Biotechnology 1996–2000. The years of controversy*. London: Science Museum Press.

Gaskell, G., Allansdottir, A., Allum, N., Corchero, C., Fischler, C., Hampel, J., Jackson, J., Kronberger, N., Mejlgaard, N., Revuelta, G., Schreiner, C., Stares, S., Torgersen, H. and Wagner W. 2006. *Europeans and Biotechnology in 2005: Patterns and trends*. Brussels: European Commission's Directorate-General for Research.

Gaskell, G., Allansdottir, A., Allum, N., Castro, P., Esmer, Y., Fischler, C., Jackson, J., Kronberger, N., Hampel, J., Mejlgaard, N., Quintanilha, A., Rammer, A., Revuelta, G., Stares, S., Torgersen, H. and Wagner, W. 2011.

'The 2010 Eurobarometer on the life sciences', *Nature Biotechnology* 29(2): 113–14.

Geller, G., Bernhardt, B. A. and Holtzman, N. A. 2002. 'The media and public reaction to genetic research', *JAMA* 287(6): 777.

Genetics and Public Policy Center 2007. *U.S. Public Opinion on Uses of Genetic Information and Genetic Discrimination.* Washington, DC: Genetics and Public Policy Center.

Görke, A. and Ruhrmann, G. 2003. 'Public communication between facts and fictions: On the construction of genetic risk', *Public Understanding of Science* 12: 229–41.

Hampel, J. 2012. 'Die Darstellung der Gentechnik in den Medien', in Weitze *et al.* (eds.), pp. 253–285.

Haran, J., Kitzinger, J., McNeil, M. and O'Riordan, K. 2007. *Human Cloning in the Media: From science fiction to science practice.* London: Routledge.

Ho, S., Brossard, D. and Scheufele, D. 2008. 'Effects of value predispositions, mass media use, and knowledge of public attitudes toward embryonic stem cell research', *International Journal of Public Opinion Research* 20: 171–92.

Holliman, R. 2004. 'Media coverage of cloning: A study of media content, production and reception', *Public Understanding of Science* 13(2): 107–30.

Jasanoff, S. 2005. *Designs on Nature. Science and democracy in Europe and the United States.* Princeton, NJ: Princeton University Press.

Kitzinger, J. 2008. 'Questioning hype, rescuing hope? The Hwang stem cell scandal and the reassertion of hopeful horizons', *Science as Culture* 17(4): 417–34.

Kohring, M., Görke, A. and Ruhrmann, G. 1999. 'Das Bild der gentechnik in den internationalen medien – eine inhaltsanalyse meinungsführender zeitschriften', in Hampel, J. and Renn, O. (eds.) *Gentechnik in der öffentlichkeit. Wahrnehmung und bewertung einer umstrittenen technologie.* Frankfurt/ New York: Campus, pp. 292–316.

Maio, G. 2006. 'Cloning in the media and popular culture', *EMBO reports* 7: 241–5.

Marks, L. A., Kalaitzandonakes, N., Wilkens, L. and Zakharova, L. 2007. 'Mass media framing of biotechnology news', *Public Understanding of Science* 16(2): 183–203.

MIT 2011. *The Third Revolution: The convergence of the life sciences, physical sciences and engineering.* Washington, DC: MIT Washington Office.

National Science Board 2012. *Science and Engineering Indicators – 2012.* Arlington, VA: National Science Foundation.

Nerlich, B., Dingwall, R. and Clarke, D. D. 2002. 'The book of life: How the completion of the Human Genome Project was revealed to the public', *Health* 6(4): 445–69.

Nisbet, M. C. and Lewenstein, B. 2002. 'Biotechnology in the American media: The policy process and the elite press', *Science Communication* 23(4): 359–91.

Petersen, A. 2001. 'Biofantasies: Genetics and medicine in the print news media', *Social Science and Medicine* 52: 1255–68.

Reis, R. 2008. 'How Brazilian and North American newspapers frame the stem cell research debate', *Science Communication* 29: 316–34.

Roach, S. 2013. 'Stem cells: What happened to the radical breakthroughs?' *The Observer*, 11 August 2013. Available at: www.theguardian.com/science/2013/aug/11/stem-cell-research-bioengineering?CMP=twt_gu (accessed 15 November 2013).

Rödder, S. 2009. 'Reassessing the concept of a medialization of science: A story from the "book of life"', *Public Understanding of Science* 18: 452–63.

Ruhrmann, G. 2012. 'Das öffentliche bild von biotechnologie und die kommunikation von evidenz', in Weitze *et al.* (eds.), pp. 287–301.

Schäfer, M. S. 2007. *Wissenschaft in den Medien. Die medialisierung naturwissenschaftlicher themen.* Wiesbaden: VS-Verlag.

Ten Eyck, T. A. 2005. 'The media and public opinion on genetics and biotechnology: Mirrors, windows or walls?' *Public Understanding of Science* 14: 305–16.

Ten Eyck, T. A. and Williment, M. 2003. 'The national media and things genetic: Coverage in the New York Times (1971–2000) and The Washington Post (1977–2000)', *Science Communication* 25: 129–52.

Turney, J. 1998. *Frankenstein's Footsteps: Science, genetics and popular culture.* New Haven, CT and London: Yale University Press.

Weingart, P., Salzman, C. and Wörmann, S. 2008. 'The social embedding of biomedicine: An analysis of German media debates 1995–2004', *Public Understanding of Science* 17: 381–96.

Weitze, M.-D., Pühler, A. Heckl, W.M., Müller-Röber, B., Renn, O., Weingart, P. and Wess, G. (eds.) 2012. *Biotechnologie-Kommunikation: Kontroversen, analysen, aktivitäten.* Heidelberg: Springer.

Wellcome Trust 2009. *Wellcome Trust Monitor.* Available at: www.wellcome.ac.uk/About-us/Publications/Reports/Public-engagement/WTX058859.htm (accessed 15 November 2013).

Wieland, T. 2012. 'Rote Gentechnik und Öffentlichkeit: Von der grundlegenden Skepsis zur differenzierten Akzeptanz', in Weitze *et al.* (eds.), pp. 69–111.

# 12 The inescapability of knowing and inability to not know in the digital society

*Richard Watermeyer*

## Introduction

This chapter considers the notions of 'knowing and not knowing' and the 'right' either way in the context of knowledge produced in an era of information/scientific transparency, openness and ubiquity; knowledge co-production; and upstream science governance – characterizations perpetuated through the global proliferation of information communication technologies. The protagonist, or *antagonist* of discussion, is 'dialogue' and the two or multi-way conversations that exist between multifarious public constituents and constituencies through which information flows and knowledge emanates. Discussion focuses specifically on dialogue produced and reconstituted in online and/or digital realms and the notion of a *polylogue* – an infinitely populating lattice of informational conversants or carriers unimpeded by the fetters of geographical separation or time – so prodigious and diffuse and so successfully networked and recruited, that the individual is impotent to disengage from knowledge transactions. In this context the right to know or not to know is not only diminished but effectively neutralized. In this chapter the polylogue is approached, in the first instance, as an enabler of the public's right to know but discussion moves on to consider how the digital society compromises, if not subjugates or entirely removes, the right of the citizen to choose not to know.

## The public, science and policy

In the UK in the 1990s, the relationship between science, politics and the public was complicated by a series of embroilments involving the bovine spongiform encephalopathy (BSE) crisis; concerns over genetically modified (GM) crops; and measles, mumps and rubella (MMR) vaccinations. The 1990s also marked a shift in the conceptualization of the 'public understanding of science', moving from a focus on 'understanding' to 'engagement' (Bauer *et al.* 2007). A House of Lords deposition

(2000) reported a 'new mood for dialogue' and an emergent discourse of 'science and society' where the public's relationship with science was re-envisaged as less cursory and more confident and critical than had been previously courted. This transition marked the emanation of the public wanting not only to ask questions of science but 'have their voices heard' (Stilgoe and Wilsdon 2009: 20). In this evolving context, the public's relationship with science reconfigured from passive recipients to active collaborators.

A turn towards 'upstream' engagement (POST 2006; Rogers-Hayden and Pidgeon 2007; Royal Society 2006; Wilsdon 2004; Wilsdon, Wynne and Stilgoe 2005) instigated an expectation that forms of interaction between scientists and public communities, traditionally top-down and transmission-based, change to become participative and bilateral; with the public instated as scrutineers and consultants active from the inception to the conclusion of the knowledge-generation process. Going 'upstream' represented a direct challenge to a 'deficit' paradigm of the public's understanding of science, identified within the Royal Society's *Bodmer* Report of the mid-1980s, which characterized the public as for the most part scientifically illiterate, detached and disenchanted (Irwin 1995; Irwin and Wynne 1996; Wynne 1996; Gregory and Miller 1998), and lay knowledge as incommensurate with and inferior to scientific expertise; disqualifying the lay public from participating in issues of scientific governance (Wynne 2003). Conversely, proponents of upstream engagement promulgated the efficacy of lay knowledge or 'lay expertise' and the contribution of lay experts in the advancement and regulation of new science and technology (Irwin and Wynne 1996), particularly where social, cultural and ethical concerns and critiques were conspicuously unattended and absent. The intercession of lay experts in matters of scientific interest was therefore intended as a means to make science more socially robust. The aspiration of public/scientific synergy was accordingly argued by science, technology and society scholars to begin by first recognizing 'the fluidity, porosity and constructedness of the boundaries established between them' (Wynne 1996: 62). These scholars anticipated that upstream engagement would cause scientific and public communities to develop a more fluent and stable basis for collaboration, thereby dispelling what Wynne (1996) referred to as the 'scientification' of issues with notable normative and political aspects. In the upstream vision, the public voice would be endorsed as a licensed authority capable of making an active and substantial contribution to the proliferation of new scientific epistemologies and what Jasanoff (2005) called 'civic epistemologies'. Lay experts were consequently reframed not only as competent handlers of scientific knowledge (Durant 1999) but also able contributors, concurrently dismantling the edifice of scientific technocracy and universalizing an opportunity for public choice in matters of scientific governance and policy.

The purpose of increased public involvement in science governance was also predicated on 'substantive' and 'instrumental' rationales (Fiorino 1990) – 'substantive' in that lay determinations of science were seen to profit decision making (Fischer 2005; Stirling 2006), 'instrumental' in that the manifestation of the public's involvement would confirm the openness of scientists to public scrutiny and the legitimacy of scientific process (Marris *et al.* 2001). Upstream advocates furthermore correlated the mobilization of the public as a critical voice or critical friend of science to what Funtowicz and Ravetz (1992) called 'extended peer review' or a means of reconciling issues of scientific risk and as a catalyst enabling scientists to be more reflexive, proactive and prospective in delivering on public needs.

A dialogical interface between expert and non-expert public groups continues to be popularized as a mechanism that:

- liberates science from the insularity, secrecy and technocracy of scientific governance (see Jasanoff 2005; Bucchi 2009);
- makes science relevant, user-friendly and integral to public discourse and by extension justifies and sustains the work of scientists and considerable tranches of dedicated public funding (Wilsdon and Willis 2004);
- catalyses new forms of knowledge worker – the 'public intellectual' (Burawoy 2005) and 'citizen scientist' (Bonney and LaBranche 2004)
- concomitantly enriches and diversifies the perceptual horizons of science; and
- facilitates economic prosperity through an integrated, fluid, multi-interfacing network and 'information/network society' (Stehr 2002; van Dijk 2006; Fuchs 2007).

This is the reported potential of dialogue. However, a closer inspection reveals a multitude of inconsistencies that challenge the patently promissory rhetoric of upstream engagement and reveals what I refer to as a *false dawn of dialogue* in public engagement in science and technology (PEST). Despite the ubiquity of scientific and technological knowledge, which Stehr (2002) comments as having penetrated every sphere of public life; the materialization of an information abundant, 'network' society (Castells 2000; van Dijk 2006); and the democratizing potential of new 2.0 online media platforms that facilitate 'individuals making active information-seeking choices' (Priest 2009: 224), lay experts arguably remain deficit members within the public/science interface, devoid of 'intellectual capital' (Bourdieu 1998) and ironically displaced by 'information poverty' (Haider and Bawden 2007). The potential of dialogue as a democratizing principle is furthermore constrained by upstream detractors who signpost a raft of factors for resisting dialogue, such as high financial cost (Andersson *et al.* 2005); the unpredictability of process and outcomes (Oakley 1991); uncertainty and risk (Watson 2007); inappropriate use of experts' time (Taverne 2005); and a failure to deliver on the rhetoric of social inclusion, social cohesion and democratic governance (Cooke and Kothari 2001).

Whilst there remains continuous investment in public dialogue as a democratic intervention fostering more knowledgeable science citizens and better science policy, evidenced most especially in the UK through the 'Sciencewise' programme, these kinds of excursions into the public's scientific literacy are compromised by environmental and budgetary limitations, where conducted face-to-face. A major issue for public dialogue activities is that the interactions they spawn are restricted by issues of geography and time. Public dialogue projects may be frequently isolated, unconnected and ostensibly superficial or impoverished processes in knowledge creation and transaction. These are closed events, less processes of dialogue, where processes are taken to be continuous and evolving. The potential pathway to greater knowledge through interactional and creative collective deliberation may be also intentionally forestalled and regulated according to the interests, sensitivities and investment of dialogue sponsors whose control and choreography of the informational basis of dialogue is intimate, unwavering and rehearsed. A route to expediting and unshackling the flow of information and therefore the contestation; revision and co/re-production of new knowledge and the faculty of choice among citizens as knowledge agents, potentially occurs in a different interactional context – the World Wide Web.

### Mobilizing the right to know: the *polylogue*

In the age of the Internet, information is both ubiquitous and instant – instantly populated, repopulated and instantly retrieved. Currently, Web 2.0 technology allows information and knowledge to be not only redistributed but reinvented through participative frameworks (Watermeyer 2010). Experiential knowledge, or what Collins and Evans (2002) call 'interactional expertise', may occur within a new dialogue continuum that disrupts the historic arrangements of scientific power and authority, identifying and drawing new rules for public dialogue. Web 2.0 thus represents a new dialogue eco-system which opens up the possibility of science dialogue to different types of social actor with potentially disparate socio-political orientations and frameworks. As a melting point for the articulation of a myriad of social and ethical values, 2.0 instruments such as blogs and Twitter postings present an opportunity for more informed and agile science citizenship whilst concurrently enhancing the dissemination pathways of scientists and the fluidity of their interface with lay expertise. The proliferation of virtual dialogue is, it would seem, evidence of the dissipation of the siloing of knowledge, replaced instead with what Dunleavy (2012) has called a 'republic of blogs'.

As an interactional space the Internet is increasingly the *modus operandi* for information exchange within the scientific community, facilitating project management, conference organization and dissemination (Trench 2009). Concurrently, as a repository of scientific knowledge, the Web has enlarged and diversified scientific readership by challenging traditional publishing channels and pursuing open access in digital formats of academic journals (Gartner 2009). Web 2.0 as a participatory forum is also a means for scientists and scientific institutions to communicate directly with public groups, bypassing the mediation of science journalists (Chalmers 2009) and/or other knowledge brokers capable of misrepresenting or prejudicing scientific information. In the 'social networks of science' (Watermeyer 2010) the *polylogue* emerges. The polylogue differs from the dialogue in that it intimates not only a multiple of conversationalists but a multiple of conversations occurring and regenerating at any one time. The polylogue may occur through a variety of communicative mediums evidenced in social network media such as blogs and wikis, and further scaffolds, ameliorates and accelerates dialogue by means of audio-visual facilitation and enhancement.

The social dimension of 2.0 technologies cannot be underestimated in linking individuals and building dialogical communities of choice that are global and continuous. Unlike formal dialogues which are in part a process of event-making, one-off, stunted and fragmentary, the fluidity of online interactions provides for a more integrated, informed and efficient republic of choice makers. Polylogues are also a means for multiple elaborations of scientific inquiry and a room for prolonged meditation, facilitating not only the lay public's but scientists' choices. It is perhaps no surprise that online social media are increasingly touted as a means for scientists to increase the reach and significance of their work.

The polylogue thus represents a unique opportunity for the online citizen to emerge as a scientific citizen or citizen scientist in a counter-economy of dialogue, beyond the control and sanction of dialogue sponsors and regulators wishing to contain and maintain oversight of the trajectories and jurisidiction of dialogue and informational movement – or ensure that dialogue is risk-averse and neutralizing. It is also within the polylogue that science assumes a plurality of meanings and uses, determined and regulated by large numbers of self-governing lay experts. In one way this is the realization of the dialogue ambition – intersecting and overlapping discussion of science beyond science institutions – freely bought into, dissected, deliberated and potentially even improved upon by numerous if anonymous lay parties.

Where traditional forms of science dialogue suffer from the disequilibrium of power and political capital, Web 2.0 may be seen to facilitate non-hierarchical debate through a process of disintermediation, or, in other words, the obsolescence of an overarching or repressive singular dialogue framework, narrative, agenda and evisceration of the dialogue moderator. However, online public dialogue in science is not without risks or drawbacks.

Where the content of scientific information is user generated the potential for the misrepresentation of science enlarges and concurrently the right of access to the 'right' knowledge. Content may be prone to inconsistency or factual error caused by unscientific, subjective interpretations. It may also be manipulated by online authors seeking to align scientific 'truths' or re-imagine 'facts' to complement a partisan agenda or personalized politics. A paucity of online regulation and the intractability of 2.0 domains mean that the propagation of false science is a significant risk and one which may further inure the credibility of scientists and harm scientific dialogue in its totality. Web 2.0 is also fertile ground for the culturing of what Durodié (2003) calls the 'quasi-expert' and the unfortunate emergence of bad science dialogue.

The polylogue may be inchoate, fragmentary and seemingly representative of a multitude of scientific perspectives, but it may coalesce and obsess around the same concerns treated in face-to-face dialogue. The sheer abundance and heterogeneity of the digital public, the multitude of its different, often competing and conflicting agendas may also cause for dialogue and citizens' knowledge choices to stall. Furthermore, scientific disagreement left unresolved by argument or referral to empirical evidence may produce what Pellizzoni (2003a; 2003b) refers to as 'radical uncertainty'. In this sense, the wealth of subjective accounts may serve to thwart dialogue as much as enrich it, for the plurality of dialogue agents or dialoguers may be so numerous as to make dialogue erratic and incomprehensible. The polylogue as an online phenomenon may also ultimately recruit the same scientifically inclined or interested individuals that populate offline events and in effect duplicate discussion. The main difference is the supposed lack of a top-down moderator, whose absence stimulates a more spontaneous, critically in-depth and reflective discussion. A lack of moderation makes the polylogue, in the shape of, for example, a blog, not only a site of informal dialogue but 'uninvited dialogue' where the critical voice of dissent, censured in official environs, is given air.

Science in the public domain remains more often than not less dialogic and more top-down. Indeed Irwin (2006) notes that deficit-informed expressions of science continue unabated, conflated under the nomenclature of public engagement (see also Rathouse and Devine-Wright 2010). Others suggest that so-called dialogue exercises are actually a camouflaged iteration of the deficit model (Lehr *et al.* 2007). The prevalence of a deficit model occurs perhaps as a consequence of unswerving confidence by policy-making and risk-managing institutions in the methods of scientific knowledge production. Inflated expectations and over-reliance on the scientific community has the effect of excluding alternative accounts of science that are relegated or disqualified for being 'lay'. Despite the continued, high-profile investment in dialogue processes[1] the public appears no further forward in claiming a licence to operate as accredited contributors of scientific discourse and as choice yielding agents.

The potential of informed choice making is compromised by a raft of other structural and organizational tensions, inconsistencies and ironies. Dialogue activities make sometimes impossibly high demands of their participants to make fair and credible assessments, particularly where public knowledge of new science is limited. Where science and technology is emergent, an information gap of public knowledge may cause speculation, which, magnified by the media, may result in sensationalist copy and hype. The early engagement of the public when science is formative may be not only premature but alarm-inducing and cause what Rogers-Hayden and Pidgeon (2007: 335) refer to as the 'amplification of concerns about risk'. Debates may consequently focus more or less exclusively around issues of scientific risk. Upstream dialogue may in this way result in issue making or the creation of imaginary or projected concerns and increased if misplaced public anxiety. This may cause to further increase the disconnect in the relations between scientists and the public and may also cause dialogue to become increasingly a process of scientists' apologies or acts intended to diffuse the public's anxiety.

The polylogue ultimately follows more faithfully the pursuit of the scientist in asking new questions, rather than the policy maker in demanding new solutions. It also importantly provides a space for 'uninvited'

---

[1] In 2012, the Sciencewise programme received an investment of a further £3.6m over a three-year period from the UK Secretary of State for Business, Innovation and Skills, Vince Cable. See http://blogs.bis.gov.uk/blog/2012/03/09/the-great-science-and-engineering-adventure/ (accessed 9 April 2014).

dialogue. The question remains, however, how to mobilize 'uninvited' dialogue in ways that might bear pressure on organizational and governing powers. At root there remains the question of how 'publics or counterpublics' (Warner 2005), emergent through multiple conversations, in multiple contexts, in multiple times, can critically and constructively talk to power and enact choices as public citizens and decision makers in science.

## Retracting the right to know

The ubiquity of official (expert-sanctioned) and unofficial (user-generated) science information that seeps through the porosity and perpetuity of cyberspace presents the potential for 'online-users' – whose own demographic may be equally polymorphous – to interface, appropriate, triangulate and (re)purpose the informational cornucopia as increasingly efficient and insatiable knowledge consumers. Indeed the intensification of the digital interface implies that public citizens as knowledge agents are becoming more seasoned, versed and ostensibly more proficient and dexterous in their navigation of the digital knowledge ecosystem. In fact, it may not be premature to speculate a culture of connoisseurship, especially among future generations 'born online', as informational orienteers and diagnosticians of knowledge in online domains. The greater the extent our lives are conducted online, the more likely we will calibrate and modify our social behaviours and skills in alignment and complementarity with digital modes of knowledge production and knowledge-based choices.

The copiousness and borderlessness of information transmission and exchange is in this case matched by the limitless online activity of the scientific knowledge consumer, whose right to know is taken as *a priori* in the context of a globally networked information society, where information that interrupts and/or enriches pre-existing knowledge is instantly and continuously accessible, thanks to SMART technology, from any geographical location at any time.

Technological advances are increasingly and rapidly altering the behaviours and expectations of knowledge consumers. This is evidenced across formal educational spheres, where students of every stage and with accelerating frequency are attending to the business of learning, primarily if not exclusively, via technological/digital learning apparatus. With greater investment by educational providers in forms of distance, online and therefore mass teaching platforms such as Massive Open Online Courses (MOOCS), the manner in which knowledge is distributed, shared and produced is rapidly shifting from an accent on technologically *enhanced* learning to technologically *driven* learning. The parameters of how we learn and what we learn are consequently redrawn to complement the rampant ascent of technology into every facet of our information-based lives. Concurrently, the globalization and marketization of educational systems, mobilized in large part through technological innovation, and especially conspicuous in higher education contexts, has altered our relationship with learning, insomuch as learners are primarily categorized as paying clients or customers of an educational experience. Consequently, technological innovation has radicalized the experience of knowledge, certainly in formal or credentializing contexts, and the way we view ourselves in relation to the acquisition and handling of new knowledge. Concomitant to this relational change is an attitudinal one, where technology is seen to have democratized and personalized knowledge. As an example, personal genomic online providers such as 23andMe represent the availability of opportunities for knowledge of the most specific and individual kind.

Technology has brought about the conditions with which information can be accessed and shared openly, transparently and freely – without restriction or censure. The idea of openness, in a normative democratic stylization, is the zeitgeist and/or shibboleth of the second decade of the new millennium, where rhetoric in science and policy settings equates good, democratic and responsible scientific enterprise and policy making with transparency and public cooperation. In a similar fashion a notion of 'informed choice' is the buzzword of public constituencies entering into a relational contract with an educational provider or health-care supplier or otherwise in the catch-all act of being an active citizen.

Active, and thereby responsible, citizenship, much like responsible innovation, is analogous with public constituencies being cognisant, engaged and invested in the multiple (expert) discourses – ethical and scientific – affecting (the democratic constitution of) the public sphere. The public's capacity to promote and safeguard the interests of the public sphere is therefore likened to the fluidity and permeability of information and the capacity of public citizens to translate information into knowledge and their manipulation of knowledge as social, economic and political capital. In other words, the public sphere is representative of the unimpeded generation, distribution, exercise and recycling of knowledge within a multi-stakeholder network.

The public sphere itself is made more heterogeneous, eclectic, equitable and efficacious – where the identity and behaviour of stakeholders (i.e public constituents or active citizens) are provided with the opportunity and scope through the digital interface to broaden and intensify. The public sphere in this instance is furthermore extended and elaborated, where exported online as an innumerable confluence of voices. This con-fluence, which I have referred to as the polylogue is significant not only as a conduit for, or distributor of, knowledge but as a crucible for rumin-ation, contestation and potential co-production of knowledge.

In the milieu of open science, open policy and open science policy the ideal of democratic knowledge distribution and co-creation (upstream engagement) is potentially compromised by a need to know too much, or, in other words, a danger that too much might be known and that intensive knowledgeability might culminate in negative outcomes. Such may be the case where 'crowd-sourcing' dilutes the veracity and cred-ibility of the knowledge under consideration. Wikipedia, as a well-known version of the crowd-sourcing model, offers a lucid example of how multiple informational authors can confuse, contradict and ultimately distort the reality and reliability of any presented knowledge. Readers of Wikipedia entries ought to access and buy into the knowledge pre-sented judiciously, cognisant that the authenticity of associated claims is not always guaranteed. The quality of knowledge that is crowd-sourced may therefore be questionable. Conversely, crowd sourcing provides an opportunity where multiple stakeholders can engage in critical discus-sion of a knowledge claim and engage in a process of extended testing, where new knowledge is subject to the scrutiny of multiple actors and not only designated or licensed experts. This kind of critical, deliberative engagement with knowledge at a mass level is therefore also synonymous with knowledge production as a process of cooperative interface and col-laboration with various stakeholders who may be distinguished by their respective levels of lay or scientific expertise. How expertise and identity is delineated and segmented transparently is, however, problematic in digital domains where the identity of contributors/authors is (intention-ally) concealed.

A significant stumbling block therefore in considering the right to know or not to know in digital domains is the lack of identity owner-ship and the intentional obfuscation and/or concealment of identity by online constituents. Informational contributors in online domains may frequently and easily disguise their identity so that online disclosures are not attributable to offline identities. In this context, who is saying what and who is listening is entirely speculative. Whilst this kind of behaviour tends to characterize blogs as online discussion forums, communication portals such as Twitter are much more revealing of their authors and provide the reader with sufficient clues and/or intelligence when making estimations about the value and credibility of their pronouncements.

The popularity and significance of digital social media such as Twitter should not be underestimated, not least for the efficiency and speed with which communities are linked to myriad informational resources. However, the speed of disclosure on social media may be seen as detrimental where the desired release of information by a first author is intended to be gradual and/or drip-fed. For example, many high-profile, ethically complex public consultations, such as that recently administered by the Human Fertilisation and Embryology Authority into mitochondrial transfer, revealed that the authority was especially concerned about the threat of 'informational leak' through online social media. At the open authority meeting, public attendees were strictly reminded not to disseminate any of the meeting's outcomes until after the meeting. I have witnessed an increasing trend for what we might think of as intentional Twitter black-out. Anecdotally, this seems linked to degrees or stages of knowledge ownership or the gradual dissemination of knowledge, where the knowledge under question has been appropriately verified.

Issues of informational ownership are made more complex and problematic where ownership corresponds to financial investment and where knowledge is understood as intellectual property with a commercial basis. In this context, a tension exists in terms of disseminating knowledge to the widest possible user group but in terms that do not undermine the profitability of said knowledge or the extent to which it might be commercially exploited. The debate around open-access publishing rages on. What remains integral to this debate is the central question of who owns the knowledge. This leads me to make a final consideration of knowing and not knowing and the right of this in an increasingly digitally mediated world.

The right or *capacity* of the individual as active citizen, consumer and contributor in a global knowledge society to opt in or out of the process of knowledge production is effectively removed where contemporary life as a 'liquid modernity' (Bauman 2000) is conducted within a digital or non-physical knowledge ecosystem; where the connectivity of persons and the continuity of their myriad networks is absolute. To opt out of the 'digital society' is to not exist, insomuch as Facebook, Twitter and other forms of social media and online networks signify and corroborate our claims to existence, where large proportions of our time – dedicated both to the pursuit of social recreation and work – are spent and manifest as, and arranged through, digital interactions. In work and employment terms, who we are is our personal and company website profile; our LinkedIn page; our Twitter postings; our Facebook 'wall'. Business communications and transactions are ever more routed through cyberspace in commercial and retail terms. Cyberspace is where we conduct our (online) banking; where we buy our groceries; arrange our holidays; procure services. Increasingly, it is also where our children play and grow up.

And the basis of all of this is the incessant production, transfer, exchange, and recycling of information and ever-changing knowledge.

We are thus faced with the inescapability of the global information network. To exist offline and/or 'off the grid' is for the vast majority fantastical and absurd. Evidence suggests that the average owner of a SMART phone looks at her/his device, on average, 150 times a day or every 6.5 minutes (Meeker and Liang 2013). The reality of our being 'plugged-in' is incontrovertible. SMART mobile devices such as phones, tablets and laptops are the modern social, cultural and economic compass – quite literally under the terms of GPS – and our means of orientation through the maze of the information society.

As tools of orientation, mobile SMART devices are also the means for our everyday domestic and work-related diagnosis. As super-computers in the palm of a hand, these devices provide instant and permanent access to an endless abundance of information which is constantly being accessed and retrieved, taken and applied in offline circumstances, and quite likely thereafter returned to an online realm. The distinction between our offline and online realms is becoming ever more blurred, where informational fluidity and instancy, brought about by the mobility and ubiquity of SMART technologies, informs our actions, behaviours, decisions, and our understanding and knowledge of the world (offline and online) we inhabit.

The impossibility of policing or regulating the global web is well reported and renders strategy for delimiting the dissemination and flow of knowledge, even sensitive and/or highly confidential knowledge, as largely impotent. Indeed, national authorities find themselves compromised by individuals and agencies who believe a part of their responsible citizenship is in 'outing' these kinds of information. We need only look at the cases of WikiLeaks founder Julian Assange, and the recent case of US soldier, Bradley Manning, to consider the ways in which individuals assert the significance of total transparency.

We might then surmise that the right to know or right not to know is in the age of the digital, information and network society, a redundant question or one with a self-fulfilling answer.

## Conclusion

As we increasingly transfer our interactions with information and informational gatekeepers onto online domains, our experience in receiving, assimilating, synthesizing and producing new knowledge raises significant questions in terms of our (public citizens') capacity as choice-wielding agents. In the first part of this chapter, I spoke of how an emphasis in the open governance of science has intensified the focus on our inter-communication and interactions with scientific knowledge as democratic citizens. The polylogue was discussed as a site and process of democratic knowledge sharing and creation, yet, as a social and cultural practice, a site disposed of the same inequities encountered in offline settings. The polylogue may be seen simultaneously as a process of mobilization and displacement of the public's capacity and right to know.

The ubiquity of information in online domains is not without risk, where ubiquity equals saturation and where a saturation of information engenders disenchantment, fatigue or ennui. Indeed, the openness and free availability of information may actually harm the knowledge process, where knowledge consumers become distracted, lost, disengaged, lazy and susceptible to bad science and bad knowledge. Furthermore, even where online knowledge consumers are deemed to be increasingly more judicious in their behaviours, what of the ways with which they distribute and disseminate knowledge?

The most profound but ostensibly most futile question is whether *all* information is suitable for open access and dissemination in the digital age? This question problematizes a right to knowledge as the basis of democratic citizenship; where such citizenship is perceived and promulgated as the epicentre of science in society. It is futile because the very essence of the Internet is that all knowledge, its producers and receivers, are connected and inseparably so. More profitable questions might be not about our right to know or not to know in the digital age, but about how we make sense of what we know, what we need to know and what we do not need to know. Discussion of these questions has never been so necessary.

## References

Andersson, E., Warburton, D. and Wilson, R. 2005. *The True Costs of Public Participation*. London: Involve.

Bauer, M.W., Allum, N. and Miller, S. 2007. What can we learn from 25 years of PUS survey research? *Public Understanding of Science* 16(1): 79–95.

Bauman, Z. 2000. *Liquid Modernity*. Malden, MA: Polity.

Bonney, R. and LaBranche, M. 2004. 'Citizen science: Involving the public in research', *ASTC Dimensions* May/June: 13.

Bourdieu, P. 1998. *Practical Reason*. Stanford, CA: Stanford University Press.

Bucchi, M. 2009. *Beyond Technocracy: Science, politics and citizens*. New York: Springer.

Burawoy, M. 2005. '2004 American Sociological Association Presidential Address: For public sociology', *British Journal of Sociology* 56(2): 259–94.

Castells, M. 2000. *The Rise of the Network Society. The information age: Economy, society and culture*. Vol. 1, 2nd edn. Oxford: Blackwell.

Chalmers, M. 2009. 'Communicating physics in the information age', in Holliman, R., Thomas, J., Smidt, S., Scanlon, E., and Whitelegg, E. (eds.) *Practising Science Communication in the Information Age*. Oxford: Oxford University Press, pp. 67–80.

Collins, H. and Evans, R. 2002. 'The third wave of science studies: Studies of expertise and experience', *Social Studies of Science* 32(2): 235–96.

Cooke, B. and Kothari, U. (eds.) 2001. *Participation: The new tyranny*. London: Zed Books.

Dunleavy, P. 2012. 'Introduction from the LSE Impact of Social Science Project Team' paper presented at From Research to Policy: Academic Impacts on Government Conference, 12 March 2012 at the Institute for Government, London, UK. Available at: http://blogs.lse.ac.uk/impactofsocialsciences/2012/03/29/resources-research-to-policy/ (accessed 21 November 2013).

Durant, J. 1999. 'Participatory technology assessment and the democratic model of the public understanding of science', *Science and Public Policy* 26: 313–19.

Durodié, B. 2003. 'Limitations of pubic dialogue in science and the rise of the "new experts"', *Critical Review of International Social and Political Philosophy* 6(4): 82–92.

Fiorino, D. J. 1990. 'Citizen participation and environmental risk: A survey of institutional mechanisms', *Science, Technology and Human Values* 15(2): 226–43.

Fischer, F. 2005. 'Are scientists irrational? Risk assessment in practical reason', in Leach, M., Scoones, I., and Wynne, B. (eds.) *Science and Citizens: Globalisation and the challenge of engagement*. London: Zed Books, pp. 54–65.

Fuchs, C. 2007. 'Transnational space and the "network society"', *21st Century Society* 2(1): 49–78.

Funtowicz, S. O. and Ravetz, J. R. 1992. 'Three types of risk assessment and the emergence of post-normal science', in Krimsky, S. and Golding, D. (eds.) *Social Theories of Risk*. Westport, CT: Praeger, pp. 251–74.

Gartner, R. 2009. 'From print to online: Developments in access to scientific innovation', in Holliman, R., Thomas, J., Smidt, S., Scanlon, E. and Whitelegg, E. (eds.) *Practising Science Communication in the Information Age*. Oxford: Oxford University Press, pp. 98–111.

Gregory, J and Miller, S. 1998. *Science in Public: Communication, culture and credibility*. Cambridge, MA: Perseus.

Haider, J. and Bawden, D. 2007. 'Conceptions of "information poverty" in LIS: A discourse analysis', *Journal of Documentation* 63(4): 534–57.

House of Lords, Select Committee on Science and Technology 2000. *Science and Society – 3rd Report*. London: HMSO.

Irwin, A. 1995. *Citizen Science*. London: Routledge.

Irwin, A. 2006. 'The politics of talk: Coming to terms with the "new" scientific governance', *Social Studies of Science* 36(2): 299–320.

Irwin, A. and Wynne, B. (eds.) 1996. *Misunderstanding Science: The public reconstruction of science and technology*. Cambridge: Cambridge University Press.

Jasanoff, S. 2005. *Designs on Nature: Science and democracy in Europe and the United States*. Princeton, NJ: Princeton University Press.

Lehr, J. L., McCallie, E., Davies, S. R., Caron, B. R., Gammon, B. and Duensing, S. 2007. 'The role and value of dialogue events as sites of informal science learning', *International Journal of Science Education* 29(12): 1–21.

Marris, C., Wynne, B., Simmons, P. and Weldon, S. 2001. *Public Perceptions of Agricultural Biotechnologies in Europe* (PABE) Final Report. Available at: http://csec.lancs.ac.uk/archive/pabe/docs/pabe_finalreport.pdf (accessed 18 November 2013).

Meeker, M. and Liang, W. 2013. Internet Trends. Available at: www.kpcb.com/insights/2013-internet-trends (accessed 18 November 2013).

Oakley, P. 1991. *Projects with People. The practice of participation in rural development.* Geneva: International Labour Office.

Parliamentary Office of Science and Technology (POST) 2006. 'Debating science', *Postnote* Number 260. Available at: www.parliament.uk/documents/post/postpn260.pdf (accessed 18 November 2013).

Pellizzoni, L. 2003a. 'Uncertainty and participatory democracy', *Environmental Values* 12(2): 195–224.

Pellizzoni, L. 2003b. 'Knowledge, uncertainty and the transformation of the public sphere', *European Journal of Social Theory* 6(3): 327–55.

Priest, S. H. 2009. 'Reinterpreting the audiences for media messages about science', in Holliman, R., Whitelegg, E., Scanlon, E., Smidt, S. and Thomas, J. (eds.) *Investigating Science Communication in the Information Age: Implications for public engagement and popular media.* Oxford: Oxford University Press, pp. 223–36.

Rathouse, K. and Devine-Wright, P. 2010. *Evaluation of the Big Energy Shift, Final report to DECC and Sciencewise-ERC.* London: Sciencewise.

Rogers-Hayden, T. and Pidgeon, N. F. 2007. 'Moving engagement "upstream"? Nanotechnologies and the Royal Society and Royal Academy of Engineering inquiry', *Public Understanding of Science* 16: 346–64.

Royal Society 2006. *Science Communication: Survey of factors affecting science communication by scientists and engineers.* Available at: https://royalsociety.org/~/media/Royal_Society_Content/policy/publications/2006/1111111395.pdf (accessed 18 November 2013).

Stehr, N. 2002. *Knowledge and Economic Conduct.* Toronto: University of Toronto Press.

Stilgoe, J. and Wilsdon, J. 2009. 'The new politics of engagement with science', in Holliman, R., Whitelegg, E., Scanlon, E., Smidt, S. and Thomas, J. (eds.) *Investigating Science Communication in the Information Age: Implications for public engagement and popular media.* Oxford: Oxford University Press, pp. 18–34.

Stirling, A. 2006. *GoverScience Seminar 2005 – Outcome: From Science and Society to Science in Society: Towards a framework for 'co-operative research'.* Luxembourg: Office for Official Publications of the European Communities.

Taverne, D. 2005. *The March of Unreason: Science, democracy, and the new fundamentalism.* Oxford: Oxford University Press.

Trench, B. 2009. 'Science reporting in the electronic embrace of the Internet', in Holliman, R., Whitelegg, E., Scanlon, E., Smidt, S. and Thomas, J. (eds.) *Investigating Science Communication in the Information Age.* Oxford: Oxford University Press, pp. 166–80.

Van Dijk, J. 2006. *The Network Society*. London: Sage.

Warner, M. 2005. *Publics and Counterpublics*. Brooklyn, NY: Zone Books.

Watermeyer, R. 2010. 'Social network science: Pedagogy, dialogue and deliberation', *Journal of Science Communication (Jcom)* 9(1): 1–9.

Watson, D. 2007. *Managing Civic and Community Engagement*. Maidenhead: Open University Press.

Wilsdon, J. 2004. 'Science is moving upstream', *Science and Public Affairs* December: 11.

Wilsdon, J. and Willis, R. 2004. *See-Through Science: Why public engagement needs to move upstream*. London: Demos.

Wilsdon, J., Wynne, B. and Stilgoe, J. 2005. *The Public Value of Science: Or how to ensure that science really matters*. London: Demos.

Wynne, B. 1996. 'May the sheep safely graze? A reflexive view of the expert–lay knowledge divide', in Lash, S., Szerszynshi B. and Wynne, B. *Risk, Environment and Modernity: Towards a new ecology*. London: Sage Publications, pp. 44–83.

Wynne, B. 2003. 'Seasick on the Third Wave? Subverting the hegemony of propositionalism', *Social Studies of Science* 33(3): 401–17.

# 13   The food we eat: the right to be informed and the duty to inform

*Michiel Korthals*

## Introduction: the evolving gap between food production and consumption as the context of the desire to know

One of the most salient features of human evolution is the continuing reduction of time needed to produce, prepare and digest food (Wrangham 2009). This evolution reveals simultaneously one of the main ethical paradoxes of food: humans have become what they are now due to the continuing reduction of food processing time (time-saving cooking mechanisms), and this enables them to be severed from food (production), to forget about food (production), even to degrade food (production). The evolutionary advantages in the reduction of food collecting, producing and digesting time create also the risk that people become both alienated from food and subordinated to the corporate production of food. In the end, many people no longer know what to buy and what to eat – but of course they must eat. They know how to unpack a prepared box or how to put its content in the microwave, but no more. This gap between consumption and production and the complexity of food production make the sector a very inaccessible one; each food item is processed and traded many times before it lands on the shelf and even producers at the beginning of these processes do not know what happens later. Alienation is the core word here; it derives from the gap between food production and food consumption. However, nowadays many consumers *feel* alienated and lose trust in the food sector (Berg 2011); some want to go back to the earlier situation of food self-sufficiency (Pollan 2006); others want to find relevant knowledge, discuss new ways of food preparation and food production, and even become involved in new types of production (Stolle and Micheletti 2013). Indeed, it is not very fruitful to overcome this disconnection by returning to the ways of food production of two hundred years ago: new technologies have developed, new types of relationships between farmers, processors and consumers have emerged, and the role of food in our social life has changed (to name just a few factors).

Therefore many political and ethical approaches propose to overcome this alienation with new connections between consumption and production. Food ethics, the discipline that besides other issues also includes the issues of the right to know and of labelling, had a serious start with a number of quite pressing social concerns that consumers, policy makers and others expressed about the present-day food production system. In the next section, the most urgent of these concerns will be discussed. These concerns fit in with the more general social trend that people want to be taken seriously, expect answers to the problems they are concerned about and to take action when necessary. 'In modern times, science has always spoken to society .... But society now "speaks back"' (Nowotny *et al.* 2000, p. 50).

In the food sector the right to know gets full prominence, and deserves therefore full support and even protection. This is contrary to what is the case in the medical sphere, where the right not to know often needs more attention. Consumers that do not want to know about the intricacies of their food items can simply refrain from looking at the available information. The right to know means that consumers can choose one type of food instead of another, according to their own ideas and values. Modern consumers can make different choices but an 'opt out' (as in medicine) is only possible at the cost of starvation. Interesting questions also include who has the duty to inform consumers (as the mirror act to the right to be informed), and how far does the consumer have a duty to search for information? About this last issue I can only spare a few words, because it opens up a whole new subject of what kind of duties, morally speaking, people have when they make their food choices concerning modern, Western life and food styles, which have such devastating effects on poor people and the environment. Food choices and more generally food styles are seen by many as purely individual expressions of personal autonomy that cannot be overburdened by a duty to find out what the ethical impacts are of these so-called personal choices on the rest of the world and nature. I will restrict myself here to the subject of the right to be informed and take into account those that think otherwise.

In this chapter, I will discuss the knowledge people have and want to have about the food they eat, the information strategies to consumers, the labelling strategies, and the knowledge policies of stakeholders. First, I will introduce consumer rights, the right to adequate, nutritious food and the right to buy food on the basis of informed food choice. Secondly, I will discuss some ethical considerations that underpin these ideas about consumer rights, but also make it clear why for a modern consumer it is a very difficult task to get relevant information to exercise those rights. One of the reasons for this is that food industries use all kinds of scientific and non-scientific strategies to seduce consumers into buying their products and consumers are vulnerable to these clever strategies. The food industry does not always take its duty to inform consumers seriously. Thirdly, I will discuss the pros and cons of labelling as a new kind of knowledge and information structure conscious consumers ask for. Labelling seems to be an important strategy to assist consumers in their informed food choice, but the sheer quantity of incoherent information and the lack of transparency of the labels are often a hindrance. Trust is therefore not always restored. Finally, some other ways to obtain knowledge will be discussed.

### Consumers' rights

As early as 1962, the Kennedy government in the USA appealed to the rights of consumers in a rather broad way in the Bill of Consumers Rights (Reisch 2004), which was incorporated into the EU consumer policy programme. These rights were: the right to safety; the right to be informed; the right to choose; the right to be heard; the right to representation; and the right to adequate legal protection. The right to food achieved in 1966 its full meaning in the International Covenant on Economic, Social and Cultural Rights (Article 11), as the right to available, accessible and adequate food. Adequate means 'culturally acceptable'. After the Rio Convention (1992), in which the overall importance of sustainable production was agreed upon by most nations, and the formation of the European single market, the 'ethical consumer' and diverse consumer concerns came to prominence. As is stated in General Food Law (178/2002/EC), which defines producer (food chain) responsibility, active consumers are to be informed according to their rights. However, their concerns are multiple and often ambiguous. In ethics, consumers' rights can be justified from at least three different perspectives that frame, in different ways, consumer sovereignty. A deontological position, that strongly advocates undeniable sovereignty, can be traced back to the German philosopher Kant. In 1785 he stated:

Laziness and cowardice are the reasons why such a large part of humanity, even long after nature has liberated it from foreign control (naturaliter maiorennes), is still happy to remain infantile during its entire life, making it so easy for others to act as its keeper. It is so easy to be infantile. If I have a book that is wisdom for me, a therapist or preacher who serves as my conscience, a doctor who prescribes my diet then I do not need to worry about these myself. I do not need to think, as long as I am willing to pay.

(Kant 1995)

As consumption choices are included in one's autonomy, consumers should determine their own food (diet); as a consequence, the markets should follow these consumer preferences. In fact, this argument is one of the strongest arguments against the conceptual distinction between consumer and citizen, because it makes it clear that in the market, the autonomy of consumer, not producers, should prevail. As is clear from Kant's quotation, he presupposes that an adult is educated, has capabilities, and has (reliable) information on the diets with which he or she wants to comply. Moreover, this view presupposes also that production systems and markets deliver the goods and services such an autonomous person prefers.

However, consumer sovereignty can be justified from a utilitarian perspective also, although in a different way, as is clear from John Stuart Mill's statement in 1863 on freedom:

The only freedom which deserves the name, is that of pursuing our own good in our own way, so long as we do not attempt to deprive others of theirs, or impede their efforts to obtain it. Each is the proper guardian of his own health, whether bodily, or mental or spiritual.

(Mill 1975)

Again, from this perspective, the autonomous person should be enabled to strive for his own good through education, regulation, reliable information and responsive markets. However, from a utilitarian perspective, governments are justified in balancing the overall costs of letting consumers choose and of letting experts on healthy food decide what actually constitutes healthy food and nutrition. There is not an inherent principle of consumer sovereignty which applies here.

Thirdly, from a pragmatist approach, originated by Peirce, James and John Dewey, the right to food is not only the right to fill bellies but more specifically the right to live with food production processes that reflect substantially our various life and food styles (Keulartz *et al.* 2002; Korthals 2004). Our various life and food styles, connected with cooking and farming practices, give rise to different preferences and interests with respect to information: for example, some people want to know more about animal welfare, others about the impact on health of food items and others about taste (Coff *et al.* 2008).

### Roles of consumers and their interests in knowledge

The roles of consumers in the food sector can be various, and the same applies to their interest in types of knowledge. Consumers can exercise their rights by boycotting products, or *buycotting*, which means buying specific products that correspond with ethical values, by leading a lifestyle totally oriented to ethical consumerism and by participating in the production of their own food (Stolle and Micheletti 2013). In all these situations, consumers need to have information about food products and their production processes.

However, to get the relevant information corresponding to the respective role and values, consumers are confronted with all kinds of information strategies from the industry and other stakeholders. Companies can be seen as having a duty to inform according to consumers' rights (and not according to their own interests). The budget of communication and marketing departments of the big food companies are often more than a third of their total budget and their daily messages to consumers are innumerable. They are way larger than the budget of non-governmental organizations (NGOs) or governmental agencies. Added to this continuous conscious and subconscious information offensive is the labelling information done by NGOs or the government. For instance, Ecolabel Index listed 432 ecolabels – ranging from 'salmon-safe' to 'bird-friendly' – across 246 countries and 25 industries (ecolabel.com). What has been called choice stress is the result (Mick *et al.* 2004). Besides that, the information given by industry is often wrong and frequently misleading or irrelevant. Health claims are often mendacious; the EU food agency recently disapproved of more than 80 per cent of them. The information is often misleading; for example, when the label says 'less sugar' the product can still contain more calories than necessary. The industry researches the connection between consumer mood and buying behaviour, and constantly (ab)uses via the packaging the often wrong connection people make between food labelled as healthy and its calories and nutritional value (Bowen *et al.* 1992; Wansink and Chandon 2006). 'For example, we found that people believed that a combination of three "healthy" foods had 28% fewer calories than three "unhealthy" meals; although in reality the combination of healthy foods contained 34% more calories' (Chandon 2012). For many consumers the information given is irrelevant because they do not have an interest in calories or proteins but in information about taste and issues of the production process, like animal welfare or fair trade (Bouwman *et al.* 2009).

## Information about food, labelling and certification

Information about food composition and food quality and about the production process is impregnated with values and therefore not a purely objective, neutral message that is scientifically proven. Information is given via labels, advertisements or other mass media messages, but also via subconscious messages. Labels refer to standards which express qualities of the product and the production process (Busch 2011). All kinds of normative choices are made before a standard of food information is established; facts that look so simple, like the number of calories, are impregnated with values, in this case because a calorie is something different before or after cooking, in the stomach or outside, and even mentioning calories is a normative decision. In most cases these underlying values that determine the quality of the product are not made explicit, and here starts one of the main contentious issues in the confrontation between consumers and producers.

Given the lack of reliable information about food, food codes such as a traffic-light system of red (for instance, for unhealthy), orange and green (for healthy choice) can have a positive function for Western ethical consumers who want to know more about the production of food. From an ethical point of view, the mandatory labelling and certification are legitimate strategies to implement the consumers' right to know. It is therefore strange that in some countries labelling of, for example, genetically modified food is still forbidden. In California, for instance, the mandatory labelling of genetically modified food has not been accepted after a big protest campaign by large agrifood companies like Monsanto and Pepsico (California Proposition 37, 2012). If seen as reliable, labelled food can provide a sense of connectedness between consumers, their food, and the people and place from which it came. As Luetchford notes, 'in ethical consumption the aim is to break down and demystify the distance between parties in the exchange and accentuate the relation between them' (Luetchford and Carrier 2012, p. 20).

There are several types of labelling schemes. Some labelling schemes are the product of the marketing department of a food company, and are often seen as no more than that: marketing tools; or they may be voluntary, market-based regulation schemes for public-demanded or state-mandated labour and environmental standards. These schemes are seen by many as the least reliable. Often labelling schemes are introduced, monitored and maintained by certification agents (or third-party certifiers); they are independent of the companies involved, but not without an interest (see below). Finally, NGOs develop labelling schemes, for example with respect to animal welfare or fair trade (such as Max Havelaar, for *inter alia* fair-trade coffee, rice and cotton). All of these schemes have their advantages and disadvantages. In an open society with impartial mass media, good journalists and critical NGOs they can be discussed; many NGOs criticise, for example, the different types of scheme as types of 'greenwashing' and 'fairwashing' (see also Bartley 2011). For example, they criticise these schemes for seeming to be positive alternatives to the regulations of developing countries, when in reality they encourage bad government or they allow governments to cede their sovereignty in the case of the food sector to the demands of Western labelling organizations. Food codes are sometimes more in the interests of those organizations than in those of the developing country workers or ecology. Moreover, new technologies to authenticate food are being developed, like laser-based isotope detection systems to identify the origin of food items, and critics can make use of these technologies. The effects of labelling schemes for producers and the production process, however, can also be that more profound reworking of the institutions of the food sector in the sense of more justice and better governmental oversight are not taking place (Busch 2011). For a more radical food information system, see below.

### Certification by a third party

A typical strategy to build credibility with respect to a particular food chain is to organize certification by independent bodies based on codes and standards. This strategy is encouraged by policy makers and NGOs and is usually done by establishing quality criteria and through paperwork and random verification. Sometimes the verification is quite meagre; moreover, the quality standards are the result of selecting certain values (such as saving the rainforest) and neglecting others (such as indigenous people living in the forest).

Well-known labels such as Max Havelaar are difficult to understand because they apply certain criteria that for the business involved are transparent and relevant, but for the consumer quite contradictory and full of exceptions for many producers. Often labels issued by the certification authority originate from requirements that meet the needs of the clients and not the preferences, wishes and ideas of consumers and farmers: 'In most instances, certification is voluntary and administered by private bodies that depend on the support of firms and must compete with other certifiers for credibility and recognition' (Bartley 2011, p. 442). Moreover, and not usually known to consumers, producers can often only participate if they make a financial contribution. Nevertheless, such labels gain the trust of certain consumer groups because according to them there is nothing better. A premise of many certifications is that consumers do not understand the science behind the standards, and just want to buy something that gives them an 'ethical good feeling'. So, certifications often prey on ethical feelings of doing something good.

### Increasing and decreasing trust

Trusting or not trusting information on food starts with the concrete relations people have with, for instance, bread, milk, potatoes and cabbage and with themselves and their co-eaters. These concrete relations concerning the daily choices of food incorporate various values, like the ones connected with family and friendship, with nature, and with global and fair justice. The right to know is therefore never only an issue of having access to knowledge but is also about the knowledge interests people have and their trust in the knowledge producer.

In Europe consumers are experiencing nearly every month a food scandal, and in the surveys one can see how trust in food companies slowly declines (Eurobarometer 2006, 2012). Whether it is about an illegal mix of beef and pork (or horse meat) sold as beef, a fair-trade sugar labelled as coming from Brazil but in fact coming from India, a health claim that is just fraudulent, people feel that companies are often not honest and become cynical about labels and information. The meat adulteration scandal of 2013 in Europe (Wikipedia has an informative entry about this) is one of the many events that decrease consumers' trust with a drop in sales of frozen food as a result. In Europe, according to the Eurobarometer 2006 and 2012, the distrust of consumers in information given by companies is high.

The problem is, however, that according to most social scientists, trust is absolutely necessary for a society to survive. Well-known economists, psychologists, sociologists and scholars of religion have analysed trust and written in-depth studies about it. For example, Niklas Luhmann argues that 'a complete absence of trust would prevent (one) even (from) getting up in the morning' (Luhman 1982, p. 20). John Elster (1987) describes trust as the lubricating oil of the social machine. Robert Putnam (2000) says that a high level of confidence maintains a cooperative society, with efficient public and private institutions. Francis Fukuyama (1996) even tries to show that societies with more economic confidence score better. Trust is a relationship not based on power. Also it is not a contract between two more or less equal parties who agree to do something for each other and fulfil this agreement. It is an unequal relationship, without an exchange of equivalent activities. Trust is a special relationship, in which three parties are involved: the person who gives trust, the one who is trusted and the ones who are not trusted. A credible person behaves in such a way that he or she can be trusted, compared to others who cannot be trusted. Merely saying 'trust me' is insufficient.

Annette Baier has presented some topics (she calls them principles) that steer trust in this sense. As stressed, it is a balance between considerations of what a citizen consumer wants to eat and to provide to family and friends, and her other, super local considerations. A perceived appropriate balance can build trust. In terms of Baier, the principles of trust are:

The first principle (Principle M) forbids manipulation of others by deliberately raising false expectations in them about how one will respond to something one wants them to do. The second (Principle D), requires one to take due care not to lead others to form reasonable but false expectations about what one will do, where they would face significant loss if they relied on such false expectations. The third (Principle L) requires one to take steps to prevent any loss that others would face through reliance on expectations about one's future behavior, expectations that one has either intentionally or negligently (that is by infringing Principles M or D) led them to form.

(Baier 1994, pp. 133–4)

On the basis of these insights, one can conclude that the examples of giving wrong, misleading or false information are indeed breaches of trust, in particular conflict with Baier's principles M and D. Moreover, the often different, opposite and partially overlapping information claims and labels weaken the credibility of the position of the claiming or labelling agency and as a consequence also of the sector as a whole. The example discussed in the following section illustrates this point.

A violation of a code of ethics or code of conduct of a company, even a partial one, be it by individuals, departments or the company as a whole, is extremely damaging to the credibility of the company, but also of the whole sector. Trust is therefore not blind acceptance: 'Well placed trust goes out of active inquiry rather than blind acceptance' (O'Neill, 2002, p. 76). The active inquiry covers also the circumstance that trust given to a labelling scheme or a company implies that trust is not placed in another body; the consumer will always have to make a choice, no one can take that away from him or her.

## Problems of information: the example of health advice

Advisory information about a food item suggesting a healthy diet faces three problems when it comes to trust and credibility. First, the majority of European consumers are interested in aspects of nutrition other than health, such as taste and social experience. Food scientists and producers overestimate the importance that consumers attach to the health information given to them. Then there is the complexity of the bodily impacts of food products. These are so complex that a negative and positive effect of a particular food for health or the environment can be identified. Usually this problem is solved by simply saying nothing about the other, adverse, effects, or to design research in such a way that the desired outcome can be proclaimed. Science can always demonstrate a positive effect of a certain food ingredient. However, credibility is undermined by 'pimped' claims. Finally, recommendations for a healthy diet can have a negative impact on the environment in which health and sustainability are not always in harmony with each other. Here, very little research has been done and so there is not much knowledge about these cross connections, except in the case of fish. The advice that many (non-) governmental agencies give is to eat more fish. However, if people actually complied with this recommendation at least twice as many fish would need to be caught, and at the current rate of consumption the seas are already quickly losing their fish stocks (Jenkins *et al.* 2009). The complexity of food production and the concentration of economic power in the hands of a small number of companies make contemporary arrangements that focus exclusively on nutrition or sustainability not only risky, but also lacking in credibility. Conflicting information about whether or not a food item is healthy or sustainable reduces confidence in products and institutions.

### Co-production as an alternative strategy to regain confidence

An alternative strategy to labelling focuses on the restructuring of the entire area in which decisions are taken about nutrition, sustainability and health, so that the mutual influences can be identified more easily. When the effects of food production on health and the environment are identified, because the barriers between these different areas are demolished, assessments about production processes can be made earlier and better. The government has an important role here, if only in the restructuring of ministries so they can make connections between these aspects. Besides that, food consumers should be allowed by governments and business to check the origin and quality of foods themselves as much as possible. Modern mass media and technologies allow this kind of information to be available.

Moreover, the role of consumers in contributing to local production through, for example, urban gardening or Community Supported Agriculture, should not be underestimated because this allows them to become acquainted with the intricacies of the balance between *inter alia* local and super local biodiversity and health. It is the active participation of consumers that enables them to have their own views on food risks and on the necessity of balancing the numerous values connected with food, such as health, animal welfare and sustainability (Allen 2012). Moreover, participation enables people to place trust in professionals that can be directly checked in cases of doubt. The Internet and other social media make it easier now to connect consumer organizations and NGOs, as well as the producers themselves; it allows the building of a collective memory of what is seen as good food.

### Conclusion

In the medical sphere, there is a continuing discourse on the status of the right to know and the right not to know, due to the special character of medical knowledge. In the food sector the discourse about these rights is different, due to the fact that a choice for a particular food item and the connected knowledge can be refused or neglected without personal disadvantages. Here the right to know and to be informed *about the aspects of food one is interested in* has much more prominence. Moreover, the right to know is never just a case of having access to knowledge but is also about the relevant knowledge, depending on the interests people have, and their trust in the knowledge producer. Various ethical approaches support this right to know; however, to really understand this right in its contextual meaning, it is necessary to consider the practices in which consumers and producers are involved.

The right to know has its mirror in the duty to inform, and here companies, governments and civil societies play a role. However, the food sector, the one which has here the foremost duty, is an incredibly complex bowl of spaghetti, full of black holes, sometimes due to the strategies of producers to make information inaccessible and to defend their interests (Roberts 2008). It is a 'bizarre bazaar' (Busch 2011). Perhaps the gap between consumers and the production of food can be bridged by labelling and certification schemes, but these are in many cases not sufficient to structure the food sector into a fair and integrated business that responds to consumers' and citizens' interests. Market-driven and third-party certifiers (labelling organizations) are often not living up to their promises. The right to be informed can also be given shape by consumers and their organizations in developing knowledge and information schemes (as a kind of crowd communication system) by using modern mass media such as apps. Moreover, in participating in agricultural processes, for example in Community Supported Agriculture, consumers can organize their own knowledge about what they think is ethically legitimate to eat.

### References

Allen, W. 2012. *The Good Food Revolution: Growing healthy food, people, and communities*. New York: Penguin Books.

Baier, A. 1994. *Moral Prejudice*. Cambridge, MA: Harvard University Press.

Bartley, T. 2011. 'Certification as a mode of social regulation', in D. Levi-Faur (ed.) *Handbook of the Politics of Regulation*. Cheltenham: Edward Elgar Publishing, pp. 441–51.

Berg, L. 2011. 'Trust in food in the age of mad cow disease: A comparative study of consumers' evaluation of food safety in Belgium, Britain and Norway', *Appetite* 42(1): 21–39.

Bouwman, L., Te Molder, H., Koelen, M. and Van Woerkum, C. 2009. 'I eat healthfully but I am not a freak. Consumers' everyday life perspective on healthful eating', *Appetite* 53(3): 390–8.

Bowen, D. J., N. Tomoyasu, M. Anderson, M. Carney and A. Kristal 1992. 'Effects of expectancies and personalized feedback on fat consumption, taste, and preference', *Journal of Applied Social Psychology* 22: 1061–79.

Busch, L. 2011. *Standards: Recipes for reality*. Cambridge, MA: MIT Press.

California Proposition 37 2012. 'Mandatory labeling of genetically engineered food'. Available at: http://ballotpedia.org/wiki/index.php/California_Proposition_37,_Mandatory_Labeling_of_Genetically_Engineered_Food_ (2012) (accessed 3 December 2013).

Chandon, P. 2012. 'How package design and packaged-based marketing claims lead to overeating', *Applied Economic Perspectives and Policy* 35: 7–31.

Coff, C., D. Barling, M. Korthals and T. Nielsen 2008. *Ethical Traceability and Communicating Food*. Dordrecht: Springer.

Elster, J. 1987. *The Cement of Society. A study of social order*. Cambridge University Press.

Eurobarometer 2006. *Risk Issues*. A report to the EC Directorate General for Research from the project 'Life Sciences in European Society' QLG7-CT-1999-00286. Available at: http://ec.europa.eu/public_opinion/archives/ebs/ebs_238_en.pdf (accessed 9 April 2014).

Eurobarometer Special 389 2012. *Europeans' Attitudes towards Food Security, Food Quality and the Countryside*. European Commission. Available at: http://ec.europa.eu/public_opinion/archives/ebs/ebs_389_en.pdf (accessed 9 April 2014).

Fukuyama, F. 1996. *Trust: The social virtues and the creation of prosperity*. New York: Touchstone Books.

Jenkins, D., J. Sievenpiper, D. Pauly, U. R. Sumaila, C. Kendall and F. Mowat 2009. 'Are dietary recommendations for the use of fish oils sustainable?' *Canadian Medical Association Journal* 180(6): 633–7.

Kant, I. 1995. *Was heisst Aufklärung, idem*. Darmstadt: Werke.

Kaplan, D. (ed.) 2011. *The Philosophy of Food*. Berkeley, CA: California University Press.

Keulartz, J., M. Korthals, M. Schermer and T. Swierstra 2002. 'Ethics in a technological culture. A programmatic proposal for a pragmatist approach', *Science, Technology and Human Values* 29(1): 3–30.

Korthals, M. 2004. 'Before dinner: Philosophy and ethics of food', Dordrecht: Springer.

Luetchford, P. and J. G. Carrier (eds.) 2012. *Ethical Consumption: Social value and economic practice*. Oxford: Berghahn Books.

Luhman, N. 1982. *Trust and Power*. London: Wiley.

Mick, D. G., S. M. Broniarczyk and J. Haidt 2004. 'Choose, choose, choose, choose, choose, choose, choose: Emerging and prospective research on the deleterious effects of living in consumer hyperchoice', *Journal of Business Ethics* 52(2): 207–11.

Mill, J. S. 1975. 'On Liberty', in J. S. Mill *Three Essays*. Oxford University Press, p. 18.

Nowotny, H., P. Scott and M. Gibbons 2001. *Rethinking Science: Knowledge and the public in an age of uncertainty*. Cambridge: Polity.

O'Neill, O. 2002. *A Question of Trust*. Cambridge University Press.

Pollan, M. 2006. *The Omnivore's Dilemma: A natural history of four meals*. New York: Penguin.

Putnam, R. 2000. *Bowling Alone. The collapse and revival of American community*. New York: Simon.

Reisch, L. 2004. 'Principles and visions of a new consumer policy', *Journal of Consumer Policy* 27: 1–42.

Roberts, P. 2008. *The End of Food*. Boston, MA: Houghton Mifflin.

Stolle, D. and M. Micheletti 2013. *Political Consumerism: Global responsibility in action*. Cambridge University Press.

Wansink, B. and P. Chandon 2006. 'Can "low-fat" nutrition labels lead to obesity?' *Journal of Marketing Research* 43: 605–17.

Wrangham, R. 2009. *Catching Fire. How cooking made us human*. London: Profile.

## Websites

Compassion in World Farming www.ciwf.org.uk/

Environmental Working Group www.ewg.org

European Society for Agricultural and Food Ethics www.eursafe.org

The Fair Food Network www.fairfoodnetwork.org/

Food and Agriculture Organization of the United Nations http://fao.org

Food crisis and the global land grab http://farmlandgrab.org

Food Ethics Council www.foodethicscouncil.org/

Grain http://grain.org

Grist. A beacon in the smog. http://grist.org

Natural Resources Defense Council www.nrdc.org/about/

People are starving, but there's enough food. Co-exist. Morgan Clendaniel (ed.) www.fastcoexist.com/1678651/people-are-starving-but-theres-enough-food

# Index